An English Psychic in Hollywood

An English Psychic in Hollywood

LUCINDA CLARE

EBURY
PRESS

First published by Ebury Press in Great Britain 2006

1 3 5 7 9 10 8 6 4 2

Text © Lucinda Clare 2006

Ebury Press, an imprint of Ebury Publishing.
Random House, 20 Vauxhall Bridge Road, London SW1V 2SA

Random House Australia (Pty) Limited
20 Alfred Street, Milsons Point, Sydney, New South Wales 2061, Australia

Random House New Zealand Limited
18 Poland Road, Glenfield, Auckland 10, New Zealand

Random House (Pty) Limited
Isle of Houghton, Corner of Boundary Road & Carse O'Gowrie,
Houghton 2198, South Africa

Random House Publishers India Private Limited
301 World Trade Tower, Hotel Intercontinental Grand Complex, Barakhamba
Lane, New Delhi 110 001, India

The Random House Group Limited Reg. No. 954009

www.randomhouse.co.uk

A CIP catalogue record for this book is available from the British Library

Cover design by Two Associates
Interior by seagulls.net

ISBN: 9780091905491 (from Jan 2007)
ISBN: 0091905494

Printed and bound in Great Britain by Mackays of Chatham plc

Copies are available at special rates for bulk order.
Contact the sales development team on 020 7840 8487
or visit www.booksforpromotions.co.uk for more information.

For Daniel

who redefined Love for me

now I know Love can be human as well as divine

Acknowledgements

I want to thank the people who made this book possible.

My mother, Ann Galloway, for putting me in the lotus position aged four and encouraging my passion for the esoteric; my father, David Galloway, for his philosophical mind and Irish soul; and both of my parents for their unconditional support for me as an artist which has been the foundation of any courage I have had; my sister Natasha Galloway for helping me in the early years with writing contracts, and still being the funniest person I know; my brother James Galloway for being a fellow artist and US/UK hybrid – after a decade in the States we can translate words and feelings together.

Angela Donovan, who trained me as a psychic and gave me the new chapter to my life, allowing me to pay her in daffodils and doughnuts; Julia Cameron, for her wildly effective methods to inspire artists, and Abigail Brown, for the afternoons on her New York roof garden, where she planted the seed among her plants that I could write as well as act.

My first writing group in Hollywood, Alene Dawson and Hunter Senftner, who listened to early drafts with unconditional enthusiasm; Dominica Cameron-Scorcese who always appears at the right moment with the right words; Heidi Wall and the A-Teams who taught me to both dream and focus; my friend Michael Hague who was kind enough to introduce me to his agent; Maggie Soboil for reading the very first chapter breakdown and encouraging me to write this book; Sophie Heyman for our weekly inspirational stream of consciousness writing sessions that taught me writing could be fun; my great and generous friend Caroline Muir who introduced me to her agent, Clare Conville at Conville and Walsh.

Without Clare there would be no book. With Clare I won the karmic lotto. Inspirational, intelligent and profoundly intuitive she is everything you dream of having in an agent; Patrick Walsh and Alfie – Patrick for his enthusiasm and insight, Alfie for his greetings. Kevin Conroy Scott as a fellow hybrid gave me faith that I could write the book I wanted to; Jake Smith-Bosanquet who always goes out of his way to help me; Sue Armstrong for fielding and organizing my frantic transatlantic requests; Edward Hibbert for bringing London to LA in our meetings over soft-boiled eggs with soldiers; and all the team at Conville and Walsh.

In the early stages of the book, Sally Abbey taught me to stand up for what I believe and Angela Mackworth Young to stand by what I believe. When I met Fiona MacIntyre, my commissioning editor at Ebury, I knew I had met the woman who would shepherd the book I dreamt of making out into the world. Her insightfulness, heartfelt honesty, humour and gentle insistence on making the best book possible inspired me to go all out. Her assistant Joy (Chambers) lives up to her name; Claire Kingston for her editorial clarity, and willingness to see the whole picture; all of the marketing and sales teams; Debbie McNally for showing me how promotion could be passionate and possible; and Caroline Newbury in publicity who inspires me with nothing but confidence.

Whenever I had emotional hiccups in the process of writing the book, there were three wise men. The first, Arthur Kopit, who brainstormed with me for five hours, and when I was in a panic about editing, wondering which stories would stay wrote "it will show you." That piece of paper was sellotaped above my computer. Similarly when I had my very own Act 2 crisis point, Al Watt, with his great mind and listening heart would always guide me through in our intense writing sessions. Finally, and most significantly, my husband Daniel for his kindness and deep generosity, who despite four screenplay deadlines of his own, always made time to read, edit, discuss, inspire and finally push me out of the nest to be a writer.

Lastly the readers and listeners, plucked from my soul tribe. My dearest friend Kate Mays who patiently heard chunks of text as she was nursing her first baby and I was an overcaffeinated wreck, shrieking problem passages down the phone. Our daily heart-to-hearts showed me the wisdom of unconditional love. Sharon Saks Soboil, who deciphered my handwritten original diaries and told me she cried in all the right places; Kim Kimbro who laughed in all the right places. Martha Chang for her great eye and practical championing; Bridget Foley and Stephen Susco, for reading the original manuscript and motivating me to see the best in Americans; Will Robertson for his friendship and courage, daring to come into the haunted house with me; Chrissy Iley for her fantastic humour and friendship; Cornelia Ven den Houdt, Kaiulani Kimbrell and Ramon Termens for their insightful comments; Patrick Butcher, a profound and hilarious healer who took away my migraines and neuroses as the deadlines increased. And my Hollywood soul teamsters, Kellie Lovelace for her belief that I could do anything; Scott Schwenk for inspirational talks; Rachel Zabar, fellow book devourer and mind adventurer; Joy Renaldi for her kindness, Camilla Outszen Ransen for her gentleness, glamour and guidance; James Mays and Tom Bresnahan, the new breed of men who dare to feel deeply; Seana McGee and Maurice Taylor who teach by example, and inspire many of us to be living embodiments of my favourite quote: "No matter how vast the darkness we must supply our own light" – Stanley Kubrick. And my beloved Ammachi who shows me unconditional love and selfless service in action.

Three special mentions. Dr. Peter Newton and the kind nurses of Cedai Sinai for saving Daniel's life, and Damon McElhone for helping find Twiglet when she went missing, Delaine Yates who called me ever day for five months when Daniel was ill. They helped save three of the books main characters.

To my closest friends who have watched and loved me for two decades. Natascha McElhone for her faith in me as a writer; Orla Brady for her belief in me as an actress; Agneishka Springate-Bakinski as my psychic companion; Malcolm Freeman the 21st century Percival, Jason Morrell for his incedible sense of humour and kind heart, Howard Blake, for his fascinating mind and generous soul and David Miles, the inspiration for Jimminy. And those now in spirit, Erik, Arkie Whitely, and Naniel Deveraux. I still feel your nudges and presence.

And finally, to all the clients who came to see me. Thank you for trusting me. I hope I helped you with your dreams, you helped me with mine.

Foreword

This is a story based on my life as a psychic.

All the stories in the book are true, or based on true events and some of the most outrageous and unbelievable stories are told verbatim. But in order to protect the people who put their trust in me, I have changed names, occasionally professions, amalgamated psychic readings, created characters who are composites of several people, interwoven stories and altered timelines. So, if you are wondering who the outrageous characters in this story might be, don't bother! While not a photograph of my life it is an impressionistic painting. The only exception is the ghosts and Spirits, they appear unaltered and are entirely real!

Introduction

There's an Oscar in the middle of the road. He's eleven foot high, made of plaster, and like the lady in the Louvre, he seems to be smirking. Well, eighty million people are going to watch him be touched up today – maybe it's a smile of anticipation. Meanwhile, my three beloved hounds are anticipating their Mighty Mutt treats and Hollywood Boulevard is closed. I slug my soy decaf latte and, in a huff, hurry to my secret shortcut home. I leave behind banks of photographers, a red carpet and all the movie stars you could ever hope to see arriving in silk, sequins and hybrids.

I zoom up a backstreet towards the hills and home. A girl is standing in the middle of the road. Hungry. Broke. Help me. That's what her cardboard sign says. A small brown dog sits next to her. Maybe her only friend. I give her some money and the smile she gives me is the smile of someone who hasn't given in to despair yet. Underneath the scabs on her face, I can see the face of a girl who got on a bus, came to Hollywood, threw the dice and didn't win – she's a street away from the Oscars, but didn't quite make it there.

I turn into the Hollywood Hills – amazingly there are people walking on the streets. It's usually deserted, but not Oscar Sunday. Women with huge heads on tiny bodies balance themselves on their Jimmy Choos and the overdeveloped arms of men in dinner jackets. TV Oscar parties. Industry wisdom is that if you're not nominated you're in the nosebleed seats, so it's better to watch it on telly.

I open the door to my house, out scuttles the pool guy, on his way to a party. Champagne in one hand, script in the other.

'Big producer at the party – and I've got a screenplay in development, about being a pool guy … You know I do Paris Hilton's pool …' he raises his eyebrows and jumps into his battered Chevy. My God, I have Paris Hilton's pool guy – what has become of the Brit used to the rain and irony? Is this now my claim to fame?

I open the door to my house and am greeted by a knowing smile: my Buddha statue, who's watching the telly, along with all my friends. I pour some glasses of fizzy apple juice and hand them out. I have a mini-cross-section of the Hollywood commu-nity assembled: my lawyer, a Hollywood must for all the legal brouhahas; a black policewoman from the LAPD who I did readings for in a horrific rape case, and now a friend; an extremely glamorous actress, the type that is gorgeous and skinny even in a bulky towelling dressing-gown – she's standing in one now having thrown herself in the pool for a compulsive dip (she ate a carbohydrate); a movie star, the sort who gets chased in cars and ends up having her face on the cover of super-market rags; a writer, struggling to make the mortgage; a painter, waiting for her break – undoubtedly brilliant, we all have one of her canvases, but not recognised yet. I put the organic fat-free popcorn on the table and we all gather around the rap-king-sized screen.

The plaster Oscars are still glistening and now they're taking us inside. One of my best friends is here with me as well, watch-ing with us; she's English, holding her baby boy, my godson.

Even he looks riveted and is quiet. She and I give each other one of those secret complicit looks that ex-pats in Hollywood give each other – the 'we're a long way from Kensington' looks. I remember we watched the Oscars together when we were tiny, in the late seventies, on my mother's bed – supper was a plate of After Eights and we'd leave chocolate prints all over the Biba bedspread. Now we're sipping Pellegrino.

People are winning and losing now. Looking brave when they lose, or clapping extra hard. And the winners, a lot of them seem to revert to childhood – their voices go higher and squeakier. 'They're regressing,' I whisper to my friend. We're in Hollywood now. We know therapy terms. They become like little children, crying and thanking and stuttering, although a few stand firm and make political statements that help the world. As I am watching this parade of psyches, an evil thought crosses my mind: if I sold the secrets I knew about this crowd to the *National Enquirer* I could pay off my house. A winner's name is called out; my lawyer and I both cheer. Then he catches my eye and, in that sixth-sense way that people who are paid to protect the reputations of others have, we share a look. He knows I know about his client. That he's a sex addict who was thrown out of treatment because he broke into the offices and was on an online porn site. The camera randomly pans through the celebrity audience, and I see several industry heavyweights who visited me when I worked as a psychic; my psyche plays tricks with me as I see the lurid rag headlines superimposed over their new noses and jawlines:

OSCAR WINNER'S WIFE STABBED HIM WITH A FORK

AFTER POLTERGEIST PROVOCATION!

SEX GOD ON SCREEN SCREWS MALE PROSTITUTE
IN SOUTH AMERICAN SLUMS!

EMMY AWARD-WINNING DIRECTOR'S WIFE ADMITS SEX
WITH GHOST BETTER THAN SMALL-DICK HUSBAND!

I catch my lawyer's eye again, as his client is thanking his wife. I realise I could never tell anyone all the stuff I know. It wouldn't be spiritual. Would it?

The last winners now, although the PC announcement is, 'And the Oscar goes to ...' and everyone's tallying up their scorecards for the pot – to see who can win. I haven't entered. I sigh with relief. Prediction was my profession here for a while and it's a busman's holiday, so I'm not playing and because they're my friends they understand.

The Oscars are over and my friends are off to parties. The actress kisses me goodbye and whispers, 'They're like birthdays, aren't they? They force you to take stock and see where you are in your life.'

Later that evening when everyone's left to find the best parties, curled up on the sofa with the dogs, I can't help thinking what fun it would be to tell my story. What a giggle to tell everyone what it's really like behind all the glamour and glitz. What it was like being 'psychic to the stars'. I look at my Buddha statue and he seems to be willing me to do it.

I start writing.

Magic in the Genes

I come from a long line of cheese-haters. For generations the Clare family loathed cheese. One of those eccentric English things. As perplexing as morris dancing. We even had a cheese confirmation day. Confirmation that we were one with our clan. For generations, every Clare baby was fed a crumb of cheese and for generations every Clare baby had spat it out. Family cheers accompanied the splendid projectile vomit. And then it was my turn.

The family gathered around. My mother picked up a yellow crumb and the cheese approached the christening bonnet, but instead of the familiar rejection … it disappeared. My grandmother searched in the folds of my christening dress; the family imagined my mother must have dropped it. Another morsel was fed to me. This time there was a loud gulp. Then a stunned silence. Tremors of shock went through my parents and the onlooking relatives, cheese-haters all. I was a cheese-eater! An outcast!

And cheese was only the beginning.

Like other babies, I dutifully woke up my parents in the middle of the night, except I didn't cry – the noise that woke them up was ... laughter. My mother's use of the expression 'She's off with the fairies' took on a whole new meaning as she watched me listening to silence and gurgling to no one.

By the time I was five, I was still different. I only had one friend: Piglet, my guinea pig. She looked like a small version of Dougal from *The Magic Roundabout*, all hair and heart, and I loved her completely. One day Piglet's little furry body stopped moving. She was dead. That was what Mummy said.

'What's dead?'

'Well, darling, Piglet has gone to sleep for ever and ever.'

'She'll never wake up?'

Mummy shook her head.

'So I'll never see her again?'

'No. She's gone to heaven. We have to say goodbye to Piglet now.'

And we did. Or at least I tried to. Because she was tiny, we buried her in a very small home: my old crayon box. I marked the spot with buttercups and tried to imagine Piglet in heaven, but I couldn't. I could still feel her around me. When I told my parents, they exchanged the same worried looks they'd worn on the disastrous cheese confirmation day. What was wrong with grown-ups? No wonder they all wore glasses. They couldn't see properly.

At eleven, while my friends were starving themselves and screaming along to the Sex Pistols, I was stuffing myself with Stilton and analysing their sun signs. By the time I was thirteen, I was christened the 'white witch' by my peers, as I 'guessed' the names of their dead spaniels and Labradors, saw ghosts at boarding school, the whole shebang. At fifteen I read tea leaves, cards and palms, but by seventeen, I was reading Iris Murdoch, Virginia Woolf and Camus. My hair and lipstick were bright red – and I had politics to match. I turned down a place at Cambridge to read English because, I declared stalwartly, I'd had enough of privilege and writing irony in the margins. (And the fact that I'd met a beautiful man with Elvis eyes and Jesus words, telling me that I must follow my dreams to be an actress, might have had a little bit to do with it.) The man was my soulmate! Minor inconvenience: he was gay ... so he became the other kind of soulmate – the type that stays. Jimminy became my best friend.

At eighteen, I had two dreams; to fall in love with my soulmate (handsome and straight, please, Spirit) and to be an actress. Jimminy and I were dream-chasers together. We lived in Paris on a boat, where I trained with Marcel Marceau as a mime. Not a field renowned for its career opportunities, so back to London we went, where we both trained to be actors – another rip roaring career choice – for three years at the Central School of Speech and Drama – Olivier and Judi Dench's old one. Loved it. But by twenty-two, out in the world as actors, Jimminy and I were trauma-bonding: he had as many boyfriend problems as I did. We would sit in dreary English cafés and, over egg and beans, dream of being actors in a Hollywood of Hockney pools with a man we loved in a water-bed next to us. Maybe there's something about saying the same lines again and again on stage that makes you start doing it in real life too:

Me: Jimminy, I've met him! My soulmate!
Jimminy (cynical): What's he like?

Me: (saviour face): He's bankrupt/criminal/just left his wife/
manic depressive/recovering heroin addict/total fuck-up
BUT (pseudo-spiritual face) I knew him in a past life/he's in
therapy/he's a genius/we're astrological soulmates/we're
meant to be together.

So that was the first half of my twenties, until it ended with me
curled up in a foetal position reading one of those 'women who
love men who don't give a shit about them' books and weeping
into my Flake wrappers.

For the next two years, in a stunning reversal, instead of trying
to help desperate men I decided to help desperate women. Not
between the sheets but between takes. I returned to my childhood hobby: reading tarot cards and palms for all my actress
buddies. Filming in Ireland, I held a séance in a haunted house;
doing a grim northern tour of Molière, the only laughs we got
were our own squeals of delight as the cards told us that the
play was going to close early; advertising beauty soap and
shivering in our undies, we found more dignity in looking at
our futures than facing up to our present. I was the on-set
mystic. Jimminy, who it has to be said was going through a
very black period, was dressing as a giant prawn to advertise
a seafood restaurant and was sniffy in the extreme. But then,
in a remarkable turnaround of his own – brought on by his
despair at ever finding work – he sneaked off to see a medium!
Mediums are to tarot-card readers what Marmite is to
Vegemite: the real thing. And that filled me with fear. It was all
very well fiddling around with cards, I did it for fun, but a real-
life Madam Arcati medium – I was terrified I'd be chastised by

her for meddling in spiritual worlds without knowing what I was doing, so even though I was desperately curious to meet her I didn't. Instead I did what I always did when I felt cowardly and annoyed with myself: put on too much make-up, dressed up and went out to a gay nightclub. I'd given up on ever finding a soulmate at this point and wanted to have fun with men in frocks, dancing to Abba.

To my dismay, on that particular night the club was hosting an event for Elite models. Not great if you're feeling wobbly about your wobbly bits. Everyone, men and women, was ogling the models ... except for a devastatingly good-looking photographer, who was staring at me. The other photographers madly shot film of the astonishingly beautiful supermodel. Who seemed to be grinning at the photographer. Hmm, redhead with freckles and an Italian body or an Amazonian supermodel? Obviously no competition, but the sexy photographer, to my utter surprise, focused his camera straight at me and stole a photograph. Then he slowly lowered his camera and smiled at me. And what a smile.

Twenty men dressed in Calvin Kleins and sweat were strutting their stuff on the catwalk. My sexy photographer was doing his stuff too. He had it all going on. He had a copy of the Buddhist sutras jutting out of the back pocket of his faded denims, designer stubble and a Marlboro in his mouth. I watched as one of the male models backflipped as a finale and I involuntarily let out an exuberant whoop.

'Is he your boyfriend, then?' whispered a gravelly Australian voice in my ear. I knew it was him.

'I don't have a boyfriend,' I said with mock sadness. 'Do you?'

'I don't.' And he started laughing. Not gay. That good-looking and not gay. My lucky night.

'Well, we'd better do something about us not having boyfriends, hadn't we? Coffee tomorrow? Tonight?' And he took another photograph of me, this time laughing at him.

'Hi. Steve,' he said, shaking my hand. Hi. I liked that. The more I looked at him the more I liked. And he danced to Abba with me. That was so uncool it was cool.

Over four coffees at Pâtisserie Valerie the next day, I discovered that sexy Steve was the exact opposite of me. Which made him even more attractive. He was an Australian, no-nonsense kind of guy who had little interest in psychic stuff – he even guffawed when I asked his sun sign. Him: Aquarius. Me: Leo. Opposites.

'So if you're not into all of that stuff then why did you have the Buddhist sutras in your back pocket?' I asked intently.

He smirked. 'That's my chick crack, isn't it? My pick-up tool. Admit it, didn't it make it easier to say yes to coffee?'

I hesitated before flirting: 'So you're a shallow playboy just pretending to be deep, then?'

Then, very seriously, he said, 'I'm not pretending to be anything any more. I think the truth's sexier, isn't it? What do you think?'

And suddenly I felt safe and sexy at the same time and told him what I really thought – all the truths about my life, my unfulfilled dreams, my unasked-for psychic power – and he listened, and he wasn't broken and didn't need fixing like all the others had before him. And I told him what a relief it was that, although I was psychic, I no longer had to have all the answers for the people I loved.

'Perhaps it's about living in the question ...'

'Is that Rumi?' I asked.

'Yeah. Hafiz or Rumi. One of them,' he said, shrugging and giving me the foam off his cappuccino.

That was it. A humble hunk that knew who Hafiz was.

Of course, I told Jimminy. But, unbelievably, he was all starry-eyed about the medium he had seen and couldn't really take it in. Secretly I suspected the prawn episode had sent him over the edge. He spouted about how she had predicted he was going to get a lead at the RSC. I felt a teensy bit sorry for him and put it down to hitting his Saturn Return, the grim twenty-ninth birthday, and ran back to Steve. And together Steve and I ran at life as if we were eating it up at top speed. We lived in our Soho pad; the curtains were drawn most of the time, we had sex, ate pomegranates off each other, had sex, read Rumi … In the days I watched him at shoots, in the evenings he watched me on stage – and I watched my lovestruck thoughts about him every morning in meditation. And then we hit a road bump. Well, a pothole. OK. The road just stopped and hung there in the air, like in that bus movie with Keanu Reeves. We were back in Pâtisserie Valerie. He looked particularly like a sex god that day.

'I have leukaemia.'

That slow-motion thing people talk about, it's true. My brain kaleidoscoped into different fragments.

'Leukaemia? You have leukaemia?'

'Yes. I was diagnosed six months ago.'

Now I was in freeze-frame.

'I thought it was going to go away. But it gets worse, I'm afraid.'

My brain was a roundabout, spinning around, and I had got

off. The part of my brain that gives signals to the mouth to open and talk did not seem to be operating.

'It's fatal. They've given me three months.'

'When was that?' My voice was working again.

'Two months and sixteen days ago.'

There was absolutely nothing to say for at least a minute.

'Why didn't you tell me before?' I asked.

Silence.

'I don't know. That's why I had the diamond sutras in my pocket. I was searching for ...' and he said the next phrase with a deep bitterness, 'redemption.'

And that was when I felt the rage. Rage at the monstrous unfairness of it. That afternoon he collapsed and was admitted to hospital. I was told to go home.

The doctors gave him five days to live. I needed faith so I could be strong and help Steve. Like a migrating swallow, I returned to Spirit.

I stood outside the door of Jimminy's psychic. The medium. Diana O'Leary. She had seen the resurrection of Jimminy's career – he was, as she had predicted, miraculously, now at the RSC. Maybe she could rescue Steve from his death sentence. I prayed to the one who had given her the powers,

'If you help Steve, I promise I will be less selfish and help others more, but please save Steve.'

The door opened a crack and I was welcomed by a toothy smile.

'Come in, darling.' The famous Diana O'Leary was blonde by choice, with an aristocratic English voice and an Irish face that looked as though it had loved a lot. She whisked me over to

a big mahogany table, put a cup of tea down in front of me –
which I noticed as I sipped it was exactly as I liked it: milky with
no sugar – and then, still smiling, sat down opposite me. She
closed her eyes and went into a trance, then snapped them open.

'Who is Steve?'

Thank God I was here.

'He's ... my boyfriend.'

'Has he been and gone?'

A terrible anguish went over me.

'Will he die?'

'Well, we all die,' said Diana. 'When it's our time ...'

Then suddenly she looked perky.

'I feel good for him ... Would you like me to tell you everything I can see?'

I nodded. 'I'd rather know.'

'You and he are soulmates ... just not the marrying kind.
You're soulmates who met each other to heal old wounds. You
gave him faith in Spirit and he gave you faith in love.'

Oh God, she was using the past tense ... He was going to die.

'And there's good news here – wonderful news! Steve is
going to get well. And he's going to have a child ... with a girl
called Emma.'

And perhaps God had already answered my prayer to be
less selfish, because in a flash I cared more that Steve would
live and find love than whether or not it was with me. It was
also the most absurd statement, as he had been officially diagnosed as infertile by London's best cancer doctors, following
his chemotherapy. But my faith was stronger than my fear. I
kept listening.

'Two more things. I'm happy to say your dreams are your
destiny. You will act, and live, in America. There's also writing

and film-making shown for you. And they're saying you will not be doing this alone.'

A strangely mischievous smile crossed her face.

'And you have the Great Gift, and I would be delighted to train you as a psychic, if that is what you would like.'

It would have been daft to wonder how the hell she knew about that at this point. I beamed. We both knew my answer.

'Until next Thursday then!'

A year later, Steve had moved back to Australia. He had a spontaneous remission of his cancer and moved in with his best friend from art school, whose name was … Emma. And they had a child together. I got a card from him:

'Thank you for everything. Go find your happy ever after! All love, Steve.'

Meanwhile I had spent a year of Thursdays finding my own happy ending to the England chapter of my life. I trained to be a professional psychic. I had to unlearn a lot. I unravelled my traditional English education and replaced it with a completely esoteric one. My education had giant holes in it at best and lies by omission at worst. I was not a Christian with one shot at salvation; I had a thousand lives in front of me and behind me. Biology had lied to me. Where were the textbook explanations for the rainbow-coloured halos I saw daily around women's Kensington silk scarves? Where were the X-rays that showed not just disease but also the psychic X-rays of cysts and tumours that started growing in grief and fear? History had failed me too: my education had centred on kings and queens conquering lands. Totally ignored were whole movements of men and women who had gone in search inner rather than outer lands.

The Rosicrucians, the Indian mystics and the Order of the Golden Dawn. I loved literature and drama, but the ghosts or spirits I was encountering daily had largely been portrayed as silly floating, whistling sheets or zombies on revenge missions. Over that year, spirits became my friends. I followed their promptings and, however ludicrous, took action. I mean really ridiculous things, like sending a photograph to a Hollywood casting director because I wanted to star in a film over there.

While I was busy trying to create my future, my past was catching up with me. I had sent a photograph. And I had received one. From my parents. They told me the history of the photograph before they unveiled it. It had arrived before I was born. Out of the blue, a long-lost relative had sent my mother and father a letter with a photograph of my great-great-grandfather, Jack Clare. In it, he is presiding over a séance at the Glasgow spiritualist association, with Sir Arthur Conan Doyle on one side and a ghost on the other. Yes, the white blob captured was 'plasma' or a spirit. Clearly there was something more in the letter.

My great-great-grandfather Jack was one of eleven children. They were all cheese-eaters. The origins of the Clare cheese ceremony were at last becoming clearer: all eleven of them were psychic. Like me. Had prophetic dreams, saw ghosts, healed the deer in the grounds of the family castle where they were a magical crew. They had the gift. Like me. My parents thought the gift had died out, hence the celebrations when babies for the last five generations had rejected the cheese. Because with the gift came a curse. Of this eleven, all had doomed love lives. Ten of them never found love, and Jack's wife died very young. That was why my parents had looked so worried on the cheese confirmation day – it was confirmation that, although I might have won the lottery as far as predictive powers went, I was going to be on a losing streak if I was looking for love. This was my legacy. They said they knew I had finished my training with Diana, and now was my leaping-off moment. They had waited as long as they could; they were, in effect, the couple in the wedding congregation who, when asked, raise their hands when the priest asks if there any objections. I could still turn away from the gift ... and avoid the curse.

Well, it certainly explained my disastrous romances ... and Steve had had a narrow escape. It must be true. Then I had one of those rare magical moments in life when we do the brave thing even though we are afraid. I had promised God: save Steve, and I'll help others. So I turned towards my promise and hugged it like an orphaned child. I married myself to my psychic powers, even if it meant it was the only wedding I would have. I would trust Spirit to take care of me. I think it was probably the hardest decision I ever had to make. There was enough flak just admitting to being psychic, without the added weight of the curse, but I made it. And in a very 'we've conquered empires' sort of way, I set my jaw and marched forward.

I 'came out' as a psychic. Diana took me with her to the Chelsea Hallowe'en ball. She set me up under a dinosaur paw, and I did my first formal psychic readings for the aristocracy: debs with heroin problems; lords with no cashflow looking for a message from the great beyond to keep them in velvet slippers; an Oxford don whose lover has just gone mad and who needed heart help where brain help had failed him ... on and on, until midnight.

Walking out into the London rain, I felt happy. I had, just for the night, fulfilled the promise I had made to God if he saved

Steve's life: to help people. Curse be damned. Diana came and hugged me goodnight. She had a mischievous grin on her face.

In the taxi, I got in a panic. I leant out of the window and grabbed her hand. I had the strangest feeling I wouldn't see her for a long while.

'Don't forget to check your phone messages, darling ...' she dashed for a cab and disappeared into the dark and drizzle.

I got back to my flat in Soho. Fought off a little loneliness and before going to sleep I remembered I'd promised Diana to check my messages. I pressed play and this is what I heard:

'Hello, my name is Al; I'm calling from Hollywood. I saw your photograph and résumé in a casting director's office and I'm interested in you playing the lead in my film. I'm sending you a script to see if you're interested.'

I wiped away an inexplicable tear, and then a new one that had just formed. What a night.

The next day the script arrived. I loved the title, *How Did It Feel?*. And all my preconceptions about Hollywood flew out of the window, as on the cover was a quote from Baudelaire that read, 'Thanks be to God who gives us suffering as sacred remedy for all our sins.' A bit Catholic, but it had a vaguely karmic ring to it too, which I loved. Most importantly, it clearly wasn't going to be some cops-and-cocaine-and-two-chicks kind of trash. I sat down just to read the first couple of pages and didn't get up until two hours later. It was one of the best things I had ever read.

After jumping around the flat with excitement I decided to ring Al, the director, and tell him how brilliant I thought his script was and that I would do anything to be in it. No, I couldn't say that – I'd sound desperate and needy. I wondered what time it was in Hollywood … Oh shit, 4 a.m.! Too late: a groggy voice answered.

'Hello?'

'Oh my God, I'm so sorry. I got the time wrong … I'll let you—'

'Is this Lucinda?'

He knew my name. Maybe I really was in for a chance with this part.

'Can you come for an audition next week?'

'I'd love to; I'll see you then. And tell the writer he's a genius.'

'It's a she and I'll tell her.'

I was so nervous that I was fiddling with the script, and suddenly a photograph fell out – of an absolutely gorgeous man. Pacino's double: dark and stormy eyes and a naughty grin.

'The leading man's a bit of all right,' I joked.

'Er, that's me actually. I just wanted you to know I wasn't some creepy guy who—'

Now I felt very embarrassed. And I didn't want him to think I might fancy him.

'Well, actors' photos always make us look better than we really are, don't they? And we all look better on telly than in real life.'

There was a slight pause.

'Do you not look like you did in the Irish show I just saw on PBS?'

Oh God, that show in a corset was coming back to haunt me again.

'No, I'm a dog in real life.'

'A dog? I'm afraid if that's a surreal joke I'm not getting it – it's a bit early in the morning for me …'

Get off the fucking phone, Lucinda, you idiot.

'No, it's an English expression meaning I'm pig ugly.'

'Not very nice to dogs and pigs, is it?'

'You know, it isn't, is it?' I said, laughing.

And we chatted away easily for half an hour about animals and the part and the US and London.

Then we went professional.

'I'll get the producer to FedEx you a ticket.'

'And I'll let you go back to sleep.'

My ticket arrived the next day. It was Hollywood style: fast, efficient and glamorous! Jimminy waved me goodbye at Heathrow as I set off towards the next chapter of my life!

2
Welcome to Hollywood

No one tells you how beautiful Hollywood smells. Standing just outside the airport doors, night jasmine and hilly herbs wafted over the piles of Prada luggage. Not, alas, *my* Prada luggage; it belonged to the Los Angelenos arriving home. Apart from the unique and beautiful smell, all the clichés met me at the airport. This was LA, where grey hair is rare and age-appropriate dressing doesn't exist. There were no shades of grey at all. It was cartoon land: all the colours were cheerful and straight out of a child's colouring box. Yellow hair, white teeth, blue sky, gold sun. And there seemed to be two sizes for women: tiny or obese. The tiny ones – who looked like out-of-work porn stars – were the norm, blonde double-Ds with line-free faces and Angelina Jolie pouts. They shuffled along in their Uggs, their twig legs poking out of candy-coloured minis as they yakked into their miniature cells. Then there were the Americans not from LA. They were cartoon-obese, wearing romper suits, with brisk hair and golfing shades. Standing waiting for the car to pick me up, I marvelled at the white teeth, brown legs and silicone smiles.

Not only did I look out of place (I was the only person wearing black and a cardigan) but I felt it. I had everything the wrong way round; my unbleached teeth were bright yellow, and my wintery legs were neon white. My shape was neither starved nor inflated in peculiar places. But this was a familiar feeling, the fear of not fitting in. Not being the right shape, in any way. But then everything about America was different. As soon as you got off the plane, you had to spend money and were greeted by the threat of violence. Unlike in any European country I had been to, you had to cough up for a trolley; and, as a non-American citizen, you had very mean-looking security guards scowling at you, their hands hovering near their guns like John Wayne. There was a reason non-citizens' green cards were called alien resident; we were aliens.

Waiting for the car, I felt even more amazed by the differences. I had trusted my English agent who had warned me not to rent a car, and so had organised one to pick me up – Brits are inevitably so jetlagged upon arriving that they are unable to drive on the right side of the street. Tales also abound of tipsy Brits tripping off the plane and ending up in metal tangles in their rented cars. Finally, I spotted a placard with 'MS CLARE' written on it, held up in the hands of a tall, ridiculously handsome black man. Hovering next to him was clearly some sort of industry person, in sunglasses and a Sundance T-shirt. I stuck out my hand politely to her and she enthusiastically hugged me hello, which actually made me feel genuinely welcome. The Blair Underwood lookalike, David, was the driver. Before we even got to the car Shelby told me she was a recovering alcoholic and had been desperate for a drink before I arrived, but she had prayed to her Spirit guide to help her. I smiled. Welcome to la-la land, where the social contract insists that the art of subtext is a dying one. But strangely, I got a sort of warm, toasty feeling that maybe I could fit in here after all, and black cardies be damned. Shelby was actually not a one-off; I had been doing my research on the plane and had read that the US is a country where 80 per cent of people believe in Spirits. She then pointed enthusiastically to our car, which was so exaggerated that it too looked as if it had driven straight out of a cartoon. This ecological monstrosity, otherwise known as a stretch limo, finally came to a halt at the curb next to us. It was like a small metal train, it was so long. It epitomised the Hollywood ideal of more money than sense. I smiled politely, loaded my ancient old bags into the spanking new boot and we whooshed away from edge of the curb.

Leaning back in the leather seats, I was desperately curious to see the LA landscape for the first time, so I opened the tinted windows to look at the movie-set palm trees and feel the warm wind. Shelby promptly leant through the glass partition and said chirpily, 'Do you need more air?' before turning on the air-conditioning until a small hurricane was blasting into the back of the car.

The car was so huge I had to yell back to be heard. Being British, it didn't occur to me to get her to turn off the air (rude), so I gathered my woolly even closer to me.

'Is that OK now?' mouthed Shelby through the icy blasts.

'Fine,' I lied merrily.

As I looked at her cheerful, tanned face, I had an eerie sensation. Peering down the limo interior, I saw a white misty veil hovering over her head, accompanied by a little black smudgy cloud of worry. I realised that I had not, in Diana's words, 'shut down' psychically, probably due to tiredness from the flight, and was being given spontaneous psychic images. I was looking at a wedding veil.

'Are you OK? you a little … ill or something … do you need some more air?'

Terrified I would be buffeted out the window if the air-conditioning got any more intense, I shook my head. 'No, I don't need more air, thank you,' I said in an oddly detached voice. I was trying to decide whether I was up for giving a reading after the bone-crushing flight. Spirit won out.

'Do you mind if I tell you something?' I hurried on, feeling a psychic message wanting to be heard and following the code of asking for permission.

I suspected Shelby, being American, was used to what seemed like an instant confession. And, coupled with that, she was clearly adept at transporting vaguely unbalanced actresses who announced that they needed to share random information.

'You go right ahead. Go for it,' she said reassuringly. Funny. If it had been England I don't think I would have jumped in with a question like that; I'd have joked around and been ironic and clever for a while, before leaping into a Spirit message. But here I felt strangely free.

'You mustn't worry about your boyfriend, the man you're going to marry. He is your soulmate. You're worrying without reason. They're giving me the shiver; it's a sign from them that you're with the right man …' I held up my arms to show the goose pimples on them.

'I'm having the "soulmate shiver".'

'Who's they?' said Shelby, staring at my arm and deciding I was not unbalanced but round the bend.

'I'm sorry,' I apologised, with no cause, in the standard British way – it was actually like Tourette's, the way I apologised in America. 'I'm sorry,' I carried on, embarrassed, '"They" refers to Spirit. I'm psychic actually ...'

I had said the magic word.

'OOhh!' she shrieked. 'How fabulous! Tell me more! I didn't realise Spirit guides talked! Yes, I do have a fiancé, and I have been worrying because we're about to get married ... but please keep going!'

'Will you tell me what you see for me?' said David, the limo driver who had been earwigging. His shades glinted at me with anticipation in the driver's mirror. To seal the deal he rubber-necked his photogenic face far enough round to give me a perfect paid for smile as we swerved down La Cienaga, towards Beverly Hills.

'Absolutely,' I said with my own imperfect grin.

As we drove through streets where even the homeless people were beauty knockouts, I concentrated on Shelby's life. Spirit was on that evening, so Shelby was thoroughly reassured that her fiancé was the one for her, especially because I was given his name (Jimmy), and to her this was utterly magical and a divine confirmation of their destined love. Her reassurance also came from the hot-wire from Spirit that she had known the guy before in a previous life, so what looked hasty by social standards (engagement after four weeks) was just playing catch-up by soul standards. The recognition they felt was in sync with Spirit laws – she had felt it on a soul level as soon as she saw him. She shrieked with agreement. 'I knew I recognised him, I thought first of all it was because he had a bit part in *Beverly Hills 90210* ... but this is much more it! You have to come to the wedding shower this weekend!' She blew kisses through the partition and added, 'Honestly, thank you. I'm just relieved to know I wasn't making it all up ... You know, it's hard sometimes, isn't it, to tell the difference between a psychic hunch and complete delusion, especially with hunks.'

While she was excitedly on her cell to her beau, I turned my psychic radar on the limo driver. As I was soon to learn in LA, everyone – and I mean everyone – is an actor/writer/producer/ director in the making, and David was no exception. So I gave him advice on his script (about an out-of-work actor who is a limo driver to the stars and ends up becoming famous) and his acting career, which, despite his rabid faith in Jesus landing him a guest-star role on *The Shield*, had clearly defeated our good saviour's scope – hence his presence behind the wheel. David was transfixed. 'Man, that's cool. I just auditioned for the shield ...'

'Well, hang in there. You're going to be offered a part where you wear a uniform; you're going to play a soldier ...'

He was staring in the rear-view mirror as I continued, taking dictation from his disembodied granny – 'Your grand-mother Arlene says you are to be congratulated for staying in reality and getting this job to pay the bills ...' – when another kind of reality hit, literally, as we heard a sickening metal crunch. A small, furious man uttering expletives jumped out of his Hummer.

'You arsehole! What the fuck were you doing?!'

The pint-sized fury rapped on the window.

David puffed himself up as the tinted glass silently slid down. 'You have a problem, man?'

The red-faced dwarf screeched. 'You're goddamn right I

have a problem. You ran into my car!' Then he stared at his face really hard.

'David?'

'Brick?'

'What the hell are you doing driving a limo? You were a series regular a couple of seasons ago?'

'Gotta pay the bills, man,' said David, smiling at me.

'All that cash gone so fast ... you still into that Vegas thing?'

David shrugged. 'It went pretty quick, man.'

Brick examined his Hummer's front bumper and said to no one in particular. 'Love this thing.' Then he turned his attention back to David.

'Come and see me ... we can get you out again, you can book.'

David smiled and took the card. Then, in an act of supreme generosity, David indicated me and said, 'You need to meet another actor ...'

He explained to me: 'Brick used to be my agent when I first got to town.'

Brick was smiling the shark's smile, his face colour matching his name. 'Brick, this is an English actress come here to audition for the lead in a movie.'

Brick peered into the back of the endless limo.

'What's the name of the movie?'

I told him.

'Who reps you in the UK?'

I told him that too.

Clearly Maddy's boutique agency passed muster, as he persisted: 'You have an agent over here, kid?'

He was only a few years older than me, but I loved being called kid, so I smiled and shook my head.

'No one over here cutting your deal?' He thrust a little card in my hands. 'Give me a call tomorrow. You've got a great look, give me a call. Tomorrow.'

Bemused that he could see me at all in the cavernous, dusky limo, I nodded. Then David got out of the car and he and Brick traded business cards. Shelby was rolling her eyes and saying 'only in Hollywood' to me as David darted back to the car, and after rather desperately rummaging in the glove compartment, triumphantly pulled out a creased picture and résumé and handed it to his old agent.

We drove away with Brick merrily waving goodbye to us. Shelby credited her Spirit guide; David thought it was Jesus; and I knew it was just the beginning of the insanity of Hollywood.

It was way past sunset by the time we turned off Sunset into the Chateau Marmont, the fabulous hotel I was being put up in for the week I was here. Despite the prang, Shelby and David were grateful for their spontaneous readings, and as we said goodnight, hugs all round, Shelby insisted I come to her Sunday wedding shower and David gave me a schedule to his church's Sunday service. Because of my new Vivienne Westwood boots, I chose the wedding shower.

After lying on the bed and obsessing about the audition the next day, endlessly calling room service to practise my New England accent, I eventually crashed out in my beautiful 1920s hotel room at 2 a.m. I slept fitfully, dreaming I was filming on a set with Al Pacino, being kissed sweetly by him, and that David the limo driver had written the script.

D Day. Audition day

I woke up to the sound of lawn sprinklers, swiftly followed by a gunshot. Confused, I called the front desk, only to be told categorically that there was no gun shot, ma'am. You didn't need to be psychic to know the front-desk guy was lying. The day before I had felt like I was in a magical realism film, and today I had been catapulted into a film noir. Everything in Hollywood felt so tricky and unreal. Especially the food. I sat in the hotel restaurant and tried to order breakfast. By the time the waitress had finished the bread choice – 'wheat, rye, white, sourdough, pumpernickel, English muffin' – and the milk – 'full-fat, low-fat, half-and-half, skimmed' – we apparently needed a translator for my reply: 'Brown bread and normal milk.' We spanned the cultural divide when, spying the script, she wished me good luck for my audition. I thought I was making progress until the coffee arrived in a bowl big enough for a Great Dane along with an entire basket of bread. I cowered as she threatened to reel off the encyclopaedic egg choices, ordering 'over easy' just because it was first on the list, even though I had no idea what it was. In the end I was so nervous – as I knew I had to a) audition and b) fit into my tight black trousers – that I couldn't eat the fried eggs anyway, as I knew I would throw them up straight away.

Two hours until the audition

I listened to JFK speeches for the American accent and then Martin Luther King speeches for inspiration. I thanked their Spirits and prayed for courage in my own battlefield, the audition. Then, eyeing the agent's card, I decided to check him out and call as I had promised, in case it could help nab the part. To my surprise, I got through the gatekeepers and had Brick on the line.

'You're the chick in the limo with the accent.'

'That's me,' I laughed.

'When's the audition?'

'In a couple of hours, actually.'

'So give them my number, OK? I won't let 'em fuck you around – I can help you out, kid.'

It was a hugely prestigious agency, one of the ones every actor dreams of being represented by, so I happily said yes to the line that was being offered me. Clearly I had made an impression on him.

'And what the hell's your name again?' Or maybe not.

'Lucinda.'

'Well, listen, Lizinder, give my assistant your numbers and we'll stay on top of it.'

And he was gone. I felt simultaneously elated and crushed as I stuttered out my full name and number at 'the Chateau', as the assistant referred to it.

One hour to go

Desperately tried to paint my nails and pluck my eyebrows, as all Americans seem to have perfect arches and neat little nails. Then changed my mind and wiped off all the nail polish as I am auditioning for the part of a non-vain writer. Realise I am a vain actress and this is Hollywood, and repaint my nails. Realise I am completely uncentred spiritually and meditate to get centred. Stop meditating as I am playing an uncentred character. Put on ridiculously uncomfortable lucky audition shoes. Decide to wear my hair up, as I want to look fierce and intellectual, which is right for the part. Feel strangely confident and ready for probably the most important audition of my life.

Half an hour

Car arrives. Sadly not sweet David driving. But happily, new driver informs me, David has an audition courtesy of Brick. As we draw out of the driveway I spot a determined Mexican scrubbing the drive, where a suspicious brown stain that looks remarkably like blood is staining the stones and reputation of the Chateau. But right now I am an actress in Hollywood, on the way to an audition, and my priority is to concentrate on my lines rather than worry about being a witness to some random early morning shooting. We drive on.

Fifteen minutes

Approaching the audition, I allowed myself to dream. I had a strong psychic hunch that I was meant to play this part, but at the same time, logically, it was such a long shot. Besides, I remembered Diana's wisdom. About our possible futures, she had one phrase: 'It is written.' She believed our souls had already chosen our destinies, and that our lives were entirely preordained. I loved the thought because then I relinquished control and I hated it because I relinquished control.

Ten minutes

Staring out through the windows at the palm trees, I started to laugh. Last night's LA limo reading had taught me that perhaps I belonged here, as everything was controlled. Most of the palm trees, that quintessential emblem of LA, were in fact transplanted from the Sahara Desert in the city's early days. Somehow, that gave me permission to be a transplant too, an English actress, who was psychic, pretending to be an American writer. In reality, doing psychic readings was almost identical to acting, so it was not hard to prepare. I had to eliminate fear, listen to my inner voices, and trust. If I allowed logic to guide me in either art form, there would be no psychic readings and no acting performances, as both required a huge suspension of disbelief and immense faith. And logic would kill the magic of either. I closed my eyes and returned to Diana's wisdom: 'As a psychic, your prayer is to be of service, in whatever role you find yourself, doing readings, as an actress, or unemployed, pray to help others.' I prayed to be of service in the audition.

Five minutes to go

Waiting in lobby of super hip hotel the Standard. Forget being of service. New prayer is that all the beautiful girls lounging around the hotel lobby are Eurotrash, hanging out waiting for their rock-star boyfriends, and not stunning actresses in competition with me for the part. I resisted psychically snooping to find out, knowing that I would be breaking a psychic code: only ask for information for the greater good. This would slip into the lottery-ticket category, utterly self-serving. Final preparation. Imagining I was married, like the character, I slipped on my fake costume wedding ring.

Zero hours

Right, I'm ready to go. This is my big moment, the moment I have been waiting for. I stand up, close my eyes to say a last prayer, and quickly realise why people normally pray on their knees and not in silly shoes as I lose my balance and tip straight into a man walking past me. I clutch his arm to steady myself and find I am looking into the face of a breathtakingly beautiful man with black hair and blacker eyes, a face that's a cross between a bullfighter, a teddy bear and a god. Infinitely proud, entirely lovable and a whirlwind of power. 'That's the kind of man I want to marry' ticker-taped across my head as I clutched his arm. I knew I was smiling at him, because we were both caught in what looked and, more alarmingly, felt like an old-fashioned clinch. I managed to stand up straight, my face still kissing distance from his, and reluctantly removed my hand from his steadying arm, giving a throaty 'thank you' and a last flirty look as I turned on my high heels to disappear into the safety of the audition room. However, he caught my hand, tightly, smiled a smile full of his own sexy wickedness and amusement at the situation, and said, 'Hi, Lucinda.' Confused that he knew my name, I squinted and smiled back. Then, with growing horror, I realised that the man I was having this sexually charged moment with was in fact Al, the director I had come three thousand miles to meet for the part. Clearly I hadn't recognised him from the photo he'd tucked in the back of the script. He looked completely different up close, and, like a lot of movie stars, he was both better looking and smaller in real life. I rearranged my face into the best expression I could manage for actress meets director, rather than vamp flirts with stud, and managed a 'Lovely to finally meet you', but the full-on sexy feeling wasn't going anywhere. This was a total professional faux pas on my part, but Al, perhaps used to the effect he had on women, or perhaps just out of an innate kindness, gently pointed in the direction of the audition room. 'I came out to find you and bring you in.'

As I walked in, I felt him walking close behind me, so close I could smell his Eau Sauvage. I still felt a sort of psychic charge in the air, which, mixed with audition nerves, made me feel faint. I was bought down to earth by a sweaty palm pumping mine up and down. I stared at the kind of man who gives Hollywood a bad name. He was so oily he practically left a grease mark where he was standing. I christened him the Snake. Shelby, who I was delighted to see, was in complete professional mode and, indicating said grease ball glinting with gold, said, 'This is the producer.'

'How do you do?' I said politely.

'You're English,' said the Snake perceptively.

'Which is perfect for the part, because the role is almost British; she's from New England,' said Al as he indicated the chair he wanted me to sit on, in front of the camera. Then Al leant over, indicating where he wanted to start the scene.

'Let's just go from here ...' It crossed my mind that we both knew exactly where the scene was supposed to start from – the beginning – and I wondered if he had used the line as an excuse to lean over me. I ignored the thought and sat down in front of the camera. 'Let us know when you're ready,' said Shelby softly.

I took a deep breath. And froze. It was bad enough that I had just fallen in lust with the director, but, on one of the few days when I desperately needed to be focused on acting, worse was to come. I felt a bizarre psychic shiver and, to my horror, a Spirit voice started whispering to me! Transfixed, I listened as it whispered, 'You will live in America, in Hollywood ...' I realised for the first time ever I was being given predictions for my own life! It whispered, 'You will marry a writer who has been divorced three times ...' I must have had an alarmed look on my face, as I suddenly overheard Al whispering to the producer, 'Don't worry. She's preparing ...' And the interruption jolted me once again into the present. Which made me furious ... which luckily was exactly what the character was supposed to be feeling. In an irritated way, I nodded to Shelby that I was ready and, with no trouble at all, as the camera started rolling, I launched into the furious monologue. Al, to my surprise, was acting as well as directing and was reading the part of my husband. Which actually made it even easier for me to be in a rage, as it was he who had stopped my psychic voice. In the moment of reconciliation in the scene, he leant forward, touched me on the knee and stared intently at me. Suddenly, tears streamed down my face, deep, lost, soul tears, which I had stored up, probably for years, and which had chosen this perfect moment to appear. The scene was over. Al touched me on the knee again and said quietly, 'That was great.'

I stood up and the Snake uncoiled himself and stood up too. I took this as a good sign. Until he opened his mouth.

'You know, you should wear you hair down, it makes you look younger.'

He was looking at my photograph, where I looked very Renaissance woman with long red hair, and then looking back at me with my careful character-study hair up. I was speechless. This was the result of bearing my soul. Al was clearly mortified. But he smiled at the Snake in that conciliatory way that artists smile at the money and resolutely repeated, 'You did great.'

Shelby also sprang to the rescue. 'Yes, great job!' she said enthusiastically.

But the Snake carried on. 'The look of Kate is important,' he said, nodding to everyone. 'I think she's a blonde. And we are seeing a lot of models for the part ...' he left this hanging in the air. Any moment now I expected to be asked if I was prepared to have a nose job. 'We'll let you know ...' he said grandly.

Al walked me to the door. 'We'll let you know very soon, these are the call-backs, so you'll know in the next couple of days.'

Very formally we shook hands. And I walked out. That was it. Ten minutes. All of that preparation for ten minutes. I walked out into the sun. And I was a total wreck.

Thank God, the hip hotel had a cab rank. I jumped in the taxi and just sat there for a moment. For the second time that day, tears suddenly streamed down my face. I really didn't know exactly why. Relief at having done the audition, perhaps, mixed with a feeling of terrible sadness that maybe that was as far as I would go with a part I was in love with. What I didn't want to think about was that I might never see Al again. I had such a strange feeling of familiarity, the feeling of having picked up where we must have left off, in another time; a sort of karmic intensity that made me feel afraid for my heart. But it was ridiculous to be in love with a director with whom I had spoken exactly four words. I just sat there. The cabbie was obviously enjoying having the meter running and not moving, until he was honked at loudly.

'Where to?' he asked in a Russian accent.

'Anywhere you can walk on the streets,' I said.

'Melrose Avenue,' he smiled.

Before driving through LA I had actually thought people were exaggerating when they said, 'No one walks,' but they weren't. The streets looked like sets, devoid of walkers, and I desperately needed to feel lost in a crowd of people. No wonder everyone accused the Los Angelenos of being self-obsessed; most of them were stuck in cars all day with only their own company and none of the hustle of anonymous humanity to rub off against them.

I sat back in the cab and, wrenching off my ludicrously uncomfortable audition shoes, fell into my own self-obsessed moment. Once barefoot and out of pain, I tried to analyse what had just happened. I desperately wanted to do the part, and I wanted to work with Al. I just knew he was a brilliant director, and that was obviously what the attraction was about. Besides, the psychic voice had clearly said that I was going to marry a writer, and Al was a director. Now if I was going to live here ... I allowed myself a surge of excitement; that meant probably I would get the part. Why else would I live here? I totally trusted the Spirit voice, but I felt a psychic huff coming on. I needed more information. It was horrific to just get a tidbit, and I didn't want to be eyeing up every writer I met as a possible marriage candidate – the Writers' Guild needed to be protected. What I really needed were some more details from a fellow professional.

'Where do you want me to drop you?' interrupted the cabbie.

I looked out of the window and, for the first time, saw real people actually engaging in life and walking on the streets. I was at Melrose Avenue. The King's Road meets Carnaby Street. Tattoo parlours and shabby-chic stores. I got out and wildly overtipped the driver in confusion, as all the dollar notes are the same size and same colour. Then I looked up at where I was standing. Underneath a gigantic pink neon sign that flashed PSYCHIC. Clearly, it was just the sign I needed in every way, the answer to my prayers. I would get the clarity I sought from a fellow psychic. I walked up some shabby stairs to her office.

A girl in tears hurtled past me, and down the stairs. Before I could react to this, a surly Spanish man jerked his head in the direction of a grubby white plastic sofa: 'Wait here for my wife.' Unwittingly, I was now forced to watch what was what was clearly the crescendo moment of a Latin soap opera. I was not the only unhappy participant in this event. His two hungry toddlers were trying to get his attention by hurling small metal trucks at the grotesquely huge plasma TV, but the man swatted the missiles out of the way as he slurped on his supersize Coke and stared at the breasts of the soap star. The deaf-mute, big-breasted heroine of the soap (a Brazilian supermodel: no Spanish, only Portuguese, therefore deaf and dumb) was standing, silicone mouth open, as her Mexican mariachi lover galloped towards her atop his white stallion. Despite the staggering odds against him hoisting his love on to the horse – her gargantuan breasts a considerable handicap – she was nonetheless heaved off her feet by her lover, and we watched as, wobbling slightly, they galloped into the sunset. Forever searching for signs that referred to my own life, however obscure, I took this to mean that a *Playboy* model would get the part I was up for, but at least I would find love in the end. At that moment the woman who was going to help clarify exactly who that would be made her entrance. It was, in keeping with the rest of the day, not exactly what I had been expecting. She was straight out of Central Casting for a psychic. A scarf, hoop earrings, long nails, and wildly obese. I silenced my screaming doubts; the poor thing probably had a thyroid condition and did the whole costume thing for the tourists.

I followed into her dark den. Wasting no time, she grabbed my hands with her curly talons and growled with a very low, some might say demonic, voice.

'What do you do?'

Not a good sign. Starting with a question. I stifled the impulse to ask for my money back as she was supposed to tell me that and I replied, 'I'm an actress.'

I didn't want to be associated with her idea of psychic. I feared her costume was as near as she was going to get to being psychic. She confirmed my fear by fishing for information.

'So ... you live here, don't you?'

'No, I live in England.' I shook my head.

She lifted her finger to silence me. 'Wait ... I was about to tell you that ...'

I was beginning to feel annoyed. Then, suddenly, she looked excited. 'I feel something about your acting career ...' and then she blurted out, 'You are cursed!'

I'd been out of work for a couple of months, but I thought cursed was laying it on a bit. She was loving it.

'Bad spell on you. All you need is candles, it will go away, and you will be famous.'

I guess that was what people came to hear. I narrowed my eyes. I wondered what the price of fame was.

'How much are the candles?'

'Three hundred dollars each.'

I was staring at several very ordinary candles in glass jars that could not cost more that a couple of dollars each.

'You need three.'

I got up.

'Very bad luck if you leave, very very bad indeed. I was born with a veil over my head, a black veil, and I am genuine psychic and I can reverse your bad luck.'

I was about to lose my temper, and instead I practised the spiritual principle of containment. As my reward for containing my outrage, my energy that was about to explode went back inside me and I was granted a psychic flash of her life.

'Your son is standing in the corner of the room. He has a balloon for you.'

Without blinking, she said, 'Very true. Today is my son's birthday. You see him?'

A young boy who was in Spirit was standing in the corner of the room. I nodded.

'Does he have a message for me?'

'He died when he was sixteen … from drugs. He says you mustn't blame yourself.'

She nodded again, without emotion.

I carried on. 'He is here with you in the readings and he can help you.'

She looked down. She knew damn well the candles were a complete ruse and she was a crook. It was the before moment in *Ghost*, and she was Whoopi. However, this was real life, and I wanted to reprimand her. However, those in Spirit are rarely vengeful like that (unless they are in Hollywood horror films), and her son was no exception. He whispered to me, 'Don't judge her. That would be us playing God.' Then he showed me a final message for his mother. A big red heart and a cake with twenty candles.

'He loves you and says today he would be twenty.'

'Very true,' she said again. We were both aware that was about the only truthful exchange we had shared.

Then, looking at me, clearly not hearing Spirit voices, she pronounced, 'You should dye your hair blonde and get very skinny; they care about this over here.'

I got up. The compassionate, human part of me felt sorry for her, for the death of her child. And, in a way, I felt I had to respect the wishes of her dead child and not judge her. And however annoyed I was with her, the person I was most livid with was myself, for being such a mug.

As I walked out of the fake psychic's office, I almost tripped over a peroxide head bobbing up and down between two hands. It was the girl who had run out in front of me earlier, incapacitated by hysterical tears. She was still crying her eyes out. Instinctively I knelt down next to her.

'Are you OK?'

She looked up at me, her face streaked with cheap mascara.

'Goddamn bitch! I hate her. I paid her three thousand dollars.'

'What!' I shrieked. The poor girl had been fleeced. My attitude of compassion and transcendent spirituality came to a screeching halt. 'What happened?' I urged.

'I was an idiot. I bought candles after my last audition because she said I was cursed, and this time she did this ceremony to banish all negativity from my life. Then she ordered me to take her to my bank so I could give her more money. I refused … and she told me I'd die in a plane crash.'

I was absolutely livid. However sorry I was for her that her son had died, it didn't give her licence to be a thief and to be living proof of the reason most psychics had a bad name. I felt my urge for justice surfacing again.

'I'm not going to report it … so don't tell me to …' she said, reading my mind. 'I just feel like such an idiot …'

In an instant, even though she was a complete stranger, I knew I could help her.

'Listen to me,' I said, 'that woman is a crook, she's hurting people, and she tried the same trick on me. It's not your fault. She's in the wrong. And you are like a rape victim who doesn't want to report her because you blame yourself.'

Then, for the second time that day, I felt my psychic self start to overtake me.

'This comes from another time, this feeling of guilt, you know …' I started.

I realised the rape analogy I had given her was not accidental; I was already picking up secrets from her past. I had to gain her trust very fast, and, having just been to see the crap psychic myself, I knew it would look odd if I suddenly announced I was psychic. How would I explain that I been duped too? If I were a genuine psychic I would have steered clear. I didn't want to get into a long story about my psychic blind spot, that I could help others but not myself, so I edited the truth. I didn't want to admit that I was also a desperate actress waiting to hear about a part, who that morning had met a man who I thought could be my soulmate. But if I doubted my own psychic hunches, that probably wouldn't fill her with confidence. So instead, I lowered my voice and told her a different truth, but still a truth, I rationalised to myself.

'I'm actually a psychic myself. I've worked on a couple of police cases, and I'm here to find out who the fakes are.'

'Really?' she said.

I nodded, feeling slightly duplicitous.

'At least you had a good reason for seeing her. I'm an actress and I just want to be told I'm going to make it,' she said. 'Not good karmic brownie points, right?'

I wanted to move on pronto from her admission as it was a little near the bone. At this point I felt so ashamed of myself I knew only an action of selflessness would realign me. 'Do you want a quick message from Spirit?' I asked, sitting down on the pavement next to her.

She nodded without saying anything. I started to take dictation from the helpful voices around me.

'They say you are not safe doing your "hands-on healing" work, your massages at home,' I said pointedly.

'I think it's all right,' she said, suddenly sulky. 'It pays the rent.'

'They say it's harmful to you.'

With a flash, I saw her as a small child being beaten viciously by her father, who was drunk, and then horrifically sexually molested in a small room in the Midwest.

I asked Spirit, 'Is it OK to show her this?'

'Yes,' came the answer.

This was the root and cause of her victimhood. 'You've had to survive a lot as a child, when you were living in that white house in the Midwest.'

I knew tiny details like this reassured her I wasn't a fraud. Her face crumpled up. She looked at me with the pain of a tormented child. Now she could tell I knew what had happened to her, Spirit had spared her having to relive the details by just giving the geographical evidence. Then Spirit flash-forwarded her life and I saw her unconscious on the floor, in a palatial apartment, older now, twenty-two or so, but still younger than she actually was now, which was about twenty-eight. A man, also drunk, was walking away, a wedding ring on his finger that I could see matched hers at the time.

'You were married before.'

'How do you know that?' she exclaimed.

'And he was very cruel to you.'

Her eyes glazed over and had a strange, far-off look in them. Then she went 'spiritual' to deal with the pain. She parroted, as though she'd learnt it in a book: 'Yes, it was all part of my life's lessons and I believed I'd been married to him before, and it was all just karma.'

Oh dear. I recognised this way of dealing with things. She was like me before meeting Diana. Doing her best but actually deluding herself about mad relationships. She was transcending before transforming, a pitfall I knew very well, having fallen into it with a thud several times myself. And I was willing to bet that the Hollywood dream of happy-ever-after was her panacea against pain.

Spirit tied the pieces of her life together in a clear way. 'You were very badly hurt as a child, physically beaten. The pattern repeated with your husband. He raped you. They say you are now trapped in a cycle and need to do emotional work as well as the spiritual work to change.'

She said nothing.

'Spirit says you cannot transcend this pain without feeling it first. Bodywork will help you get in touch with the pain.'

'Do I do that with my massages?' she said flatly. I was shown a picture of her giving hand-jobs to exploitative executives who were stringing her along with promises of parts.

'No, not the massages you give. They are causing you emotional pain. You need massages for you.'

'If I could afford massages for me I'd be fine.'

'You will be able to,' I said with great certainty. 'You will get out of the financial trouble you are in. It involves moving and changing cars.'

I paused.

She cast her eyes down and whispered to me, 'I'm in such debt. I can't afford anything, my apartment, my car – I don't know what I'm going to do. I've left everything to come here and make it in Hollywood. I don't even have an agent, no one wants me, I even thought I'd found my soulmate and that he would ... help me.'

I could psychically see that said 'soulmate' was a struggling actor, deep in therapy and busy rescuing himself before he could rescue her. I relayed this and she acknowledged it with a painful nod.

'I think I have the answer. I've been saving for months to make the trip to India.' She opened her wallet, showing me a photograph of an infamous man, an Indian guru who had been publicly served with several writs for paedophilia. Again repeating the cycle, she was attracted to a saviour who wasn't. Then I heard something beautiful from Spirit, so much greater than my petty mind's judgemental way of seeing it.

'Your devotion has been noticed. Even if you love a charlatan, your love, the love you've given, has magic and healing in it for you.'

'Is Hollywood the right place for me?' she asked with desperation.

To my surprise, I heard, 'Yes, it is.'

'I want to end there,' she said suddenly, 'on some hope. I visualise every day that I am going to be a success, you know, a superstar diva millionairess. And I will be.' She was determined. 'And I need to stay positive. I don't want to get all negative and think about the past.'

She had fallen into the classic trap sprung by the Shadow to defend itself: the Shadow was 'unspiritual'. 'Spiritual', to her, was light, fluffy, twinkly and always positive. It had the obligatory happy-ever-after filled with endless visualisations of wealth beyond compare, and an Oscar. I had a feeling I was going to come across a lot of this in Hollywood. The blonde picked herself up from the floor and said, 'How much do I owe you?'

'What?'

'For the reading.'

'No, no. You don't owe me anything. This was a gift.'

Her red painted mouth fell open. Looking at her for the first time, and seeing her face not contorted in pain, she was actually remarkably attractive.

'Wow. That's rad. I guess not all psychics are crooks then.'

That was worth doing the reading for.

'I'll pay you back somehow, I promise. I'm Astrid, by the way.'

Funny, it was that weird thing about being a psychic. I knew her entire past history of sexual abuse and emotional neglect, yet last of all her name.

'Here's my number, if you ever need any help,' and she handed me a scrawl on the back of a sushi menu. Highly unlikely as I thought that was, I took her number and spontaneously gave her mine. Then she jumped into her banged-up custard-coloured Beetle, *circa* 1972.

'Do you want a ride? I could show you the coolest part of Melrose?'

'Why not,' I said, and following my gut I jumped into the car with out-there Astrid.

Astrid was almost apologetic. 'I have to go to my waitress shift, otherwise I'd hang with you ...'

As we drove along, it was obvious to both of us that we'd already skipped the getting-to-know-you phase, trying to make polite chit-chat felt daft, so we continued soul-sharing.

'What do you think is the most important thing I should do to be more spiritual, so I don't get conned again?' she asked earnestly. Privately, I was thinking how ridiculous it was to be giving advice to Astrid which I had failed to follow myself; after all, I had ended up with the fake psychic for the same reasons she had. However, because of 'the gift', I had been cast in the role of spiritual mentor; my own inability to walk the talk was irrelevant to her. This made me sort of sad and a little lonely.

Then I told myself to be grateful. Even if I was a personal mess, I could at least help others. That was what I ought to remember.

'Listen to your instincts. Dare to look at the dark. And most importantly, tell the truth.'

'What do you mean?'

'You're an actress, right. Play the part of a truth-teller.' I knew I was telling her that because I could feel how much she had had to lie in her life.

'Yes ... I am an actress,' she said uncertainly. There was an uncomfortable pause, then she fessed up. 'Well, the truth is I was a model, and I've done a couple of workshops with casting directors. And I did a commercial. I don't have my Screen Actors' Guild card yet, but I will soon because there's a producer who wants me in his movie. And I have a script that a friend wrote whose trainer knows Brad Pitt's gardener, and if he agrees to do it then I'm going to play the part.'

She took another breath. 'That's the truth I tell most people, the "Hollywood" version. But here's the real truth:

'Basically, a couple of producers want to fuck me and in return I could take my top off and get my Guild card. And the Brad Pitt thing's just a dream. And I'm not a waitress; I'm lap-dancing in Long Beach to pay the rent.' She started to laugh.

'I actually feel better! My life's a fucking disaster but at least I'm not pretending. What about you?'

What a relief – now I could practise what I preached.

'Basically, although I'm a psychic I'm an actress too. I was put on tape for an audition this morning and I felt like a big fat ugly cow compared to all the models, and I think I fell in love with the director, who's probably mad or terminally ill if my past is anything to go by. And the reason I was seeing that fucking crap psychic was because I wanted to know if I was going to get the part, because I don't trust myself psychically even though I can see for others.'

'Police cases?' Astrid managed to let out between gulps of laughter.

'Actually, that bit was true.' For some unknown reason she found that hysterical.

I looked at out-there Astrid at that moment, who was howling with laughter, and that was the moment we knew we were going to be friends. I also knew it was the last time I would ever let her drive me anywhere again. She was the most shocking driver and we lurched to the curb.

'You need New Age retail therapy at the psychic mall. Aunt Vi's is the key to success. I got a part because I bought a bottle called "wish fulfilment", and whenever I felt nervous I just kept spraying and praying. I promise you that's why I got the part.'

'I guess it had nothing to do with the audition ...' I said teasingly.

'You may laugh, but what do you have to lose? You're not in London now; do it the LA way. There are thousands of actresses here, and a ton of negativity; you don't want to buy into all of that shit ... I'm telling you, on some level we're all telepathically linked; you want to only be emitting positive thoughts.'

I couldn't resist letting out an 'Om ...'

'Om away, baby ... and get that bottle, even if you only do it for me ...'

'Are you on commission?'

'I'm on the lookout for your soul. You looked out for mine, this is fun, and honestly it'll take your mind off waiting to hear for a while. And spraying has less calories than chocolate, which I bet is the other alternative.'

I kissed her goodbye, and over her shoulder, I saw a sign advertising psychic palmistry outside the shop. Astrid spotted me spotting the sign.

'Step away from the psychics!' she said, beeping wildly and flicking off a hapless rollerblader who clearly had the right of way. With a fruity 'Motherfucker!' aimed at the six-pack rollerblader, she turned and grinned goodbye at me, almost mowing down another innocent pedestrian and his poodle.

Now it was Hollywood retail time. And clearly time for a glittery G-string, I thought, catching sight of a fun clothes shop with pieces of string for underwear. A bag full of sparkly flip-flops, yoga pants (I was getting the lingo down – pants not trousers) and an oversize pair of rock star sunglasses later and I was feeling quite zippy. Now I had the LA look down pat, Vegas meets ashram – if I was going to stay in Hollywood I had to start with my outsides, like everyone else. I was almost a Los Angeleno bar the fact I was a redhead with a normal nose and an Italian figure.

Giddy with excitement, I lugged my new wardrobe off to Astrid's recommendation, Aunt Vi's Garden. As with most things in Hollywood, you didn't know quite what to expect. It was, of course, not a garden, and there was no aunt to be seen – only the ubiquitous stunningly beautiful ex-model, Miranda, presiding over her tiny New Age kingdom, a store filled with 108 jewel-coloured bottles glittering in the early afternoon sun. They were filled with scented coloured oils in very vogue combinations of surprising hot pink and tropical orange, or muted violet with the palest of blues. Interestingly, I read that a woman who went completely blind had created the bottles. I crossed my fingers this was not the dire consequence of meddling with the dark side. However, the bottles not only looked beautiful, they felt healing, everything to do with light and love and nothing to do with dark and hate. In case I needed further evidence of being in the right place, I could actually see, glittering in the sun, the bright-blue spirit lights that often appear to me when I am in the presence of a very healing place or person.

After all, this is where Julia Roberts has bought skin creams. I wondered whether, if I anointed myself in the bath with the magic wish-fulfillment bottle, I could not only get the part but like Julia in *Pretty Woman*, drive off into the sunset with my everlasting love and prince. Then I spotted the sprays Astrid had been talking about. They were called 'aura' sprays. Now some cynics might, upon first glance, think that the aura sprays were very expensive bottles of coloured water, at best appealing to the whimsy in us and at worst ripping us off with promises they couldn't keep. However, Miranda assured me that the bottles offered 'vibrational healing' and, to be totally honest, they looked so aesthetically beautiful that I wanted just to stare at them as objects of glory. And if I didn't buy one, I rationalised, I would blame myself if I failed to get the part. Clearly buying the bottle belonged on the list of 'doing everything I could.' Yup, I *needed* the magic bottle – desperately!

A harassed LA type barging into the store obviously thought the same. Miranda mouthed, 'Look out, it's suicidal Susie,' to me, clearly to warn that we were going to be dealing with one of those borderline personalities that are sadly so frequently to be found in New Age stores. She was a classic LA combo, anorexic and bottle-blonde. Miranda managed a polite smile; Susie countered with a hostile sigh.

'How's it going, Susie?' Miranda chirped.

'Not good. I have nine unsold scripts.' Ahh. My first view of the frustrated Hollywood artist.

'Have you tried the LA bottle? My customers nickname it the "wish fulfilment" bottle.' Miranda went into her pitch. Alarmingly, I realised this was the bottle Astrid had been raving about to me.

'The LA bottle is a fabulous aquamarine blue, the "colour of communication", because it opens your throat chakra. Perfect to seal deals.' Or get parts, I thought to myself.

Suicidal Susie grabbed it as if it was the last whisky at closing time and declared, 'This motherfucker better get me a deal,' before stropping out, streaking her neck with aquamarine oil. Watching her go, I learnt three things. One, why the hell wasn't I quicker off the mark? Susie had probably taken the last bottle. Two, clearly a lot of people in LA were barking, and I seemed to belong here. Three, I had a psychic hunch that her unsold scripts were not the real cause of Susie's misery, and psychically tuning in I started to pick up on the hidden cause. But as she was already halfway down the street, I guessed I was let off doing another spontaneous reading. But suicidal Susie was not to live up to her name today, and miraculously she reappeared. 'I forgot to pay … it's easy when you're broke,' she snarled, reluctantly shelling out. I wondered whether to butt in and see if I could help her. Then Spirit presented the perfect opportunity. Susie pulled out her astrology chart, shoved it at Miranda and demanded, 'You do readings. Can you see anything? Will I get this deal?' Did everyone in LA do readings? I wondered. Miranda shook her head politely. 'I just read the bottles,' she said dismissively. I couldn't resist. I didn't want to unmask as a fully-fledged psychic, especially with someone so scarily edgy and needy, so I said casually, 'I used to work in an astrology shop. I can tell you what I see.'

Susie almost had an orgasm with delight. Clearly, everyone in LA loved readings, and there seemed to be no bad time for them; in the back of a limo, in an audition, on a street corner; Spirit bombarded me when I was here. I'd make this one fun and easy. I stood at the counter and stared at her chart. I didn't let on that I wasn't looking at the glyphs and hieroglyphs that represented her planets and signs (which I did actually know how to decipher from my secret esoteric studies at school), because in her case, Spirit was overriding those clues, by super-imposing a misty picture of a dog over her chart. I started taking Spirit dictation: 'You had a dog, a Saint Bernard.'

I looked up to see suicidal Susie sobbing. 'Yes …' Now I was confused; she was sobbing as though her dog was dead. Miranda, meanwhile, was quietly squirting the store with the white purification spray and simultaneously offering Susie some homeopathic rescue remedy. Susie was sobbing too loudly and enthusiastically to notice.

'The dog is sad,' I said, feeling a broken-hearted St Bernard … but he was not dead. Spirit was giving messages very simply, like a small child.

'He misses you,' I went on. Now it was becoming clear to me what had happened. 'You gave him away.'

Susie doubled up and was collapsed on the bench. Clearly, she was mistaking the store for her therapist's couch, as she started repeating very fast, 'I'm sorry, I'm sorry …' Then she confessed: 'I thought I was going to kill myself!'

Miranda mouthed to me, 'Suicidal Susie.' Clearly this was common knowledge and certainly not her first admission.

Susie finished her confession, 'So I gave my dog away.'

However over-the-top suicidal Susie was, I actually felt sorry for her.

'She was a puppy and I couldn't cope ...' Now I didn't feel so sorry for her, as I psychically received more of the story.

'You never said goodbye to her.'

'I didn't!' she wailed.

'She's waiting for you to say goodbye so she can feel she belongs to the new family you gave her to,' I finished.

'I promise I will,' said Susie, filled with remorse. Then she stared at me, suddenly suspicious.

'Where the hell does it say all of that in the chart?' she said, pointing to the piece of paper I was supposedly studying to give her astrological reading. I got flustered.

'I see things ...' I started, but before I could finish she was accusing me.

'Brett told you! He put you up to this!'

I looked puzzled.

'Fuck you!' she screamed. 'I'll get my lawyer on you for harassing me, just because he wanted the dog, and I gave it away because I couldn't cope because he was fucking his secretary. I was abused by him ... and now you come laying some guilt trip on me ... Tell him fuck you from me!'

Staring at the slammed shop door, I muttered, 'Did I miss something?' Miranda, clearly used to suicidal Susie's outbursts, clarified for me.

'She's in the middle of a divorce and her ex keeps laying traps for her to prove she's nuts, some weirdness over the pre-nup.' The pre-nup was of course familiar to me from all those *LA Law* episodes where unscrupulous blondes married rich magnates and were forced to sign agreements to keep their paws off the spoils if their love went sour. Interestingly, the mere fact of signing a pre-nup, statistically, meant the marriage had a much smaller chance of survival, but I was to learn that in LA it was standard practice.

'She's in therapy too,' said Miranda. I was also to discover that in LA this was used as an excuse for bizarre antisocial outbursts I wasn't quite sure how to respond to.

'She does seem a trifle unbalanced,' I said.

Miranda nodded. 'She'll work through it.' Hopefully not with complete strangers in shops, I thought to myself cynically.

Looking at the aura soma bottles I realised I had resorted to being very British and was trying to pretend that an emotional scene had not erupted in the store. Actually, I felt incredibly guilty that it was my fault for interfering in the first place.

Miranda could see I was upset. 'Don't be phased by her, her day job's in the Pilates studio down the street so she's in here every day, and she's always blaming someone and screaming. And by the way, you're dead on about the dog; she just dumped it to get back at the ex because he was going to come and claim it.' Any spiritual precept of not hating anyone and loving one and all goes out of the window any time I hear of cruelty to animals, most especially dogs. How could anyone abandon a dog, however difficult their circumstances?

'You're waiting to hear about a part, aren't you?'

'Are you psychic?' I said enthusiastically.

'No, you've just got that look,' said Miranda perceptively. 'Listen, I know she was a bit dramatic, but I actually think you helped Susie. She's been complaining she hasn't cried for years ...'

'Oh dear, and I helped her sob uncontrollably.'

'It's good though, isn't it?' said Miranda wisely. 'It releases stress.' At least here was someone who wasn't inanely positive and respected true emotions. Then she handed me the LA bottle: 'Have it as a present. You look like you need it, and it was kind of you to try and help Susie.'

I bounced out of the shop and foolishly decided to walk back to the hotel.

Lost and blistered, I eventually found the hotel. I was so exhausted after my overwhelmingly exciting and intense day that I collapsed on the bed and fell fast asleep. But because of the jet lag, I woke up at 3 a.m. I was so anxious I couldn't get back to sleep. The man behind the desk looked at me knowingly.

'Waiting to hear about a part?' I nodded. The place was full of actors. 'I'll just check again in case anything came in.' He looked puzzled. 'You've got three messages here from Brick, asking to call him urgently. Nothing on voicemail?'

'I was too embarrassed to ask how to work it; I'm afraid I was defeated by the technology.'

'Brit, right?' I smiled. 'It's OK to ask for help, you know, it's not rude. We know you used to rule the world, but if you need a hand ...' I laughed. He deciphered the phone system for me and I ran back to my room.

Annoyingly, I had all these messages from complete strangers, asking for readings. They were friends of Shelby's and Astrid's and were eagerly asking me for my rates. Finally, I came to the message I was waiting for; the reason I'd come to Hollywood. Brick's message.

'Wanted to tell you personally, kid, but you're obviously out there causing another traffic accident. But hey, listen, they're offering you the part, seems the director's fought for you. Call me tomorrow and we'll talk about the money. I'll get you a great deal. Well done, kid.'

Dear Jimminy

Before 3 a.m., I hated Hollywood. It's all the stuff we feared. Fake blondes, fake tits, weird names like Astrid and Apple, agent's a nut, psychic's crap, and have been screamed at by a complete stranger believing she was in therapy as I was indulging in retail therapy. But ... wait for it ... five minutes ago I found out I GOT THE PART!!!!! I LOVE Hollywood now. I think the silicone women should be seen more as performance artists, don't you? And I love the sun, the swimming pools; everyone's in the business, don't feel like a freak; everyone loves psychics (did FIVE readings today!!); and despite weird first day have such a sense that anything is possible over here ...

Other BIG news is I met a great guy who appears to be single (he thinks I'm married, but I'll tell him tomorrow I'm not) and he is the director of the movie (which is a bit tacky, I think), and I heard a psychic voice tell me I was going to marry a writer (and he's not one) ... Oh dear, writing this to you maybe guy thing not going so great ... but I have the part!! More news tomorrow, how goes life with you?

Will be here a couple of months, why don't you come and stay?

All love, Lucinda

PS Don't worry about me. Meeting Al (the sexy director) again tomorrow. I'll keep you posted ...

3
Satellites

I realised it was my professional duty, as an actress, to look fabulous for my meeting with the director. (Nothing to do with how I felt about him personally, of course …) But trying on the results of yesterday's shopping expedition – yoga pants and little sparkly vest – I looked decidedly late Elvis – glittery but tubby. So I erred on the side of the East Coast writer look and trussed myself up in my sexy Vivienne Westwood tweed suit.

'Aren't you hot in all that?' asked Al curiously.

'No, no,' I lied, positively baking.

The open top of Al's BMW prevented long conversations. He had promised me the diner was only a couple of minutes away, so while he hummed along to Sounds Eclectic on the radio I tuned in psychically, but heard absolutely nothing – either because I was so attracted to him, or because he was taking the curves so fast that Spirits were left behind. So I resorted to more mundane methods, sneaking a peek at his ring finger (bare) and looking for traces of a female in his car (chocolate wrappers), finding nothing. By the time we pulled into the parking lot of the trendy café – 'the last cappuccino before the 101' – I was sure he was single. But not a writer, I reminded myself.

We walked into the hip diner and everyone turned around to stare at us, as if we were somebody, then as soon as they realised we weren't famous they returned to their skinny lattes. This, I would come to learn, was standard Hollywood behaviour: everyone craning to see who had just come in and, if they were famous, wondering how they could slip their scripts to them. Looking around the café, I realised it was entirely populated by people who could lounge around in jeans on a weekday at teatime and call it work. Guys in hip glasses pitching their ideas to eagerly attentive girls. Clearly we were not the only director-actress combo in the room. But Al was definitely the best-looking of all the directors in the place. He had that red-blooded Italian-American thing going on. Black hair. Pacino eyes. Walking behind him to our booth, I mused that men in England just didn't have that way with jeans, the American swagger and easiness of being. I even allowed myself a moment of smugness as I sauntered to our seats. I may have been the daft Brit wearing a silly suit that I was sweltering in, but I was also the English chick who was starring in a movie directed by an American hunk.

'So, you feel confident about the part?' he asked as we sat down in a red leather booth. The Beach Boys hummed along in the background, courtesy of an original 1950s jukebox. It was very Hollywood indeed. A waitress who could have won Miss World plopped two coffees down. I fought feelings of insecurity and promptly decided that fake breasts couldn't compete with real.

'I guess so,' I said, stirring my coffee a little too vigorously and idly wondering if you could read coffee foam as easily as tea leaves.

'Well, you really were the best actor for the part.'

'Did the producer think so?' I asked cheekily, knowing full well the Snake didn't get me at all.

'Well ... the producer was rather keen on the blonde who came in after you, but I vetoed her after she read.'

'Because ...'

'You know the line where you're talking about the Renaissance and how you love Italy?'

I nodded.

'She asked me whereabouts in Italy the Renaissance was.'

Although I was listening and laughing in all the right places, I found it hard to concentrate. I had never wanted to lean over a table and kiss or be kissed so much. An internal battle began: this was a professional relationship, he was the director and I was the actress, I couldn't afford to fuck this up. But I kept seeing his left eye locked on my left eye as his mouth came close to mine – no, no, I'm not going to blow this thing ... I had to force myself to think of mantras. Al was finishing up his story. He was making a great effort to make me feel comfortable, and succeeding, and I was making a great effort to look attentive and professional.

'I told the producer we also needed someone who really understood the character, someone who the audience believed was really smart. And you're English, and like most Americans, he automatically felt intellectually inferior when he heard your British accent so he went along with that.'

I laughed.

'Of course, you're married, so that was factored, in his mind, into you getting the part. Where's you ring today, by the way?' he asked, with a frown – and, possibly, I imagined, the faintest degree of hope.

'Oh, I went swimming ...' I lied, 'and took it off.'

My mind was racing horribly. They had given me the part because I was married, or they thought I was, because of the ring I wore, but it was a fake wedding ring, it was my costume ring, which had helped convince me I was married. If I confessed then ... I could lose the part because the Snake obviously wanted a real blonde babe, and Al had convinced him to cast me partly because I was married. If I took away any slender reason for them giving me the part then, God forbid ... On and on my mind went, as Al kept talking and looking at me; and I kept smiling and looking at him, and I kept dreaming of love and babies and a life with him in the City of Angels and he kept seeing shots and character development and perhaps me? NO. Get a grip, Lucinda. Spirit had definitely said a writer, remember.

'I'm really glad you're going to do this. When I first saw your photograph, I just had a feeling you would end up playing the part. You know those sorts of feelings, almost like a premonition ...'

'I do,' I said, suddenly serious.

Still staring at me, he asked, 'Do you ever have them?'

I was finding it a little hard to concentrate as I felt turned on just by the way he was looking at me.

'Are you a Scorpio?' I asked suddenly.

He laughed, breaking the intensity of the moment. 'I am. Very good.'

'I have my little psychic moments,' I said casually. Then, absolutely seriously and for no reason I could fathom, I blurted out what I had heard in the audition room.

'I had a premonition not long ago that I would end up living in the States, being with my soulmate, who I think is a writer, and we would work together.' As soon as I said it, I felt bizarrely vulnerable.

'Interesting. That's actually my dream. To live and work with my soulmate. But I thought you were married; you didn't sound like you meant your husband when you said your soulmate.' His black Scorpio eyes were staring at me again. Oops. Big fuck-up. Forgot I was pretending to be married for the sake of the part.

'I am married, just we're going through a bit of a rough time. He … he thinks he's gay.' Christ, why had I said that? I was supposed to be a spiritual person with psychic insights, but I guess I was in the landmine area of my love life. Luckily, Al seemed to have a bizarre response.

'He's British, right? I can never tell with them, who's gay and who isn't. They're all so funny, right?'

He was doing his best to get out of an awkward situation by making a joke, but this was getting seriously out of hand. I had just lied to the director for the second time. I realised the gay part had come out because the only believable person who could be my husband was of course Jimminy.

'Enough about me,' I said, a trifle hastily, 'let's keep talking about the part.'

So we did. And we talked about Italy, Spirits, grandparents, dreams, we talked about how much we both loved dogs, he showed me a picture of Lupe, his wolf husky. We talked and talked until they closed the café. He went to the bathroom, and I couldn't resist sneaking a peek at his leftover cappuccino foam. I saw a ring. Clearly a message from Spirit to stop telling porkies about being married. When he dropped me off at the Chateau Marmont, I ran into the hotel so as not to turn the incredibly obvious frisson turn into an inevitable kiss. I was after all a married woman, albeit to a fictional gay husband.

That night I had a great dream. I dreamt I was flying through the sky, like Icarus, dangerously near to the sun. Except it wasn't the sun, it was a gigantic star. Like the moon, you could make out a face on the star and it looked like Julia Roberts. All around the Julia star were little satellites, and all the satellites had faces too. Faces I didn't recognise, but they were orbiting the star. Then I realised I was in fact a shooting star, and with a human shriek I fell to earth and landed with a loud bang. I noticed I had landed in a garden and Al was digging what was either a grave or a bed of roses, I couldn't quite see. I woke up feeling thoroughly disconcerted and confused. And fuck, I was late.

I ran out and straight into my delivered-to-the-door rental car – a bug, chosen because I was intimidated by the oversized monstrosities most people drove, and besides, who wouldn't chose a car that had a built-in vase for flowers?

The satellite navigation was totally useless in my hands and I resorted to the age-old method of finding your way.

'Astrid, I'm totally lost!' I yelped. Balancing my cell in one hand, I tipped out my make-up bag, where Brick's card nestled among the old mascara. I could hear her flicking through the Thomas Guide.

'By the way,' she said, 'I started seeing someone and I think it's the real thing.'

'Really? Who is it?'

'A therapist. More real than giving blow-jobs in studio parking lots – my old use of my spare time. She's encouraging me to tell the truth and write down my dreams and it's really freeing me up.'

'I can hear that. God, I had a weird dream last night, about satellites revolving around a star.'

'I don't think you need to pay her to have that one analysed, that's the first rung of Hollywood society. New name for entourage. I like it. Satellites.'

Before we could get into her sessions she found the page number on the Thomas Guide. She told me how to get there and how to behave.

'Don't allow yourself to be bullied. Remember, agents work for us,' Astrid said in that assertive American way. 'You have the power, not him.' Was Astrid reading my mind? I was feeling very nervous about meeting with a powerful agent at a top agency to discuss my acting career. But I would be breezy and authorative like Astrid. This would be the first of many great deals. I puffed myself up: I would get what I wanted; I would not be bullied.

My self-confidence took a dive as it took me an age to find the right office and it was hard to miss. An enormous building made of glass – like the entertainment mother ship. Once in the lobby, the vibe was downright sinister; I even noticed there was a particularly nasty painting of grey and black blobs that if you squinted, distinctly resembled a girl with a knife in her back. Not a great omen. The receptionist told me to wait on the leather sofa next to a pile of *Hollywood Reporter* and *Variety* magazines. These things depressed me: they were all film-as-business, with endless weekend opening numbers and which executive was moving where. Then various actresses were ranked – not encouraging for a British theatre actress. It was like sneaking a peek backstage after a transcendent production of *Romeo and Juliet* and hearing Juliet bitching about her wages.

After a good fifteen minutes, Brick was ready to see me. He was wearing a royal blue shirt of the type so beloved of agents in

Hollywood, along with the ubiquitous earpiece and a Blackberry poking out of his pocket. Not the piece of fruit, of course, but the up-to-date machine that meant he could be contacted wherever he was. In England, we can get a beat on people pretty fast – accent, clothes, name – but here … I mean how do you react to a guy called Brick? I realised I needed my psychic perceptions more than ever.

'Great to meet you again … Lizinder.'

This, I was to learn, was the standard way my name was going to be pronounced, so I went with it. Hell, I'd already met Astrid and suicidal Susie; Brick was almost normal in comparison.

'So …' he said, sizing me up. 'Once you've done this movie you'd be great at playing young mothers.'

'Right,' I said, feeling vaguely disconcerted and knowing how positive and plentiful the young mother archetype was on film.

Then, ushering me into his office, he barked, 'Great. Great. You got the part. And it's a great script. Great script.' Clearly it was very Hollywood to repeat everything, almost as if you were trying different line readings.

'Great writer.' He nodded like a bulldog. He actually looked a bit like bulldog: determined and jowly. 'Great writer.'

By now I was intrigued: this could be the writer my psychic voice had warned me about, the guy I was supposed to meet and marry. 'What's he like?' I asked, trying to disguise my eagerness with a professional tone of voice.

'It's a she. Lives in Montana. She's the real thing. A recluse. Black. Feminist. Done lots of theatre.'

Unless Spirit was proposing a lesbian liaison she was out as a marriage partner.

He sized me up. 'You're a Brit, right?'

I nodded, wondering where this non sequitur was leading.

'You'd be great in a room. Great in a room.' Wonderful. I now had a dual purpose: I could play young mothers *and* amuse executives in meetings, which is what I guessed 'great in a room' meant. At this point I noticed a faint white line of powder under his nose. His eyeballs previously small pinpricks, were now disappearing and he was gabbling.

'I need to feng shui my office,' he said, as if his life depended on it. I was nonplused as to how the cocained chemicals in his brain had leapt from Brit in a room to Chinese room designing, or feng shui.

'I'm sorry. I think I'm losing you ...' I said, utterly confused.

Then it all became horribly clear.

'Listen kid, the chauffeur told me you were a psychic. Apparently, the reason we had an accident is because you were chatting to his dead grandmother. You need to work your magic now.'

I tried clarifying. 'I am psychic, but that's a teensy bit different from feng shui.'

Brick was not to be put off.

'But you can help me, can't you?'

In a moment of inspiration, I decided I was being churlish. How wonderful that an agent, a top agent at that, wanted to be spiritual; who was I to dissuade him from dipping his toes into spiritual water? On the contrary, I was here to be of service.

'I'll do my best,' I said valiantly, 'although this isn't really my area of expertise.' Diana would be proud of me for rising to the challenge.

'So how would we begin?' he asked gamely.

'Well, from what I know, we'd need to harmonise the energies and create a vibration of high success and prosperity, but most importantly we'd have to get rid of any poison arrows. Poison arrows are sharp angles in the room, which create harmful, poisonous, destructive and negative energy.'

I was getting into the Hollywood thing – why one adjective when four are better?

He looked at me, seemingly impressed.

Brick sniffed and rubbed his hands together with glee. Then he leant forward and said, 'Listen, I wanna fuck up those sons of bitches.' He rammed the point home. 'Do whatever you have to do. Those goddamn poison arrows? Don't get rid of them, OK. Just point them into the office next door, and send some across the hall too.'

'Why I would want to do that?

He looked at me and replied calmly. 'To help me be the best. I repeat. Make me your best poison arrows and send them in there.'

Then he got up, indicated his rivals' offices, and said 'Fuckers' in an even tone. Clearly he was under the impression that feng shui was some sort of voodoo and was hoping for some black magic.

I gathered together my psychic integrity. 'I can tell you that the point of feng shui is actually not to make poisonous arrows and create discord. It obviously goes against spiritual laws. The point is to rearrange the energies to create peace and harmonise everything.'

It was as if I hadn't spoken.

'You can do it for me, can't you? You're psychic, right, some kind of witch?'

This was turning into a full-on disaster. I had to try and dissuade him. I managed, 'I can find you a feng shui practitioner … but I don't think they'll want to …'

He cut me off.

'How much?'

'I believe you pay three hundred dollars an hour,' I said, just to put him off.

'That's expensive for a furniture mover. I can get a Mexican to do that for ten bucks.'

'Well, you're not necessarily moving the furniture physically; it's about energy forces.'

Then he said, 'Well, we'll just force those fuckers energetically to fail. I want the arrows pointing at them because I'm the best.' And he actually went into his wallet and started fingering hundred dollar bills. I sat there, totally horrified. 'I am going to fuck up the competition.' Just in case I hadn't got that part earlier. Then he laid out four hundred dollars on his desk.

'You want me to do your contract right ... so just do something to help me.' This was said as if it was the most natural request in the world. 'We have to help each other.'

I stared into the faces of various world-famous actors behind him, some holding Oscars, and I had to admit to my innermost self that I was totally and utterly flummoxed. For a moment Brick disappeared and my mind, in awe of the man and the situation, began to analyse it all. It was really extraordinary to see how powerful people a) thought they could buy anything and b) had spent so much time acquiring material wealth that they didn't know the first thing about spiritual laws. What was also bizarre was that I was an unknown actress, a minion in comparison to his clients, but because he was in awe of psychic powers, he had turned me into the power-player in this game. The fact was, I really wanted him to do my contract as an actress because I knew he was one of the best, I was cornered in a Faustian trap. In a magnificent move – clearly years of making deals made him an expert – he felt I was going to reject his offer before I could have the satisfaction of doing so, he tucked the money away back into his wallet.

'Just joking with you, kid!'

But he wasn't.

Then, with a smile, he said, 'You're staying at the Chateau, right?'

I nodded.

'Get them to call me. I'll cut a great deal for you.'

I knew our meeting was over. As I left he shouted, 'And next time you come in we'll do the entire office.'

And that was it. Apparently, that was the deal. I had a contract and a new power agent to 'cut me a great deal', as long as I became his personal 'Merlin gone to the dark side', a black-magic feng shui magician.

As soon as I came out of the building I called Astrid and told her that I had utterly failed to be assertive and had let myself be roundly bullied by evil Brick.

'He offered to be my agent under the condition that I became his black-magic psychic. I feel totally humiliated,' I insisted, with my best 'poor-me looking-for-sympathy victim' tone.

She didn't fall for it. 'You Brits are so dramatic; he's a satellite anyway,' and with that she moved on excitedly: 'Listen, I've got you an appointment with the guy I told you about, the guy who does all the stars' hair.'

'Great,' I said excitedly.

'I got you in by telling him you're psychic though – don't kill me, nothing else worked. You're not famous or rich, so it was all I had.' Astrid was clearly taking the therapist's advice, to tell the truth whatever the consequences, very seriously. 'And I'll set you up with a couple of people who can help you as an actress at Shelby's shower tomorrow. Gotta go. I have an audition.'

I was in a funk after the debacle of the meeting but Astrid's wheeling and dealing made me feel a little better. And it wasn't so bad with Brick. I mean, OK he was off his head on coke before lunchtime, and he clearly had some issues with his co-workers, but he was still at one of the best and most powerful agencies in town, and he was going to do my deal. And now I had scored by getting in to to see Ziers, scissors to the stars. Did anyone here have a normal name?

As I drove down Melrose towards the hair salon, I noticed how even the billboards catered to the industry. 'Call your agent from your Pilates class,' read one. It reminded me of a famous anti-war poster that hit the billboards in the seventies. A beautiful blonde actress sauntered past the Hollywood sign with a nuclear mushroom cloud looming in the background. The slogan read, 'Nuclear war, there goes my career!' Even the dodgy dry-cleaners were called 'celebrity cleaning'. I was beginning to get a beat on the Hollywood sales pitch. It was most definitely a gold-rush city, and fame was the gold. In fact, if LA had a colour it would be gold. It was everywhere.

To prove my point, a smiling gold Buddha greeted me inside the door of the top dollar salon. Gone were the days of scrunchies and shampoos for sale. At the counter, nestled incongruously among the eighteen-caret gold Ganesh pendants, were the latest vogue accessory: strings of sandalwood beads, usually found around the necks of renunciate monks. Spiritual renunciation was for sale, in the form of mass produced Bhagavad-Gitas (the Hindu Bible) and wooden beads. This was the new twist on success at any price. The arrival of Spiritual Materialism. Hinting that these charms really worked and bought you fame were the photos on the walls. Photos of stars from the latest magazines with person-alised thank you's above their one-second signatures. I guess this was the height of satellite supremacy. Photos dedicated to the satellite himself. Himself was running a tad late, so I took the decaf soy latte that was offered by a supercilious assistant.

Seconds later, supernova satellite Ziers walked towards me. He looked almost saintly, wearing a white linen shirt with khaki pants and silver Birkenstocks. He was black and beautiful. And surprisingly, he was bald. Sitting atop his mirror was a photo of his guru, who, unlike most Hindu nuns, had long luscious locks. Clearly she was his inspiration to shape the follicular futures of his starry clients. The guru, like Ziers's clients, was also a very beautiful woman (who, it is unkindly rumoured, has used the devotees' money to have plastic surgery). Seeing me eye his teacher, Ziers raised his diamond-pierced eyebrow enigmatically and whispered, 'God is everywhere.'

As I sat down, I was imagining God in her various forms as I leafed through *Vogue*, wondering if I would find her sprawling centrefold and wearing Rozae Nichols. His guru smiled back at me implacably and suddenly Ziers and I were talking about India. I told him of my thwarted desire to set foot in the land where my former selves had lived.

'Maybe we knew each other in a past life. I lived there, you know,' he said proudly as he snipped.

'Which life?' I asked.

'This one! And probably before that as well. I love all that karma and destiny stuff, don't you?

'My psychic says I'm black on the outside but Indian on the inside.' Then he laughed at himself, and I instantly decided he was OK. I also realised gleefully that I didn't have to keep my psychic side quiet, like I had to do in England for fear of being laughed at or judged by a lot of people. Here everything was fairly ludicrous, so as a psychic I was just part of the landscape. In Tinseltown I clearly had free rein to indulge.

'Did living in India change you?'

'Living in LA has changed me far more. In India, I saw God everywhere, in everyone. And it's a very honest place; the poverty's out there on the streets and some of the poorest people there are venerated as saints. Here they're "losers". And we're more segregated than the caste system. You go to Santa Monica and everyone's white.'

We were off chatting, anyway.

'I drove there by mistake,' I said. 'It had a really weird feeling to me, and I didn't like it actually.' In reality I had loathed it, but was being tactful as Santa Monica was one of the smartest neighbourhoods and I knew several of Ziers's movie-star clients lived there.

'You know why?' he asked. 'I believe it's built on a Native American grave site, where you're supposed to respect the spirits of the dead. But then you'd know about all that ... you have Siddhis, I hear from Astrid.' Although it sounded like a nasty venereal disease, he was actually referring to the Indian terminology for esoteric powers.

Before I could reply, he asked flirtily, 'Do you want to go blonde?'

'You're the psychic there ...' I said, surrendering to his take on me.

He nodded. 'Brave girl.' And he glopped some blue goo on my head.

'And what's your vision of LA so far? Beneath the surface? Apart from sensing the bones of innocent Native Americans we slaughtered,' he asked. Instinctively I trusted him, so I told him what was on my mind. 'I think it's a cruel city. I met a casting director at the bar of the Chateau Marmont last night ...'

He tutted. 'Everyone there's industry, aren't they? Your bill's entirely tax-deductible if you stay there, you know.'

'I didn't,' I laughed. 'Anyway, she asked me the same question you did, my take on LA, and I was bored of giving the same answer, so I said, "There are lots of slums here, aren't there?"'

'And she replied?' asked Ziers mischievously.

'She replied, "Oh yeah, but nobody lives in them."'

We were bonding, the colour of my hair was changing and Ziers and I were bonding.

'I'm embarrassed to be American sometimes,' he said, rolling his eyes.

'I can tell,' I said, gesturing at the pantheon of Indian gods and goddesses smiling at the wet heads underneath.

He looked at me quite seriously. 'I just keep representations to remind me.'

Interesting. My judgement had been too swift. He was a self-aware spiritual materialist.

'But of course I have to keep India inside of me to survive here. The values are very twisted in this town.'

'How do you do that?'

'I meditate every morning for an hour and I listen to what God tells me to do.'

Usually I would associate that phrase with Charles Manson or George Bush, neither of whom seemed to be listening very clearly to judge by their actions, but coming from Ziers the phrase was neither terrifying nor ludicrous, but bizarre and intriguing. What did he hear? Was God behind Jennifer's shag-cut, I wondered.

Then he whispered, 'I would never normally tell a new client that, but Astrid told me you were one of us – you hear helpful voices too.' Is that me? I thought. I'm one of those? 'Those' meaning people who are aware of Spirit whispering? With Astrid and Ziers as my soul tribe?

'So why are you here in Hollywood?'

To my surprise I answered, 'I met someone.'

I didn't need to do the whole film thing with Ziers.

'And I have a feeling I'm here for reasons I don't even know yet …'

'Well, trust that. You're psychic after all.' I smiled wryly. However, Ziers was on to me.

'It's easier to help other people though, isn't it? Why do you think I'm bald, can't cut my own hair but am paid a fortune to do everyone else's?'

And I could see why. He spun me round to face the mirror and I had long, straight, white-blonde hair, the colour I had always secretly dreamt of being but was too afraid of because it felt too extreme, like I was showing off or something.

'This is what God intended, for you to be beautiful. Not hiding away under all that 1970s henna. See you again!' he said, waving goodbye.

And I knew I would.

I didn't even care that I paid three times what I would normally pay for my hair. I was three times as happy. And for the first time I got 'blonde attention'. Everyone stared at me in the salon, and everyone stared at me as I picked up my car; everyone even stared at me in the Chateau Marmont, where everyone is usually too cool to stare at anyone.

I finally made it to my room. It had been a big day. By the

time I lay down, I thought how awful it must be to be famous, and be ogled at all the time. It actually gave me the sensation that I had spinach in my teeth, as if there was something wrong with me. I decided to meditate, inspired by Ziers to see if I had any psychic messages. As soon as I closed my eyes I had a feeling I should check the emails. My heart perked up when I saw one from jimminy inc:

> Pissing down with rain here. Have offer to do North Country tour of Silas Marner. Offer to come to LA far more cheery. Was it serious offer?
>   Jimminy

> Dear Jimminy
>   Very serious offer. And could you please come over and pretend to be my husband (it's a long story and no I'm not sad fag hag who thinks you're really straight, got over that when we were drunk in Paris twelve years ago).
>   Love you
>   xxxx
> PS – warning you, Hollywood full of surprises, had the deepest conversation I've had so far with the hairdresser here.
> PPS – I'm now a platinum blonde! Yippee!

And I pressed send. To my delight, Jimminy was online.

> Buying a ticket tonight.
> Love
> Your husband.

PS – we'll always have Paris ... ☺

PPS – all great changes start at the hairdresser's xxx

I woke up in the middle of the night saying lines from Al's movie. I got up to go to the bathroom and saw myself in the mirror: I had yellow hair. I didn't recognise myself. But I liked it. I went back to bed ... wanting to wake up in Hollywood next morning. I don't think I'd ever been anywhere where the possibility of a new life was so palpable.

My first morning as a blonde. I attempted to cobble together yet another LA outfit without black or a cardigan as the main stay. This time for a shower, obviously not the watery kind, but the party kind, which were a peculiar American obsession. There are bridal showers and baby showers, and baptism showers. Astrid explained how the whole thing worked: the happy bride-to-be, in this case Shelby, went to her favourite store and drew up a list of things she needed, and all her friends chipped in to help her buy it. I loved the idea. We set off in her shocking old banger to buy the presents.

'I like the hair, it's very Jean Harlow,' said Astrid with a smile.

I made a mental note to buy some fake tan.

'Thanks. I like that,' I said eyeing her new tattoo. 'What else have you been up to?'

'Auditioning, you know ...' and she tailed off. Before I could ask her, we arrived at Fred Segal on Melrose. 'The' Fred Segal, where all the glitterati go shopping for three-hundred-dollar nail polish. We contemplated getting a coffee at the picturesque café stretching along the front of the store, looking over – in Paris – the Seine, in Florence – the Duomo – in LA – the parking lot. We sat down.

Chatting to Astrid in cafés had become a familiar occurrence. No matter where we were going or what we were doing, we were addicted to chatting in cafés. Most of what I learned about Hollywood took place over cappuccinos. I was hanging on to to the best part of being European.

'I approve of these wedding showers. How great to help other people like this.' I felt all spiritual and tingly and community minded and as I said this, I added, 'It takes a village.'

'It takes a fucking American Express card,' refuted Astrid bitterly. 'I could have bought a car with all the cash I've dropped on these lists. My friend, Big-star-tiny-body, when it was her birthday, she had a list! Her birthday, for God's sake. There was practically nothing on it that was under a grand!'

We talked through a couple more lattes and joined the glitter babes inside.

I scoured for presents in the two-figure range and plumped for a contribution to the baby buggy Shelby had optimistically asked for. 'I steered clear of that,' said Astrid. 'She had terrible endrometritis and she told me her tubes are scarred.'

'Er, too much information, Astrid.' And she had the good grace to laugh. She said apologetically, 'My homework from my therapist was to keep telling the truth.'

'That should be fun,' I said wryly, fingering some three-hundred-dollar sunglasses. Then it came to me.

'Well, the truth is endri-whatever, she's going to have a boy first and then a girl.'

Suddenly Astrid was wistful. 'It must be great to be psychic, you know what present to buy, what's going to happen, life must be so easy …'

I had moved on to a turquoise coat that would have been a down payment on a Prius. 'You know that's not true,' I said seriously.

'Speaking of the future, has Al called?'

'Strangely, he hasn't,' I said, trying to hide my disappointment.

'Not a good sign. According to *The Rules*.'

'I hate that book. I think it kills love. It's the antithesis to Spirit.'

Astrid did a silly 'talk-to-the-hand' gesture from *Jerry Springer* and mouthed, 'Talk to me when you're married and I'll listen.'

'What's got into you, Astrid?'

'I didn't get the audition and I just feel like giving up, I really do. I mean I'm over thirty ...'

I gasped. 'How awful! That's right, we forget how to act after thirty.'

'Fuck off!' she said, but she was laughing. 'Maybe I'm just deluded that I'll ever make it here. Are we two sad fucks who can't get what we really want then?' she asked.

'Sadly I think we are. I want love and you want fame and neither of us have either.'

I was aware that I was doing that very female thing where, despite the fact I had a great part, I wanted to bond with my new friend and join her in being sad. And actually, I was kind of sad that I didn't have a great guy to celebrate the movie news with. The good news of getting the part, bizarrely, showed up even more acutely the absence of love. And I also felt sad that Astrid had to live or die by the sword of acting. I really didn't want to end up like that.

'Listen, we mustn't get down,' said Astrid, moving into her cheerleader role and doing the other very female thing of picking up my mood. 'Let's go for it at the wedding shower, OK. Be really positive. I might get a part and you might meet someone – something will come out of it for both of us,' she said with a renewed chirpiness.

'Which is obviously the point of going to the wedding shower – not to celebrate Shelby's life-changing day, but to get something for us, right?' I raised an eyebrow.

'Welcome to Hollywood, babe, where everyone has an agenda.'

I wondered what my agenda was. To meet the mysterious writer Spirit had predicted ... maybe he'd be waiting for me at the shower? I knew something amazing was waiting for me, and it felt like love.

So Astrid and I set off to the shower. We were dressed to kill, with fabulous frocks and daft shoes which somehow had sneaked their way on to our bodies at Fred Segal, thanks to the joys of plastic. Topped off with our matching Ziers's specials, the bottle-blondes were in high spirits. Driving with the windows open – as the air-conditioning in the Astridmobile had of course packed in – we made a pact with each other.

'I'll give you the Hollywood scoop at the shower and you give me the psychic scoop, OK?'

'Deal,' I said, using Tinseltown's favourite word.

We pulled up at the valet parking for the wedding shower.

'Does anyone ever park their own car?' I asked nervously.

'Unfortunately not. I wish I could hide this piece of shit, but at a smart party, valet's the done thing. Hollywood rule.'

'Don't give it to that guy,' I said, pointing to a shifty-looking guy.

'Why?'

'Psychic hunch. He's going to park it somewhere weird.'

'And what will happen?'

I felt a psychic jolt of energy and then the message came in clearly. 'Someone's going to run into it.'

Astrid smiled at me and, to my surprise gave her keys to the valet I had told her to avoid. I shrugged and assumed she was psychically testing me.

I gasped when I saw the house. It was a gigantic fuck-off mansion. And spectacularly hideous. It was an imitation-Tudor manor house, with slightly surprisingly fake hunting-and-hounds oil paintings as murals on the walls. Ten out of ten for kitsch. The shower was being held poolside, of course. I silently mused that this was quite unlike any low-key British bottle-of-wine hen party in a damp second-floor Brixton flat with some cookware from India, and nappy vouchers. This was an event.

'First Hollywood rule: whatever you do, don't swim; no one does,' hissed Astrid.

'At parties? Or ever?'

'Ever. It's too ... Malibu. Besides, your breasts would look weird and different from everyone else's. If you did back-stroke they wouldn't stand up like little meringues, they'd flop to the side.'

'What exactly's the point of having a pool then?'

'Tax breaks and the sexy Spanish pool boy,' she replied.

'Ancient psychic lore says that being near water helps absorb negative energy.'

'Pity the town wasn't built on a lake then.'

'Astrid, we're supposed to be positive here.'

'Look at that and tell me it's possible.' Astrid's eyebrows were raised skywards. We were greeted by a scattering of fake marble statues of well hung boys, who looked as if they were modelled on Michael Angelo's David. For some bizarre reason they were all carrying various gardening tools like some sort of porno-Pasolini. The other invitees were oblivious to the largephallused statues and were milling around the tables under sun umbrellas. Everybody's glass of champagne seemed to be at the same level and they would only pick at hors d'oeuvres that could be swallowed in one bite. People talked at each other; nobody listened, except for key words like 'got the money', 'I'm in pre-production', 'got distribution' or 'I signed ...' – fill in the dotted line with the name of the star.

We were both ravenous, and with our gracious hostess, Shelby, nowhere to be seen, we headed straight for the food. It was a vegetarian nightmare thanks to the latest fad diet, the Atkins. Various forms of meat and cream were laid out in stylish arrangements.

'Carbs are bad, you see,' said Astrid, helping herself to filet mignon, cream cheese and a Coke.

'My ancestors survived on potatoes; there's nothing wrong with them.'

'Have you ever seen the aura of an apple?' she suddenly asked.

'Is that a serious question, Astrid?'

'You're the fucking psychic!' she hissed.

'Right, and I have nothing better to do with my days than look at the auras of apples.'

'Actually, you'd learn a lot. I borrowed an aura camera, someone in California invented it.'

'You don't say?'

Stuffing her face on the steak, she ignored me.

'I'm trying to agree with you,' she said, annoyed. 'The point is, you're right. The aura camera showed the apple and it had lovely energy waves, and the meat and cheese had nasty grey auras ...'

'Then why do you eat all that crap?'

'Because Atkins keeps you skinny!' said Astrid, stuffing down a salami.

'Talk to me when you're fifty.'

'Nothing's going to happen to me, is it?'

'Don't be daft. That's not a psychic threat; I'm not like that ...'

'You'd better not be, because I'm about to make your day, English girl in Hollywood. Real movie star here, I think ...'

Before Astrid could reveal her surprise celebrity friend, we were accosted by Clingfilm girl. She embraced Astrid and clung to her like a limpet. Then she did the same to me.

'Hey Astrid, did you get the part?' asked the enthusiastic Lolita-type, dressed head to toe in black.

'Waiting to hear,' said Astrid, her fingers crossed. I noticed Astrid's truth policy did not extend to telling people she had not got the part. Lolita grimaced sympathetically.

'How about you?' Astrid asked her.

'Oh, I've given up acting, I'm too old for all that now. I'm a make-up artist.'

'How old are you?' I asked.

'Sixteen,' she said earnestly.

Astrid gave me a look to confirm whether or not the girl was really telling the truth about her age. I nodded. They hugged enthusiastically and Astrid and I walked towards the main gang.

Like in the chorus of a Greek tragicomedy, sentences from the women began to blend with one another: 'Dying to work with you', 'I have a great lawyer', 'Funny is money', 'Horror films are in', 'Action films are out' – a little further down the path – 'Horror films are out', 'Action films are in', 'I have a script for you', 'I read your script', 'Didn't have time to read hers but I'm reading yours', 'Independents are dead', 'Independents are back', 'Independents are all really studio movies', 'Studio movies are the new independents' ... 'I have the right PR person for you', 'I'm taking a break from acting', 'I always wanted to write', 'What I really want to do is direct', and on and on and on. All the clichés about Hollywood were true, but there was something wonderful about it to me. At least they cared, and were trying to get their movies made, or act or write. I had had enough of a decade of English dampness and dismal drinks parties, with two sad actors huddled together over a pint in a corner: 'It's so hard, the industry's dead over here, no one's working.' I liked this mad, gung-ho, focused community.

Astrid pulled me by the arm. 'Clingfilm girl. A sad fate. From would-be star to satellite,' she said.

'And by the way, that will be the only time you get told someone's actual age; when they're still at school,' she whispered out of the corner of her mouth.

'How can sixteen be too old? Mind you, I think she'll be a better make-up artist than actress.'

'Trust me, that's not hard. Have you seen her work?'

'No, I can just see Spirit offering her a make-up kit.'

'She's really fucked up, you know.'

'Well, so would you be if your mother had killed herself.'

'Is that what happened?'

'Yes,' I said, checking my psychic radar.

Astrid turned to me quite seriously. 'I'm glad you told me that.'

'Why?'

'Because I actually feel sorry for her now, and I'm going to make an effort to be kind to her. Which is usually a good idea, right?'

'Do you want your spiritual quote for the day?'

'Go for it,' said Astrid as she stumbled in her platforms around the pool edge.

'Before you say anything to anyone, ask yourself these four

things: is it kind, is it true, is it necessary and is it the right time? It's the Dalai Llama, not me,' I added hastily.

'Before you say anything, remember which lie you told. That's not me, it's William Goldman on Hollywood.' She looked at me guiltily. 'I know I lied about the part. I know, I know … but I just didn't want to have to feel like a failure.'

We were walking towards a group of girls. Lying on the sunchair was a very well-known sexy blonde actress. She was – another cliché – more beautiful in real life than on the screen. As we approached the group, Astrid hurriedly revealed who the gang circling the lounging star were.

'See, that's the star – my nickname for her is Big-star-tiny-body – and there are your satellites. There's her make-up artist, her stylist, masseur and private trainer. The bodyguard is hovering over there …' Sure enough, a big guy was having a field day as the only guy allowed in the hen party.

'That's her healer, I think, and I'll bet there's a dog-trainer.'

'You mean everybody here works for her?'

'Every single one of them is on her payroll.'

'Does she have any real friends?'

'Oh no, stars either have hang-arounders, staff people or fans.'

As we got closer, Astrid was ending the interminable list of people who make their living off someone else's talent. The manager, publicist, business manager, accountant and 'entertainment' lawyer.

'Then there's the litigator for all the law suits and the secret bad guy for when things get tough …'

'There is something very sad about this scenario, don't you think? Very alien. Where do the stars get their quota of love?' I asked.

'From the camera,' said Astrid.

Then, like a strong plot point in a movie, I saw something that changed everything. The recipient of my attention was sitting next to the star on the grass. It was love at first sight. She had silky brown hair, funny little eyebrows, a long nose and short legs. She was clearly a diva by the way she sat. She was the most beautiful dachshund puppy I had ever seen. That little thing was going to change my life.

Astrid strode into the group and, after furious hugs all round, indicated me. 'This is my friend Lucinda, she's doing the lead in a movie. Isn't that great!' Apparently, résumés were the standard form of introduction. There were some muted murmurs of 'great', 'well done' and 'congratulations' from the satellites. Only a girl in the latest jeans, Tammy, seemed genuinely interested. Seeing as this intro had not had the desired effect, Astrid added, almost as an afterthought, 'And she's a psychic who's worked for the police and she did me an amazing reading the other day.'

The muted murmurs turned to full-on attention. Suddenly the spotlight was on me; I even upstaged the star. That was the moment when I realised that, living in Hollywood, until I made a million on the screen I was inevitably in satellite land as an actress, but as a psychic I was in star land. I was barraged with questions that I really tried to pretend I was hearing for the first time. 'When did you find out you were psychic?' 'Can you see if people are going to die?' 'Were you always psychic?' 'Did anyone teach you?' But love couldn't be upstaged. My mind was on the dog. The star picked up the delightful diva dachshund and, in order to stay near the furry delight, I pressed my internal 'tell psychic stories' button and plunged into:

The miracle story of how Diana, my psychic teacher, helped an old friend of mine, Steve. I ran through the fatal doctor's diagnosis, the five days to live, then the one-in-a-million chance he pulled through, the 100 per cent infertility prognosis. Eveyone oohed and ahhed. Then Diana's psychic predictions – he would be a father and marry a girl called Emma. I paused triumphantly. The last I heard, Emma, babe and Steve were doing a road trip across Australia in his old car! There was a burst of applause from the crowd. The happy ending Hollywood loves. I noticed the star nodding thoughtfully, clearly impressed, as she patted her adorable dog.

I also noticed the girl who had been introduced as Shelby's sister, Cheryl, hovering behind a deckchair. Suddenly she marched into the circle and, in front of everyone, put her hand out and drawled in a super-soft whisper, 'Hi, my name's Cheryl, and I was raped in the back of a taxi cab when I was eleven, so I know exactly how you all feel.'

I stood there, stunned, my mouth gaping idiotically while I tried to find a connection between the story of Steve in the hospital and this revelation. Was it the car in the road trip that had triggered her memory, and the synapses in her brain had gone from car to taxi to, 'Oh yes, tell a complete stranger I was raped at eleven'? Or was it the circle configuration that led her to believe we were in group therapy? Or was it just that I was behind the times and the new social contract, encouraged by the instant intimacy of the Oprah age, meant that information previously reserved for therapists – or best friends in the early hours of the morning when you'd been up all night soul-talking – was now considered perfectly suitable for complete strangers? America was so bizarre sometimes, I had no idea how to react.

Luckily, Shelby suddenly shrieked, 'She's a fabulous psychic! I had a reading with her! She read for me and the driver and it was spot on! Would you do a couple of readings, as it's my wedding shower?' She shooed Cheryl away and looked up at me pleadingly, like a child. I had had a hunch this was probably going to happen, so I politely chose a table in the shade near the pool, discreetly away from the crowds, and sat down. An eager line formed. The movie star looked very curious, I noticed, but understandably went back to playing with the puppy. And discussing her eating disorder with her healer, who was encouraging her to visualise herself as a size zero. The girl in the jeans suddenly grabbed my attention and insisted on barging her way to the front. She shook my hand and said in a super-friendly voice, 'Hi! I'm Tammy, Astrid's friend, the publicist. She said we should talk about your marvellous acting career!' Then she turned to the line and bare-facedly lied: 'We have to go first, her agent arranged it.' Somehow I knew we were going to be talking about Tammy. The line settled into comparing wedding-shower gifts and sharing their marital statuses. I settled into my first proper sit-down reading in Hollywood. It was to be very instructive.

Tammy the Publicist

I could read Tammy straight off. Tammy was a winner on a losing streak who never lost the chance to remind everyone, including herself, that she was a winner. And Astrid had warned me that there's no one more determined to fathom the reason for losing than a one-time winner in a slump. As she sat down, she told me she'd represented 'huge' (her words) *celebrities* (the pinnacle of success for satellites), and put 'dangerous' (my words) diet books on the bestseller list, and now she had 'spiritual' questions for the Big Beyond, and if I gave her a good reading, she was 'very well connected and would see to it that I'd get some great press'.

Underneath the sales pitch about how successful she was – which I've noticed the truly successful never have to give – I could sense that bills were coming in and money was not, so she'd drafted a deal memo to Spirit and wanted to hand-deliver it to my door.

I had asked her to close her eyes and relax before I started the reading so I really had time to take her in. I guessed she must have had her hair done at Ziers's, as she too was wearing the high-fashion ashram look. Sandals, T-shirt with a do-gooding slogan, magical crystals around her neck and that big-eyed you-could-find-me-in-a-cult look in her eyes. She couldn't bear to sit still with her eyes closed, so she carefully rearranged the sun umbrellas so she was fully shaded, and I was in the sun. Then her cellphone went off and she answered it, pretending she was on a freeway and was about to get cut off, and I watched as she negotiated a table at a fashionable restaurant for a visiting celebrity; then she abruptly closed her cell, clearly faking a cut-off. She shook my hand and whispered, 'I'm very spiritual too,' and then closed her eyes again.

Shuffling my tarot cards (which I had grabbed as I ran out of the hotel that morning on an inner prompting), I pondered on the spiritual axiom that if it's true that each person we meet is, somehow, a reflection of ourselves, I was having a great deal of trouble looking in the mirror. Was I this vain? Had the peroxide gone to my head and was I like this? A shudder of sadness passed through me as I remembered being in the same room as the Dalai Llama while he told a very self-deprecating story about his own ignorance. And I remembered being in the same room as an Indian saint who had stood for ten years, alone in the middle of the forest, balancing on one leg in the tree pose. He balanced long enough to hear God's dreams for him, ten years, and was still humbly tuning in to God's thoughts for him every morning at 4 a.m. And I doubt he would have called himself spiritual. And I wondered what memory Tammy was going to leave for me.

Still shuffling the cards, I had a hunch she might fall into the born-and-bred Angeleno-type Astrid had warned me about, who also declared they were 'very spiritual'. Tammy fit the cliché profile. She opened her eyes again.

'How much is this?' she asked anxiously.

'It's free, it's a present for Shelby. A good cause,' I said, smiling. Tammy launched into her monologue on good causes.

'I don't believe in good causes. Most especially giving money away to help "the poor", which, as you know, is the in thing over here. Because really, we all "co-create" our destinies, don't we? I did a weekend workshop and suddenly I understood I was the most important person. I was responsible for my life. And the poor are responsible for their lives. And what about the homeless downtown in LA? Seventy thousand now! They're just not doing a good job of manifesting wealth, are they? I mean, they have access to these workshops – like Anthony Robbins, he speaks in that stadium near skid row. I mean honestly, if they were really spiritual they'd go do a workshop and manifest a home, wouldn't they?' I was struck dumb. If I were starving on the streets my priority would definitely be Anthony and not a sandwich. But she carried on blithely. 'And people feel sorry for the sick. Well, we create our illnesses as I'm sure you know. But I beat cancer. I didn't want it, so I changed the way I thought.'

Tammy had wholeheartedly adopted the idea that we all 'co-create' our destinies. This, I mused, is an empowering concept, up to a point, but callous when it is translated – as she had translated it – into the idea that all people who get cancer deserve it because they have created the circumstances that cause cancer to thrive. To me she was the victim of countless workshops that promised success through willpower and not from a higher power. It was convenient. There was no God. Tammy was God. Very LA.

Then she ostentatiously sat in the lotus position on the sun chair and mused that she also thought meditation would be helpful, slipping in the name of a 'very famous' meditation teacher she represented. She didn't meditate herself, had been planning to, but didn't have time to fit it in; she had a large altar in her home but just hadn't had time to sit in front of it as she was just too busy looking after other people's projects; but she was going to meditate, one day, because of course she was … 'very spiritual'. I wondered when spirituality had become callous self-obsession? And why were Angelenos more guilty of it than any other group I'd read for so far?

Tammy declared she was into 'advancing' her spirituality. I idly wondered if Spirit was into advancing anything but love and compassion. Luckily, we had some good psychic hits right away.

'Who's Andy? Assistant?' I asked.

'Yes, yes he's my old assistant!' she replied.

'You're going to have a connection with—' and I gave her the name of a famous writer.

She started to laugh and, genuinely happily, squealed. 'Yes! Yes! I'm meeting them tomorrow for lunch! He wants me to do his PR!'

These were the advances she was most interested in. And in that brief moment I suddenly accepted her enthusiasm and crazy self-obsession and realised she was like all of us, just wanting someone to know her and root for her. She looked like a little girl who had never been loved and now there was proof! Someone in Spirit was watching out for her; someone in the sky even bothered to take note of her lunch appointments!

'You have to be careful with coffee; you're allergic,' I continued.

She looked over the moon at this tidbit. 'I am! I am!' she said, ecstatically.

I was happy, it was infectious. But it was all too soon. The unloved Tammy took over. Her voice changed; it became nasal and high. A question surged up from inside her, the question she had come here to ask but couldn't bear to hear the answer to. She was playing games with herself, tantalising herself, wanting to ask, wanting to trust, and then out it came, guilty and demanding at the same time: 'Jimmy? Tell me about Jimmy.'

I turned my head and saw the letters J-I-M-M-Y, bold and dark, almost like the Hollywood sign imprinted on the air, and there, in the background, in the shadows, stood a blonde woman, who, if I looked at closer, I recognised. It was Shelby! Tammy's great friend. Shelby whose shower we were celebrating. And Jimmy ... the man she wanted to know about was Shelby's fiancé. I had a horrid hunch she wasn't looking out for her friend; she was looking our for herself.

'Well,' I said very firmly, 'he's with someone right now. He's about to get married in a couple of weeks.'

'Oh, I know, he's about to get married.' She let out a brief, harsh expulsion of annoyance. 'But do you see anything romantic between us?'

By now, I thought, I should have got used to this type of Hollywood-wives attitude, where romantic obsession ruled regardless of any minor encumbrance, such as a best friend's spouse.

'The point is,' she said plaintively, 'I can do more for his career than Shelby. I mean, she's an assistant, for God's sake. And he's pushing thirty, tick tick tick! He needs someone to really help him. I know the top magazine editors and I really do get invited to all the best parties. It would be such a positive career move for him if he were dating me. I mean, I know he's talented, but I can make him famous, which I'm sure is his karma. Because I'm a catch! I'm powerful! I deserve love! I'm sexy!'

I sensed that, beneath the ludicrous self-obsession and deceit, there was an attempt to get at something true. I had to try and steer her away from giving her life meaning by a) pinching her friend's bloke and b) giving her energy to another's career. But satellites grow so used to orbiting others that their identity hinges on giving up their own artistic dreams to further reflect someone else's brilliance. They are little lost moons with no light of their own. Tammy was the dark side of the moon. But most satellites lead desperate, sacrificial lives, dying in the shadow of their own goodness.

I was shocked and relieved to hear my voice completely change the subject and, taking dictation from Spirit, loudly blurt out, 'You need to concentrate on writing your book. Forget about dating for a few months and focus on that, and it's going to do very well. Great success!'

Tammy lit up like a January Christmas tree – discarded but, by God, she'd been beautiful in her day. Jimmy was history. Tammy was the future. We were all happy again. Spirit, Tammy and me. Tammy was going to pull through. All moral quandaries and differences were forgotten. We were both dwarfed by the power of the moment.

'I *am* writing a book!' She was absolutely triumphant, and shrieked, 'And it's going to be a *spiritual* book!'

Then Tammy, who Astrid had assured me was one of the best publicists in town, turned to the waiting line and screamed, 'She's fabulous!' And my fate was sealed and Astrid's plans foiled. Astrid wanted me to get help as an actress. But I was being given top-dollar free publicity as a psychic. However, to my relief, just as the line surged forward, I was gazumped. There's one thing more exciting to a group of ambitious women than free psychic readings, and that's free clothes. Thankfully I was forgotten. A tall, handsome man wearing tight leather trousers was being greeted as if he were Father Christmas, which in a sense he was, as he had arrived laden with gifts and goodies.

Shelby ran forward and embraced a barely recognisable Ziers. The ashram look had been replaced with leather queen. He spotted Astrid and me, and as he toppled forward with goodies he mouthed, 'Come and get it, girls!'

'Celebrity cast-offs,' said Astrid dismissively. 'It's part of the karmic unruliness of the universe; the rule is, the richer and more famous the actor the more "clobber" he or she is given for free. And they pass it on to their "friends", i.e., their hairdressers.' Astrid thought this was the perfect time for us to make our escape, before I was forced to do more readings and she would have to admit she didn't get the part everyone kept asking her about.

She was right. Over my shoulder, as we left the shower, I witnessed the excess of the gifts that Ziers was 'regifting'. Big-star-tiny-body was presented with a large suitcase of clothes that she accepted as though it were her due. I watched as Ziers left the remaining rabble to sort through Nintendo games, holistic creams, fat handfuls of designer sunglasses, and even a new thousand-dollar watch. Big-star-tiny-body had been presented the five-grand one, of course. Astrid had managed to grab something and held it up to me. It claimed to be a phone, although it also took photographs and played music and made films – and probably designed frocks when it was sleeping.

Secretly I was gutted, as my love affair with the dachshund had been cut short. Maybe, in the middle of all of this Hollywood hullabaloo, I had fallen in love with the dog because she was the only thing that didn't seem to want something from anyone, and was affectionate just because it was in her soul.

We came out of the party and handed our keys to the valet. There was a huddle of chatter and eventually a shame-faced valet came towards us. Astrid looked at me mischievously.

'Let's see what happened to my car then, Madam Lucinda.'

'Give me a break, Astrid.' But Spirit had come through for me.

'Sorry … mistake,' said the man.

Astrid's car drew up and we saw evidence of the mistake: a huge, streaky paint mark where a car had clearly bashed into it … and driven off. Instead of being angry, Astrid picked me up and embraced me. The valet hung his head. I knew he was really worried about losing his job. Astrid whispered, 'Well done!'

I shook my head, nonplussed.

'Excellent. Now I can get my insurance to pay for the repairs and make some money suing the valet company. What do you think?'

'A law suit?'

'Everyone in LA has a law suit … or is it bad karma?'

'It depends if you win or not,' I said sarcastically.

'You're right,' she said earnestly.

'Astrid, I'm joking.'

'I'll learn,' she said, gleefully opening the door to her newly striped car.

'Will I win?'

'You know this is not what you're supposed to use psychic powers for ...'

She looked at me pleadingly and I acquiesced. 'You won't need to get money from a court case; you'll get it from your work.'

'Why? I'm totally broke right now ... and the lap-dancing in Long Beach doesn't pay that well ...'

I could see Astrid was eager to find out more and I was totally wiped. 'You just won't need to be lap-dancing. That's what I heard. And are you sure you don't mind dropping me off?'

'I can drop you off if you'd like, it's no problem.'

I heard a voice behind me that I recognised from the screen. It was the movie star again, Big-star-tiny-body. Close up she was so beautiful I kept trying to find something about her that wasn't gorgeous, in a pathetic attempt to make me feel better. Of course I said yes to the lift, because she was beautiful and a movie star, but also because she was sad and most of all because she handed me the puppy to look after. This was the moment I knew there was a God. The puppy was in my arms. Astrid blew us both kisses, leaving me with the movie star.

'What's her name?' I asked, looking at the chocolate fur bundle.

'I'm not sure yet, I haven't had time to think of one,' she said, as she hurriedly pulled on a pair of gigantic sunglasses and a baseball cap, the uniform disguise of celebs, which just made her look all the more obviously famous.

As we got back into the car, she turned to me and revealed the real reason she wanted to give me a lift.

'So you're psychic,' she said, clearly suspicious.

'I am.'

'And you read for the police?' I could see she didn't quite believe me.

'I did.'

'So can you see anything about my future?'

I could tell it was a test and I really wasn't in the mood to be tested. In some bizarre way I realised – watching the way the valets stare at her and a fan who asked for an autograph – that, in a very minor way, being psychic was weirdly similar to being a star. Everyone wanted something from you. Normally I would have been able to use my 'I always meditate for an hour before I do a reading' excuse, but as she had seen me reading Tammy poolside that wasn't going to fly.

'While you "tune in",' she said, impressively knowing the lingo, 'I have to do a quick errand if you don't mind ...' It wasn't really a question, as she assumed I would say yes. Celebrities – I was soon to learn – often behaved like this; whatever they were going to do, they were going to do. And it meant more time with the puppy. Who I was by now besotted by. We jumped into the ridiculous SUV.

I didn't need a minute to tune in. I needed a minute to come out of my ego and into my Spirit side. I couldn't see her soul's journey yet because I was still stuck in the unimportant (in Spirit terms), i.e. her fame and beauty. To be honest, I didn't really want to give a reading; I felt kidnapped and trapped. But the dog made me want to stay. Luckily for me the fates were on our side.

'Ooh look, we're here. Just come in with me, will you, and bring the dog.'

Orders again. She was used to having people do things for her all the time. A permanent sense of entitlement.

'Is she trained?' I asked nervously.

'I spent a thousand dollars on her training, so I hope so,' she said as she darted across the road.

We were outside a store that said 're-sale designer clothes'. It crossed my mind that maybe she was about to – but I dismissed the thought. No. One of the world's most famous actresses was not going to do what I suspected. But she was. She unloaded the free loot she had acquired from Ziers and, suitcase in hand, she marched in. I followed, Twiglet prancing behind on the pink snakeskin leash.

The sales girls were very animated to see her, and started chatting with self-conscious looks on their face. We all watched as Big-star-tiny-body pulled out her loot. All the other people were sitting around with sacks of beautiful designer clothes that had been rejected, and we were riveted to see what would and wouldn't be accepted. What would make the 'yes' pile and what the 'no'. The power celebrity buys – it was unbelievable! Very, very ordinary clothes were being piled into the 'yes' pile by the sychophantic sales assistant. Then Big-star-tiny-body was handed a large wad of cash for the clothes she had got for free. The diva dachshund had clearly had enough of this fiasco and decided this was the time to show that her ludicrously costly thousand-dollar canine obedience training meant nothing to her: she delicately squatted and turned the soft white pile carpet a vivid shade of yellow. Immediately the store manager came huffing up to ban her and, just as immediately, changed his mind when he saw who was the owner of the dog. He looked almost honoured to have his carpet pissed all over by a star's dog.

What an extremely peculiar day. A deranged publicist wanting to have it off with her friend's fiancé; the very rich star taking advantage of gifts and flogging them for peanuts in her world; and me somehow roped into hanging out with her and giving her a reading. In case I forgot I was with someone famous, a blinding camera flash taken by an unabashed fan exploded in our direction. I clutched the puppy who was genuinely distressed by the lights.

'She likes you,' said Big-star-tiny-body.

'I love her.'

'What's a good name for her, do you think?'

'I'd call her Twiglet, because she's long and brown and so good you could eat her.'

'Piglet?' she said. 'That's cute. Weird but cute.'

'No, Twiglet. It's an English snack. Or Twiggy for short.'

'Oh, I know her, the model. I like it. The dog kinda looks like you.'

It was true. She had sad eyes and a long nose.

As we heaved ourselves up into the ridiculous mini-van that Angelenos insist on driving, she glanced behind us. Out of nowhere a black car with tinted windows and no number plate revved its engine sinisterly.

'Fuck. Paparazzi.'

The paparazzi looked like SAS soldiers, with lenses poking out of their car like AK47s. I was surprised by how genuinely sinister they looked. Even Twiglet looked very put out.

'I hate this,' she said, and I could see she was genuinely afraid. We just clipped a red light and left them behind, and still had a few seconds or so before the lights would change and the paparazzi would be on to her. But she absolutely froze, as if she couldn't drive at all.

'What's wrong?'

'I think I'm having a panic attack.'

And the face that adorned the screens so often as an action heroine crumpled into a nervous heap.

'I'll drive,' I said purposefully.

She sat there, dead still.

'Get out, I'll drive.' She was in a state of shock, and suddenly it was as if we were in a film and I had taken the role of Thelma. We switched seats and for a moment I almost regretted it, as the car was a new SUV.

My brother races cars and I'm used to this, I thought, which was actually true. Or partly. I was used to watching the cars. The time it took us to switch seats was the time it took for the paparazzi to catch us up.

'I just don't want any photos, not right now.'

I nodded tactfully. Unfortunately she was in the middle of a scandal at the time and the rags were extremely unkind. At that moment the paparazzi illegally overtook us, hitting the wing mirror and clipping the front bonnet.

'Los Angeles is the most dangerous city in America and more people die in traffic accidents here than in any other city, so forgive me if I just avoid an accident.'

I did an extremely dangerous illegal turn and sped up a side street.

'Do you know where you're going?'

'Haven't a clue, but you have a friend that lives on this street, right?'

She looked astonished.

'I do ... how do you know that ... wow ... so I guess you really are psychic ...'

Spotting the SUV behind us, I said, 'I'm going to do a quick circle round the block, and in a second a cyclist is going to come out of that driveway ...' An arty musician type with a guitar on his back came out of his drive. I sped up to him, 'Block the street for me, would you?'

He looked at the movie star and his mouth fell open, and credit to her she smiled her million-dollar smile at him,

'Sure thing, and I love you in …' but we were whizzing down the street by now, the furious paparazzi hooting and shouting obscenitites at the musician who was blocking the street by weaving in front of them, singing loudly and waving us goodbye.

I took a sharp right and went up the parallel street, 'Go through that garden. Your friend, she lives about halfway up the street.'

'You're good.'

'It's not me,' I said, 'it's Spirit.'

She nodded again. 'I think I can jump out like I did in that movie.'

'Sure, sure, jump out! But your dog?'

'Keep her!'

I was aghast.

'Have her! She's yours! Bye, Twiglet!' And she did a stunt roll into the stranger's garden.

'And you need your car!' I yelled, but she didn't hear me as she leapt up and dashed off to her safe house. I idled the engine, my new dog bravely at my side, snout quivering but with a fierce look on her fuffy face. Together we waited for the reappearance of the maniacal photographers; I could feel they hadn't given up and at any moment they would appear. Sure enough, there they were … I sped away, pretending the star was still with me. To my horror the gas was on empty. 'Gas station, gas station …' I prayed. I knew it was near – I had no idea of the geography of the place, I was entirely relying on my psychic hunches. 'Left and left,' I muttered to myself. Took the left and left and *voilà*! Gas station! I loved being psychic sometimes!

I spluttered into the gas station and, in the nick of time, came to a halt at the pump. The SUV crew circled around the car like vultures, one leaning his lens out so far I could almost have grabbed the camera. I took the greatest pleasure in just waving them goodbye with a smug smile of my own. Then my cell went.

'Are you OK? Astrid gave me your number,' said Big-star-tiny-body.

'I'm great,' I said, laughing.

'Listen, can you come to dinner tomorrow night? It's actually my birthday and then ...'

'I can give you back your car!' I laughed.

She laughed.

'That was really cool, like some sort of psychic action-figure chase; I haven't had such fun for ages. That'd be a good pitch you know: a psychic action-figure. Who's the director you're working with on your film, by the way?'

I nervously told her about Al.

'Oh, he's great. I'd love to work with him. Anyway, see you tomorrow and I'll find out more.'

Wow. Big-star-tiny-body wanted to work with the director I was playing the lead for.

I drove back to the Chateau feeling surprisingly exhilarated. I even knew I'd lost weight on my diet of coffee and nerves. It didn't get much more fun than this, I thought, as I jumped out of the huge car, swinging my blonde hair chirpily from side to side. Papparazzi car chases, absurd parties, this silly car I had borrowed and, by far the most important thing, the adorable dachshund diva as my new companion. And tomorrow, I imagined myself sitting at the party and telling everyone how excited I was to be doing a film I believed in. I sauntered into the hotel and smiled at the clerk. He handed me a phone message; it was from Al! 'Need to meet up again … need to talk to you about the part, how about dinner tomorrow night?' I had to catch Jimminy up.

Dear Jimminy,

Never guess who I stunt-drove for today? Big-star-tiny-body! (that's Astrid's name for her). And am invited to her birthday party tomorrow!!

Yes, really. Wouldn't happen if I wasn't psychic so not flattering myself too much. Do I have psychic written on my forehead or something? Done more readings here than ever did in England. Love it love it love it here.

Had a dream last night about a star surrounded by satellites, and met them all, but by far the most fated meeting was with Twiglet. Used to be Big-star-tiny-body's dog but she just gave her to me!!! I guess dogs are as disposable as designer clothes and I have inherited the Twig. You'd love her … when will you meet her?

Miss you.

Xxxx

PS – sexy director taking me out to dinner to talk about the part!

PPS – if I ever get famous will you be my entourage?

Then Jimminy texted me:

If I ever get famous will you be my psychic?
Love Jimminy

Fuck off.

Love you too.

I practically skipped into my room and slipped on a fax that had been shoved under my door. It read:

BAD NEWS
Tried to call you, couldn't find you. You're fired
from the movie. They want a name. That's the way it
goes sometimes. Call me. Brick.

I reread it. And I reread it again. And it didn't change. No magic was going to rearrange the letters. Then I started to laugh. I don't really know why, but I started to laugh long and hard. Steve once told me that when he had first been given the diagnosis for cancer he had burst into laughter. 'Why?' I said. 'I don't understand, it was the worst news in the world.' He had paused and said, 'I don't know. It was just so absurd. I'd never ever imagined it, and it was funny.' It was almost, he said, a spiritual experience. Or it was the beginning of one. I had stared at him without comprehension. Now I knew what he was talking about.

Very calmly, I tucked Twig under my arm, walked out into the car park, got in my car, and drove into the night. I drove until I reached Mulholland Drive. I parked in a place where Twiglet and I could see all the lights of Los Angeles twinkling below us. I needed to feel very small, with the sky above me and the city below. Twiglet was staring at me with her soulful eyes. 'It's not good, Twig,' I said in a tiny voice. And my voice sounded strange and far off and foreign to me. Then, despite the agonising feeling of disappointment and fear that was stuck in my chest, I pushed the seat back, opened the sun roof so I could see the moon and lay back. 'Why the hell is this happening to me?' I asked some invisible force. I could hardly breathe I was so upset. I forced myself to close my eyes and see if Spirit had any clues for me. I fell into an intense trance, somewhere between sleeping and waking.

I saw myself standing in front of a camera. Al was directing, but I wasn't acting a part; I was giving psychic readings. My hair was bright orange and standing up like antennae. Little blue electrical sparks were shooting between the pigtails. Then, one by one, all the people I had met so far in Hollywood stood in front of me. And they were talking to me.

Shelby, wearing a T-shirt with dancing suns on it, was throwing me her wedding bouquet and saying, 'Thank you!' Then I was flying in the air above a set, and down below was David, dressed as a soldier, screaming and shooting. Then he looked up at me and gave me a thumbs-up. 'You gave me back my hope!' he was yelling. Then I saw the fake psychic. I zoomed over her Melrose place, and she was kneeling in the corner of her room, clutching the photo of her dead son, sobbing those terrible guttural sobs that only a mother who's lost her child can cry, and I could hear her saying, 'I'm sorry, I'm sorry,' over and over again. Then a bright-blue aquamarine bottle appeared in my mind's eye, and there was suicidal Susie, floating out of it like a genie, waving maracas around and hugging a St Bernard. On and on the faces flashed in front of me, just like the visions people talk of before they die. Astrid, dancing on a cloud, Brick, with earplugs in; Ziers, with a huge gold bindi, linking arms with me; Tammy, writing furiously; clingfilm girl, painting my face with make-up. Then I was back looking at Al, but tears were streaming down my face and he wiped them away. Mysteriously, a white peacock flew past us and into the East. I flew after the peacock.

I flew through the clouds until I came face to face with a figure I recognised from my favourite Indian restaurant – a woman wearing fuschia with four arms to hug you with – and she introduced herself as Lakshmi. She was sitting on a throne shaped like a heart with white flowers at her feet. She leant forward and with intense black eyes, but very gentle voice, asked me, 'What have you done for Love? What have you done for Love?'

Then the trance dream stopped and my eyes opened suddenly, as if I had come up from the bowels of the earth. It was pitch black, and Twiglet was curled in a tight ball on my tummy. I gently disengaged her and started up the engine. I needed to drive again.

Everything that had been so clear suddenly started to fade, just like dreams do. I was driving away from the answers I had been given. Then an image of a heart, white flowers – words – what were they? Then Susie hugging her St Bernard flitted across my mind. Some great hidden truth was trying to come into focus, a clue that had been dropped in my dream. 'What have you done for Love?' That was it. 'What have you done for Love?' I suddenly jammed on the brakes. A truck had cut straight in front of me; a second later and we'd have crashed into the side. I was back in reality. Then I glanced down at the Californian bumper sticker; swirled in psychedelic letters was the word 'trust'. I reversed the car out of the impending accident, and drove very slowly back to the hotel.

I couldn't bear to be alone in my room yet, so I stopped again. If I was in a smiling mood, I would have laughed at the irony of the car, parked smack in front of the Hollywood sign, lit up by the moon. But I felt eerily calm – psychic shock from losing not just the part but a promise of a new life, as well as the physical shock of having avoided the car accident. I also felt very alive, alert and awake. And then it came to me. I knew what I had to do. Spirit had been telling me very clearly all along. Since I had set foot in Hollywood almost every person I had met I had ended up doing a psychic reading for. Shelby, David, the fake psychic, Astrid, suicidal Susie, Tammy, even Brick. That was what the vision was showing me. Maybe it really was a City of Angels, and they were hovering all around us, trying desperately to give guidance to lost souls. And for some reason, I had moved to a town where I couldn't take a step without their whispers. The film part had gone. But the whispers hadn't. And I wanted to stay here. There was a reason. I wished that it was Al, but now the film was kaput – I wondered. 'What have you done for Love?' Readings. That was the answer. Psychic readings.

If Al was mine, he would come to me; like a tsunami, it would be inevitable. If acting was for me, it would come back. But I was a sign-reader and I would have to be blind not to read the signs. Even my agent wanted help in that way. Time to be spiritual in the scariest town to lay claim to spirituality. That was my task. Twiglet and I drove back to the Chateau Marmont, slept curled up together in the foetal position, and the next day we were reborn. I checked out, not knowing where I would be that night.

4
The One You Can't Forget

Four months later ...

Thinking of you in England ... with autumn and hot chestnuts ... here it's 'fall' — although to pretend LA has seasons is as silly as pretending decaf is tasty. They don't and it isn't, but who cares, it's very LA and LA is ... well, I'm trying to find out exactly what LA is. Fluid, perhaps, like mercury you can't get your hands on it, but I suspect it has the same dangerous properties. Will let you know ... Meanwhile ... my zip code is in: HOLLYWOOD! Yes! A guesthouse in a Hollywood Hills mansion! A lot has happened in the last few months ... I have my own private garden, table complete with sun umbrella, roses and humming birds ... makes you sick! Half an hour before clients arrive. Clients! Lots of them —

making my living as a psychic now – phone going mad with Hollywooders wanting readings ... who would have thought ... (well YOU obviously, Diana!) but I still feel a bit shocked by it all, and keep just asking Spirit to help me so I don't turn into one of those loony psychics they have over here who show off on telly ... Anyway as ever I'm thinking about the future and today I can pay the rent ... thank God, any extra and I can eat ...

Thank you thank you thank you for encouraging me to put an ad in the magazines and forcing me to charge for the readings. I always send 10 per cent of all I make to India (my small bit at rebalancing the inequalities of the world in the money-mad USA) but, I also window-shop at Fred Segal's with my friend Astrid and we splurged on Twiglet who is kitted out in fake diamante. She twinkles with jewels on her meditation mat. A diva yogi! Guess this is what LA is about ... contradictions. Speaking of ... everyone seems to want to know about 'the one' (sounds familiar???) So ... I am teaching them the soulmate exercise you taught me ... BUT feel a bit of a fraud as I am not with mine ... yet ... (I keep saying 'it's already done,' hoping he will appear soon) ... could it be the mysterious Al, the sexy director I told you all about? He's been shooting in Argentina (film not pheasants). Haven't seen him since our movie fell through, but will tonight, dinner date. Acting a bit on hold at the moment I'm afraid ... but Jimminy's here (best friend and actor too) and he always encourages me ... which is great, he met someone who he thinks is 'the one' and wants advice, but

```
it's hard to read clearly for people you really love,
isn't it? You're right, I'm too close emotionally ...
    Say prayers for me, hugs to Bill and the cats,
    All love
    Lucinda
    Xxxx
```

I pressed the send button and closed the computer. It was my first email to Diana since my acting life had crashed on the night of the dark, demeaning exodus from the Chateau Marmont. No more distractions. I needed a quick cup of tea and to relax before the morning's first client. All the people I had read for in my first couple of weeks here told their friends, and then they told theirs and it was a sort of positive pyramid scheme ... and I really was swamped. As if on cue, the phone rang again – I'd need an assistant if this went on, I thought to myself rather grandly – but thank God it was not a call I was trying to avoid; it was my lovely friend, Astrid. As soon as I picked up, she insisted I pull a tarot card for her audition that afternoon, and to her delight, I pulled the wish fulfilment card. I stupidly made a joke that her wish had been fulfilled as she had finally got rid of shit face. In that rather peculiar way of Americans in therapy, she then confused a conversation with a monologue. She launched into telling me in detail exactly how she felt about her ex, shit face. And why. And what that meant about who she was. Selfishly, it suited me perfectly, as I knew I had a good five minutes before my reading in which to make active listening noises to her insistent pronouncements as I made my Tetley's. Also, I listened patiently because I loved Astrid, because she was hilarious and, God knows, she had been there for me when I needed her. I mean a true friend – especially the day I walked out of the swanky

Chateau with no papers, no money, no job and no place to live. At that point, I had the Twiglet, coupled with the incredible exhilaration that a crisis can bring on. She had offered me her life-raft, her leatherette Ikea sofa in her pad. Indefinitely. And lots of advice. And then shit face had come on the scene.

Listening to Astrid's anguished analysis of her last few days, I remembered how desolate I too had felt in LA, camping out at her pad, sleeping on the sofa. At that time … it was only four months ago … so much had changed. Astrid had advised me to follow the normal Hollywood procedure for girls in my predicament – broken dreams and flat broke – find a sugar daddy who gave good gift. She boasted about hers: MD, for Maple Daddy. SD for Sugar Daddy would have been the obvious choice, but as she was detoxing at the time (her agent wanted her at 118 pounds at five foot eight) she said she found the word sugar set off cravings, hence MD. Later he became 'shit face'. As Astrid's room-mate, I was privy not only to the perks of MD – the $5,000 Tiffany bracelet he gave her – but also to the lows: Astrid having phone sex at three in the morning as unofficial payment for the baubles. By week two of Astrid's sex-goddess role-playing (all on the phone, thank God) her wrinkly beau had revealed an unhealthy interest in enemas, and even she, who put the late-night phone sex down as 'voiceovers' on her acting résumé, drew the line at his coprophilia. Especially the night she had food poisoning, with appalling diarrhoea, and he wanted her to be on speakerphone. Not exactly an ideal room-mate situation; we were both desperate at that point. The following morning Astrid suggested blackmailing him, as he was a big muckety muck at one of the studios. She suggested that we should send the answer-machine tapes to his wife, revealing his puerile predilections. Despite the fact that I think she was unconsciously test-ing me – to see if I would hold on to some spiritual principles when desperate – we went through the sham of an election to decide on our next course of action. We voted. Twiglet had the all-important half-vote (too small for a whole one), so by half a vote Astrid's idea was vetoed. That was the morning I started the search for a new place in earnest, and that afternoon I started charging for the readings; both actions had led me to my mini-paradise in the Hollywood Hills.

Astrid was still monologuing on the phone, or coming to the end of her 'check-in' as her therapist had advised her to call it. After listening to her half-hour take on 'shit face', and how her low self-esteem had attracted him, and how she was determined to change, I peeped in with my two cents. I warned her to stay alert: she had to be careful with the dating scene in LA. I'd heard the sexual decadence was almost Roman and there were a lot of little shit faces running around like modern day Tiberiuses; on top of that, HIV meant that kinky, non-tactile was the new safest sex. Shit face was a product of his Hollywood environ-ment. No real contact. Statistically, phone sex and cyber sex were the most popular pursuits in LA … I glanced at the clock nervously; three minutes before the first appointment I had to move my mind away from sex and into the spiritual. 'Gotta go my love, break a leg and I'll call you after the readings, if I have any energy …'

It was strange how draining I found the idea of readings. With a minute to go before my first client, I knew I needed a quick top-up meditation. I had already tried at dawn, but the mystics, who swore this was the most beneficial time to tune in, as the world slept, had clearly never lived in LA. The film trucks were rattling and whizzing by before the sun came up. So I closed my eyes, as did Twiglet, and we sat, side by side, resolutely meditating together, on my orange yoga mat in the late morning sunshine. Twenty minutes flew by and then the Twig shrilly announced that now was the time not only for listening to Spirit's whispers, but also for passing on their messages. The client had arrived, thankfully late.

By now, it was mad dogs and Englishmen weather: blazing hot. Oh dear, perhaps an alarmingly apt analogy, I thought to myself as I watched a peculiar figure let herself into my garden. Maybe not quite mad, but certainly friendly with the fairies. She was wearing several layers of plastic raincoats with over-large hoods and carrying a small regiment of plastic bags. She must have weighed about 250 pounds and struggled to squeeze through the garden gate. She gripped the bags unflinchingly, so I was forced to end up shaking her wrist hello. I offered her a glass of water, as she was sweating profusely, and instead she pulled out her own 'bio-energised' drinking water from a plastic flask, because she, 'Didn't want to risk contamination.'

I felt desperately sorry for her, but I knew Spirit, despite its sometimes chocolate-box PR (pink-cheeked Marys and coy Cupids), was made of more ruthless stuff – like a diamond, it cuts through what isn't real. Spirit was into solutions, not sympathy.

Moira tucked her trotter feet under the table and told me how great the buses were, except she was always at least half an hour late. I smiled and told her she was here now and not to worry. Hearing this, she took the bags off her lap and placed them gently at her feet. This was clearly a great act of trust.

'I spend most of my time at the library, so it's nice to come here,' she said, looking round at the roses and the fountain.

I could tell she wasn't used to having an empathetic ear, so she went on, 'I spend a lot of time on the Internet. Researching.'

Then she proudly indicated her convoy of plastic bags.

'These are just some of the photos you told me to bring,' she said, as if it were quite normal to translate my, 'Bring a photo or two,' into, 'Fill a bin-liner if you feel like it.' I wondered exactly what had inspired her to fill the small dustbin bags at her feet.

'They're all photos of him.' Then she smiled impishly and said, 'Tell me about him – "the one", the love of my life.'

As I was about to start the reading I noticed a strange whiff of urine. I glanced around to see if Twiglet had been up to her usual mischief, but she was in savasannah on the yoga mat. Then I noticed a yellow stain on Moira's skirt. I took a deep breath and prayed to be told how to help her. Spirit came straight to the point.

'There is a difference between love and obsession,' I said to her firmly. She was listening. 'You're not very ... well at the moment,' I went on.

'He will make me better.'

Her aura gave off a beatific glow, but the 'He' she was gooey about – clearly a saintly Jesus figure to her, her saviour who was going to deliver her from the mundanity of her existence – 'the one', was nowhere to be seen. There was no 'He', capitalised or not, no husband, boyfriend, other or mate to accompany her. Spirit was directly contradicting her. Again, I felt desperately sad for her, but some unseen Spirit guide steered me from pity to purpose.

'You are alone at the moment,' I said. The diamond part of Spirit had won through.

'Not for long though,' she said happily and giggled. 'Tell me when the happy day will be. I've already chosen a wedding dress ... when will he ask me?'

This was confusing. No prospective fiancé was shown. Then a name popped in. And hair colour.

'Redhead.'

Moira perked up. 'Yes, yes, that's his girlfriend! That's who he's with now. But she'll be out of the picture soon.'

I frowned. 'No, they seem happy together. All is well there.'

Then a date was shown. 'September 9th.' She was very excited now.

'That's his birthday! You've got him!'

Then I gave the year.

'That's it! That's it!' She was flushed and squealing. 'I know we're meant to be together.'

'And you're Pisces.'

'But tell me about him!'

But Spirit didn't care about her obsession. They wanted to help her. 'The lesson here is self-love. Love of self ... then others. You're very clever. You will go back to college. Study again. You're starting very soon.'

This provided just a momentary distraction.

'I know he's the one for me,' Moira said simply. 'I need to know more about him.'

Again, I felt desperately sad.

'Look – I mean look at the girls throwing themselves at him ...' And out of the bags came magazines: hundreds of clippings of celebrity parties and premieres.

'Look at that,' she said, beaming, 'my man.'

Adam Sandler's face stared back at me. I was momentarily confused.

'Look!' she commanded. And she grabbed out handfuls of Adam Sandler. 'Now that's his girlfriend, Sarah,' she growled the word girlfriend, 'and this is his birthday ...' She proceeded to pull out endless scraps of paper with doodles and hearts with arrows through them.

I felt beyond uneasy. She knew I did.

'I don't have money, in case you're going to suggest I get help. You are my help. I know I've never met him but I know he's the one for me.' I felt like her mother. As the psychic I was in the mother role ... no, I was misinterpreting a message: Spirit was telling me her mother was there in Spirit ... Wake up Lucinda, you're being slow today.

'Your mother's here.' That got her attention. 'She says you're diabetic. You are to be careful because she says you're not eating as well as you could. She sees you late at night under the covers, eating. And she wants to help.'

'She's the one who wanted me to marry. I'm fifty-four now. She'd be happy if Adam and I tied the knot.' She paused, then lowered her voice and whispered, 'Well, I'm sixty-four really, but I shave a few years off so the age difference won't be so noticeable.'

As I was looking at her, one of her eyes stayed staring at me while the other drifted off to the left, perhaps into the fabulous land where she was indeed united with Adam.

'Your mother loved you very much. She wants to know about Paul. She's asking about him.' Her eyes came back to the painful present.

Moira pouted and shifted in her chair as much as she could. 'I don't love him. He's fat and he's a loser. I only want Adam.' She pulled out an oversize jumper, with the unlikely combination of emerald, olive and yellow stripes. 'Look!' she said. 'I knitted him this! He'll love it. I'm going to give it to him on his birthday. I'm going to give it to him at a premiere.'

'Let me say something that will truly help her,' I prayed. And at that moment, a bird sang very sweetly in the boughs of the tree above us. Twiglet stirred. Nothing happens by accident in the readings. Images flashed into my head of Moira holding dogs, then birds in cages, and cats, and she was smiling and wearing the green jumper herself. And she had friends around her.

'You must go down to the shelter, the animal shelter, to volunteer,' I said. 'You have so much love to give, just give it away, where it's needed.'

A dog, in Spirit, jumped on to her lap.

'You will take a dog home with you. He will change your life for the better. Just trust.'

She was listening. It was a bit of a readjustment, from A-list movie star to mangy mutt, but she was hanging in there with me.

Then a small terrier appeared in Spirit. I described him.

'Oh,' she moaned. 'Oh, that was Pinky. We had him when we were little.'

'He's with your mother and they both love you.'

'What about Adam?' she asked, as if he were her ailing son.

'Adam has a different destiny,' I replied.

'Really?' she said. 'Really? I mean, everywhere I go I think of him and I've even seen him once, and isn't that a sign?'

'It's time to say goodbye now.'

'But it's been years, I've loved him for years,' and as always, she clung on to the plastic bags as though her life depended on them – which, until then, it had.

'You can help a lot of animals,' I said. She nodded very slowly.

'I love dogs,' she said. 'Why are people so cruel? Why do they dump them? Where are the angels protecting them?'

'You're their angel,' I replied.

'But I'm hopeless.' And, at last, she started to cry. 'No one loves me,' she said. 'I have no money. I don't even have health insurance. If I died, I doubt anyone would even notice. The woman next door to me died and no one found her for four days. That's sad, isn't it?'

I nodded, but instinctively remained silent.

'I still want him,' she said through tears, holding up Adam Sandler's magazine face; he was smiling at an awards ceremony, beside a skinny blonde.

'I'm sure I love him more than she does. She's just using him.'

One of the blue spirit lights that I see in the presence of truth sparkled. 'How odd,' I thought. 'She was right!'

I said, 'She may not be the one for him.' And then I nodded, and that small agreement with her, entirely engineered by Spirit, changed the energy in the room.

'I will go and volunteer. And I am going to the library to study so I can go back to school. Tell my mother I'll be OK. I don't want her to worry.'

'You can tell her yourself. Every night when you go to sleep, you can talk to her.'

'Won't that make me seem mad?' she said, as one eye drifted off to the plastic bags again and the other eye stared resolutely down at her chest, where a badge with Adam's mug on it was proudly pinned; beside it, scrawled in her childlike handwriting, she'd written: 'You have my vote!'

'Don't worry about seeming mad,' I said quietly. Suddenly I felt exhausted and drunk dry. And like many borderline personalities who have learnt to be hyper-vigilant and alert because the world is a dangerous place to them, Moira sensed my exhaustion. The tape clicked off.

'Thank you very much,' she said, formally, as if she were leaving the doctor's. She gathered Adam up in her arms and squeezed through the door. As an afterthought she poked her head back and said, 'And tell my mom I'll go for a walk with Paul. I know he's interested in me. He's just so ... not Adam.' And she walked out of the garden and back to her life. I went back to mine, my Hollywood fantastical life, as a psychic, as an actress, and above all as a seeker of my soulmate.

For the first time in a very long while the sun over the gold coast went grey and the chill Santa Ana winds blew in. I sat in my deck hoping to clear Moira's energy. I prayed silently that every single reading that I did would help someone and their lives would be altered for ever, helping then towards happy ever afters. I closed my eyes and imagined Moira dating sweet fat Paul, finding a dog that adored her and going back to school. However, the truth was, I couldn't be certain what would happen to Moira. The thing that made me feel unutterably sad was a hunch I had, that in England Moira would have had a different fate. At sixty-four, she would not have been a freak, as she was here. She was the first person I had seen in Beverly Hills who had her grey hair. I imagined her in England, at a local community centre, with other old, grey-haired biddies, and maybe a nice old boy who could walk with her in the park. Here the nice old boys were all dating twenty-year-olds and sitting in tanning salons, gripping on to their youth in a town where it's a sin to look old. In England, at worst, the NHS would have come up with some affordable medication for her, if her obsession grew manic. But here, she could die of no health insurance, brutal isolation and terrible loneliness. This was not a town for the aged. No wonder she had something unreal to keep her going, a fantasy love.

In fact, wasn't I guilty too? Jimminy chastised me for occasionally bringing up my first love, Sexy Steve, and I wondered if on some psychic level I was using my nostalgia for an ex, to prevent my soulmate from coming in. I had ludicrous dreams of Sexy Steve and I getting back together and travelling the world, with one small adjustment; Sexy Steve no longer happily married ... Fine, I admitted to myself, I am heading out towards Moira land. It was the sex we had, I guess; multiple orgasms create obsessions, I thought to myself ... Then, what the fuck was wrong was me, why was I thinking about sex all the time?

The doorbell rang.

Watching the girl walk up the steps, a kind of poor man's Pamela Anderson, I strongly suspected that my sexual thoughts had been unconsciously preparing me for the second reading. God it was tiring being psychic sometimes, not knowing whose thoughts I was thinking, the client's or mine. Bambi walked in, or rather her breasts walked in, followed by her gigantic lips. She was dressed in a leather mini and retro boots. At first, looking at her glazed eyes, I thought she was on heroin; then I realised she was so emotionally disorientated that she could barely focus or balance herself. She sat down.

'I wanna talk about love.' The only thing that gave her away was her eyes. Big, sad, mascara-clumped eyes, but impeccable nails, hair, and costume.

I let out a deep breath and started the reading.

'I see a trapeze. Swinging back and forth.'

Bambi burst out laughing. 'I used to be in the circus!' she said. 'Will I go back?' Her voice was filled with fear.

'No. Because of your injury, to your knee.'

'So I'm stuck where I am.'

'No. You have a choice. Victims get stuck. But victims can leave.'

Then I heard a strange whirring sound, almost like a medieval rack, and a montage of images followed. They were pornographic: violent, nauseous, and shocking. Then an image of Bambi began to form among the pornographic images in my mind's eye. I looked up at her and she saved me the explanation.

'I am a victim,' she said. 'He pays me to be a victim. I am a slave of love.'

'He' was shown to me. He was the classic Hollywood suit that makes projects happen. No name came, just his car; a blue Bentley. I saw it drive away from a suburban house, LA-suburban with Roman columns and a ludicrous fountain. Then I was guided underneath the house. 'The torture chamber. It's in the cellar.'

'I know, it's very James Bond, isn't it!' Bambi said, giggling, tickling Twiglet with her pointy plastic boots.

I wouldn't have been surprised if Ian Fleming had appeared at that point, anxious to point out that his books were full of surprises, but not modern-day torture chambers where would-be actresses were lured. She had the porn-star mannerisms nailed; she was giggling, pouting, and thrusting her formidable chest at me all at the same time. But I had to connect with her soul, not with her body, which she had used for years as a shield against the awful reality of her life.

'He won't let me leave. I went back to Minnesota. But he says he loves me.'

I was shown a psychic picture of him whacking her across the face.

It's one thing to read the 'Dear Jean' page of a magazine, and sigh at the impotence of the girl who won't leave the guy who beats her to a pulp but says he loves her, but to be confronted in person by the same girl, who is counting on you to help her, is something I could only do if I allowed Spirit in. Because to really help her we needed a Spirit clue to see the underlying reasons for why she ended up in the basement of a rich fuck who beat her.

'He says he loves me,' Bambi repeated.

I looked at her intently. 'I want you to close your eyes and imagine it's ten years in the future, and you are still with this man,' I said.

She recoiled. 'But I don't want that!' She nervously kicked her foot and Twiglet yelped as the boot caught her in the tenderest part of the snout.

'Then you have to leave. You will be helped.' Bambi had picked up Twiglet and cuddled her fiercely.

'My friend wants me to stay. Cindy.'

Bambi pulled out of her bag a photo-booth picture of a girl, also in her twenties, sticking her tongue out.

'I can't leave without her.'

Spirit whirred the kaleidoscope in my head and I insistently said, 'What about your uncle? Tell me about your uncle.' This was the clue we needed. Her past had created her present. But this was unusual. Usually Spirit wants me to tell my clients. Not ask a question. However, they'd named the person. And this time it was important that she told me, important that she had a witness to her truth.

'Your uncle?' I repeated.

'He was a bad man,' she said, and her voice was suddenly tiny, like a tiny girl's.

'He lived with you, didn't he?'

'Yes, and I couldn't escape.'

This time violent images of a child's body being made to do

unspeakable things invaded my consciousness. Then I saw bars
… as if she were locked up … but she didn't want to stay on
that part of her story. She needed to get to her future to make
her feel better.

'But I did escape. I came here, and please tell me I am going
to make it. Tell me!' She reached across Twiglet and her nails
were digging into my arm.

Spirit wanted to give her evidence and hope. I took dictation.

'You're a model, right?' I said calmly.

She nodded, going back to cuddling Twiglet. 'Sort of. Part-
time. But I dance as well. And I just do the other thing, the
dancing thing, to make money.'

I had a suspicion we weren't talking ballet.

She hurried on, 'But I'm pretty enough, aren't I? Pretty
enough now to make it. I'm an actress as well.'

Something in me again commanded me to be quiet. Just
to listen.

'I'm a good actress. I act all the time. I pretend I'm happy, I
pretend I'm going to stay with the creep, then I fool him and I
escape. I'm going to get rich and leave.' But Spirit was on to her.

'Is that why you took the jewellery?'

She narrowed her eyes. 'You should understand that,' she
said, 'that's karma. He hurts me, I hurt him.'

'That's not karma, that's revenge.'

'Anyway, I've met someone else.'

'The German guy?'

'Describe him,' she said, testing me.

Sometimes I see more when I'm put on the spot, and other
times I just have to be honest and say that's all I see. But Spirit was
batting with me today. 'Tall, and you met him in a nightclub.'

Now Bambi trusted me. Just for today that meant more to

her than PC self-helpy stuff about abuse, because she was hoping for a miracle, having lost faith in her life.

Matter-of-factly she continued, 'I tried to kill myself ... but it was only once.'

'How did your friend Cindy feel about that?'

'You know I—'

'—slept with her.' I finished the sentence. It was easier to talk sex than soul for her.

'What about Cindy?' she said. 'Do you think I can leave that guy and be with her?'

As if taking dictation, I said, 'Your destiny is not to be the damsel in distress for ever.'

She suddenly lowered her voice and almost mischievously said, 'Can Cindy come in and see you? Because I really like her.' Bambi placed Twiglet sweetly on her miniature dog bed.

'Of course,' I nodded.

'Just a minute then ... she's waiting outside.'

'OK,' I said, startled, and then attempted to give a look that said, 'I'm-not-that-startled-of-course, because I'm psychic.' But I was picking up the batty energy. I took a deep breath.

Cindy, who had obviously been eavesdropping, crept in. They had been to the same surgeon. They had matching faces and bodies like dolls. But Cindy, although the same age, was a decade older in her soul.

Cindy squeezed in between me, Bambi and the tarot cards. She gave Bambi an affectionate kiss hello. The sweetest thing they had was how they felt about each other.

Then very matter-of-factly she said, 'I was eavesdropping. You're not bad. Pretty good so far.'

'Thank you, but it's not me; I just hear things.'

'Could I hear things too if I wanted to?' Bambi asked eagerly.

'Absolutely. You probably do already. We all have intuitions.'

'Yes, but she can't seem to act on them,' said Cindy laughing dryly. 'Her guy's a sadistic creep! Why doesn't she just leave him?'

'Well, that's usually because there's a psychological block, or an intellectual one.'

'I think it's my family's fault,' said Bambi tentatively.

'Hell, it always is,' said Cindy.

I suddenly felt as if I were on a chat show that was a cross between the two iconic American shows that had helped form these girls' psyches: *Oprah Winfrey* and *Jerry Springer*. Cindy, clearly an old pro at telling her tale, launched in: 'Oh honey, her uncle came to the house when she was fourteen. He hated her. He put her in a cage.' So those were the bars I had seen earlier.

Then, in a moment of spiritual confusion, I wondered if this was one of those 'You say tomato' moments, and that cage meant crib or cot.

Bambi now had two witnesses to the truth of her sordid story. She told us, 'It was a cage, well it was more like a kennel really. He locked me up in it in the garden. Said he did it for my own good because he loved me. Mom was at work, then he got lizards and cut their tails off and made me watch as they jumped around. So I thought I'd come to Hollywood, and that as well as acting I could sell my idea as a screenplay. My therapist thinks I should go to AA. What do you think?'

But Cindy wanted to be the one with the answers, and as she was probably the only genuine protector Bambi had ever had, I listened to her.

'Bambi's not a hard luck story.'

She went on. 'We both have money. We've always been able

to take care of ourselves.' She reminded me of one of those Hollywood dames, with red lips and dangerous solutions.

'We met when we were fifteen and strung out. We got clean. We started dancing. But we really wanna know, should we stay here? We could get a cute apartment together, keep working at the club ...'

A bright white light flashed in front of my eyes and I suddenly knew why they were both here. I had very important information to give them.

I looked at Cindy very sternly. 'There's a girl at the club who dances with you. The place about an hour from here. She dances between you both, I can't see her face properly ...'

Bambi and Cindy looked at each other, searching the pole-dancing line up at the club they worked at, and then Cindy exclaimed, 'Oh – Sue!'

'She has a stalker,' I said slowly.

'She has a fan ...' Bambi interrupted me. 'He's a producer and he's just really into her and he's got a bit of a thing for her ...'

'He's not a producer, he's lying. He's a stalker,' I repeated.

'But he says he loves her,' Bambi insisted.

I don't think I'd ever done a reading where every man mentioned had professed love but acted with hatred.

'You must warn her. Tell the police. He's not a fan. He's dangerous.'

They both looked serious, although Cindy still looked sceptical. 'Why should I believe you?'

'She worked for the police,' said Bambi earnestly. 'Right?'

I nodded.

'OK,' said Cindy, clearly the decision maker of the two.

'We'll tell Sue about the guy ... that he's a stalker.'

But Bambi had a faraway look in her eyes. 'If you can see these things, then that means someone is telling you. And if someone is telling you, that means someone can see what we do?'

I nodded, shying away from talking about the philosophical battles/spiritual realities I fought daily with myself.

'So if someone wants to help Sue, what's in it for them?'

I was puzzled.

She continued, 'Well, you won't gain by it, I won't and Cindy won't.'

'I guess it's just a good deed from Spirit. I think it's part of their job description. Will help, no reward required,' I said.

'So wow!' Bambi exclaimed. 'I think that's the first time I've been told to do something by someone who doesn't want anything in return, and if I do it I don't want anything. That's rad! I thought I was just going to get a whole load of predictions, but this is great. Sort of spiritual.'

'Maybe I should pray more,' said Cindy seriously.

'Tell your friend, this is really, really important,' I said, nodding.

They left together, holding hands and talking earnestly.

There was love there. Between the lesbian strippers. In whatever form it would take, it was real. Loyal and kind. But I sighed. I was exhausted and troubled by something ... someone was gnawing on my psyche. I picked up the snoozing Twiglet and walked into the cool inside of the house.

Sad Moira was still on my mind. That was it. It was easy to judge her and write her off as obsessive and mad. If I was really honest with myself, I realised she was just an extreme version of many people I had read for. People obsessed with an impossible dream. Holding a candle for someone they believed was their true love. Lying down, moving Twiglet so that she lay curled on my feet, ready for my revitalising meditation, my mind kept being flooded with concepts and ideas about this extraordinary syndrome. As if Spirit wanted me to understand it thoroughly so I would be able to help others to cure themselves of this spiritual malady ... As I closed my eyes, the name I was looking for floated into my mind in big capital letters ... THE ONE YOU CAN'T FORGET ... and it was as if I was reading a description of this condition, dictated by Spirit.

The One You Can't Forget can be your college boyfriend, your first love. He can be the forbidden one you always thought you should have. Usually he's the one you went out with, thought it would last for ever, and then you broke up. And he won't go away. Geographically, he's usually miles away, but psychically, mentally and emotionally you can't forget him. He tempts you with your past. Cue music for the impossible dream. Eventually he will become your drug of choice.

And, just like a drug, there is no immunity from The One You Can't Forget. Class, age and marital status don't deter the inner realms of your psyche from responding to his Svengali-like attraction. The most common time for hearing his siren call is either just before you are about to get serious with someone new, or after a break-up, when you are feeling vulnerable and afraid, and fear is your motivator. He is the permanent other choice and always the one on the back burner. Even if you, or he, are with someone else. It takes an inner grit not to be threatened by The One You Can't Forget. The ties between you are sticky, sweet and gummy, and hard to disentangle yourself from. You are the fly in the web.

So many times in readings, when it comes to question time,

you see women, and men, get that wistful look in their eyes and say, 'What about …?' And just the saying of the name puts them into a trance. Inevitably, the name will not come up spontaneously from Spirit, who is happy and keen always to show the new or congratulate the stable. But The One You Can't Forget is an old conjuring trick of your mind, often used, usually distracting, and always deceptive.

Have there been occasions when you've seen someone get together for ever with him? Never. By his very nature you can't have a fulfilling long-term relationship with him. An old love or old flame can return, but that does not mean he is The One. He is always marked: 'Danger'.

You even know people who have met someone once, briefly at a party, and cast them in the role. But it is always doom-laden. Because these people are creatures who like to skulk around in the darker corners of your mind, and, like vampires, they will die when they come into the light of everyday life, the life of children and garden repairs and mortgages. They are night-time party creatures.

So, if these people are so bad for us, why do we eulogise about them? And what can we do to exorcise them? Because usually the first step towards finding a real solid kiss-you-on-the-mouth mate is to say goodbye to the dream – which is really an illusion – so that the real dream man can appear. And no, we're sorry, you can't do it by contacting The One You Can't Forget and having another five-hour conversation about life and poetry and why it didn't work before, and why it could now. Banish these phantom lovers on the psychic level so you can both become free to choose. Choose someone different and sustaining and fulfilling.

The other mark of The One You Can't Forget is the long

term on and off: 'We can make it … no we can't,' which goes round and round in an obsessive love-loop until you are both exhausted, but seemingly unable to leave. Just like drugs, the only way out is cold turkey. And just like drugs, there will be a period of withdrawal and you may have to stay away from people, places or things that set off the craving. But the reward is that you will now be free to go where your Spirit voices have been prompting you, and meet those in your destiny who are there for your Highest Good.

When we are addicted to giving Spirit a photo ID of The One, they are very polite and usually won't introduce you to anyone else. Give them a break, give yourself a break and give The One You Can't Forget a break. He needs to be evicted and relocated. Then, if he reappears in your psyche, it will be where he belongs, in the compartment labelled 'past'. Possibly, you will need to demonise him first, to help with the goodbye, but give him his rite of passage and persist until he is no longer a possibility, but a dead end. This is one of the most vital steps in readying yourself for a soulmate.

I opened my eyes. Back to the so-called real world. And I heard, opening the gate to our home, someone humming happily to himself, my soulmate friend Jimminy. I had to remember that. Friends were soulmates too. Not just the one who was going to sweep us off our feet. I thought of Al again, and the first time I met him and literally fell into his arms. And I felt nervous about seeing him tonight. I hoped he would never become The One You Can't Forget. Concentrate on the present, Lucinda; stop going into the future. I focused on the present; Jimminy.

Jimminy looked like a pretend American; shades, brown grocery bags, beer in hand. Just his hair was a giveaway. It was wildly peculiar and stylish.

'Great hair! Ziers?'

'Yes indeedy. I like him,' he said, twirling his hybrid's keys.

'I know you do,' I said, smirking. I had introduced him to Ziers, the sexy hairdresser.

He sat down at the table and, though fooling around, using a silly voice, he put out his palm, saying, 'Oh madam Lucinda, please tell me, is Ziers my soulmate?' But I knew that under the jokiness he really wanted to know what I thought. Whether Spirit was delivering him with 'the one'. Why were we all obsessed with finding the one? Every self-help book insisted, 'You are the one you are looking for.' But none of us bought it. We were New Age but Old Romantics.

'Jimminy, you know it's hard to see with you. I care too much … so it clouds it.'

'It's like not operating on your family if you're a surgeon then …' he said glumly, withdrawing his palm and consoling himself with his beer.

'I'm afraid so, it's just not a good idea. Consolation prize: as your friend, I really like him.'

He disappeared into the kitchen and, in a silly voice, fake-whinged, 'Not good enough. Where's my guarantee of eternal love and not getting hurt?' He stood there looking at me, holding a fantastically stylish vase, with his brand new hair, and I wished I had an answer for him. But I smiled and shrugged.

'With the gods, Jimminy. With the gods.'

We both smiled. Then he turned the tables.

'And what of you? You're going to the swanky dinner party with the sexy Al tonight? Do you think they'll be any action?

'Oh right, you can't see for yourself. God what a drag. Remind me of the plus points of being psychic again, would you?' He finished arranging the bright pink Gerber daisies he had bought from the farmers' market, and started unloading the week's organic groceries.

'Today's meal, goats milk ice cream.'

Jimminy and I had vowed that every time we went shopping in LA, we had to try some new American thing to eat. We had had mixed success so far that week; the vegan soy caviar was a new low in California cuisine (1/10) – only because Jimminy insisted on giving it one point for ingenuity – but, surprisingly, the low-fat rye yeast-free wheat free what-the-fuck-was-in-them mountain bread wraps got 9/10. Within minutes, the chocolate cabernet goats milk ice cream was top of the list. On a complete sugar high, Jimminy did what English actors in LA do with a spare moment; he spent ten minutes attempting to say the 'give-away' words for a Brit perfecting their American accent. 'I felt like merrrrrderrrrrr when I saw the squirwl in the mirerrrrrrrrrrr.'

'Come on, Jimminy,' I jollied him along in my American accent, 'you felt like murder when you saw the squirrel in the mirror.' Jimminy was landing somewhere between a dalek and a yokel. He twanged his new kabbalah bracelet and changed the subject.

'By the way, I saw Astrid up for that sci-fi thing today,' he said cheerfully.

'I know, she called me.'

'Poor girl, she ought to give up. She never books a thing …'

'I know,' I said, tutting.

'Mind you, I was up for a wealthy warlock with two heads. Pretty depressing after the RSC. Not sure if I'm cut out for the LA acting scene … What about you? You miss it, don't you?'

I sighed deeply. 'I miss acting but I don't miss the rest of it – Brick-type agents and the awful waiting for the phone to ring … and worst of all having to shave my legs and do my eyebrows and all of that every time I walk out the door …'

'But, darling, Americans do that anyway.'

'Tell me about it. Every time I hold someone's hand in a reading they stare at my nails in horror.'

'They look like most English women's nails, unless they're going to a wedding or are married to a footballer,' said Jimminy, examining my hands, and on we chatted as we polished off the ice cream.

What I didn't admit to him was how odd it was that whenever the subject of acting came up, somehow I always gently veered off into psychic stuff. And the truth was I missed it dreadfully. It had been fifteen years of my life, four of them training, but I was having to take my own advice, the advice that came out in readings for other people most days: 'Walk through the open doors.' And right now, those doors were not just closed, they were bolted. And, I think, of all the things that had caused me the most pain in my life – my disastrous early relationships, being with Steve when he got cancer – and, on a soul level, the ups and downs of trying to express yourself for a living – acting and writing – the reason why clients loved their psychic readings was not because I knew the names of their dead relatives, or even because I encouraged them to hang in there with their artistic dreams; on a deep, deep level, they knew I empathised with them and had experienced that pain. At least the pay-off for suffering was that I could help others up the hill when I had already walked over the crest. The question that kept going around my mind was whether I had to suffer in order to help and 'be of service', as Diana called it. I knew I was thinking about this because I was going to see Al tonight. He was my tribe, the film tribe. It was just so hard to explain to people in the business that acting and psychic readings come from exactly the same place, a deep listening. And I didn't want to tell him that I was doing psychic readings. There was such a gulf between my film friends (wore black, cynical, intellectual, atheists) and my New Age friends (wore white, hopeful, intuitive, believed in God), and not only did I not know where Al fell on that spectrum, but I wasn't even sure exactly where I fell any more. And that was more frightening to me than anything.

'Time to go to the ball, Cinderella,' said Jimminy perkily, looking at our art deco clock. He was more nervous than me about the date. I had the feeling that he wanted 'us' – Al and me – to work out.

I walked to the cupboard, heading for a big cover-up shawl, and heard from the next room, 'And don't hide yourself in layers of wool … Wear the sexy boots.' I obediently picked up the boots. Gay men know best when it comes to footwear.

I took perverse pleasure in going against the LA tanned-skin 'natural' look, and went for black eyes, white skin and red lips. Jimminy came in with the Map-Quest directions to the dinner party. 'As promised for the directionally challenged.' I smiled my thanks. Then I dropped the 'I'm a psychic so I know everything' mask and hesitantly asked, 'Any advice for tonight, Jim Jims?' as I fastened the final strap of the Westwood killer boots.

'Get him to wear a condom.'

'For God's sake …'

'No. No advice. Advice just gets in the way of the moment. And of all people that's where you need to be, in the moment, not several lifetimes back or peeking into the future.'

'Thank you, oh wise one.' How fantastic and what a relief to be the receiver of advice, not the doler out of it.

'And you look fab ... especially the nails.'

'Thank you for noticing.' I had painstakingly painted my nails the colour of faded ballet slippers. That was about as American as I was going to get.

'Can I borrow your polish? I'm going to a drag stag party in Vegas, and you're not the only one on the town, luvvie ...'

I surrendered my Chanel polish. 'Borrow anything else you like ...' His eyes widened in glee. 'Excellent! When the cat's away ...' and he was nosediving into my Jimmy Choos as I waved him goodbye.

Driving down the freeway to the dinner party, seeing hundreds of other cars with just one lonely passenger in them, I realised that LA is a city for introverts, or for the sort of people who go to night classes or enroll for the Open University. The average person will spend three and half hours a day in their car. That's a third of a day. If you were an A-type personality you could speed-learn twelve languages in a year. One a month. You'd have most of Europe covered in a year. These are the kind of thoughts that go through your mind while you drive in LA.

I came to a complete stop – traffic was bumper to bumper on the Santa Monica freeway and another thought crossed my mind: why did this town's love habits feel so different from all the other cities I had lived in? Beyond the universal search for love and a friend-for-ever that we're all searching for, wherever we live, the difference here is that most beautiful people come to Hollywood not to fall in love, but to fulfil big dreams and to make it. So everyone is selling everyone on what they could be; their potential is their ticket. Therefore youth is valued, because age without material success is a sign of having missed the boat. And in most cases, it's a brutal truth that people's youthful expectations will exceed their results. Unrealistic expectations are cited as one of the leading factors associated with both depression and suicide.

Back home, I was used to a sort of European grace about failure, a kind of faded dignity to it. But in Hollywood, failure is not an option; everyone is selling everyone on a promise, and at the same time they are busy buying self-betterment because there is an erroneous belief that willpower must win. I smiled as I looked up at the billboard above the freeway, of a Barbie doll pretending to be a woman. Was everyone buying this elusive imitation of youth? Hadn't we learnt from Narcissus? The 'self-improvement industry', which ironically promotes self-acceptance as its heart, offers horrifying instant makeovers. If you change your breasts, stomach and thighs – three of the most common plastic-surgery operations and, interestingly, the parts that define us as female (to say nothing of the new designer vagina) – you will alter your destiny. Many soul-destroying studies are cited which encourage the more physically attractive to believe that they will be the most successful! I have nothing against plastic surgery per se, except when it turns out wind-tunnel freaks, and more especially when it flouts the spiritual law that says that true change comes from the inside. But in Hollywood they've got it inside out, changing the outsides instead of the insides. Bambi and Cindy could tell you that.

Despite evidence to the contrary, lots of angry-looking people stewing bumper to bumper in Hummers, I tried to remind myself that, in our souls, all humanity is wise, and even the Los Angelenos sense the soulful lie about their exterior-focused, beauty driven, society and try desperately to combat it with the inner search. The most easily available – and perhaps socially acceptable – remedy here is therapy. I have never met so many people in therapy as I have in Hollywood. In England, a raised eyebrow was the usual response to the brave soul who ventured into therapy, but in Hollywood, NOT confessing all for a sum is greeted with a raised eyebrow. However, as I knew from Astrid's rambles, therapy could miss the soul.

In fact, I mused, the reason my practice was growing so fast, was that therapy seemed to be failing to answer the soul's greatest need, the need for love or a soulmate. I think it's the Old World idea that romance still exists that people are longing to rediscover in a reading. Because their souls don't forget. They've lived too many swashbuckling lifetimes. It's magnificent that therapists can heal abuse, but tragic that they're taking the magic and romance out of life and pathologising love. Chemistry is considered passé, true love just an unrealistic myth, and physical attraction a drug not to be trusted. The traffic on the freeway began to move faster.

The end result, I concluded, as I pressed the gas pedal, is the death of the romantic date. Because everyone is in therapy, the date often mistakes their possible love mate for the therapist and the romantic social contract is thrown out of the window as neuroses are chewed over. It's not exactly sexy. It makes you long for Pablo Neruda and French men and bold, bad heroes. James Dean is long gone. Now he'd be crying and talking about his mother complex, his leather jacket gathering dust and his motorbike turned to rust. It made me weep.

Therefore, basically, I cheerfully reasoned to myself, you have a town full of wounded narcissists pursuing fame and riches as substitutes for low self-esteem. They are filled with unrealistic expectations and suicidal tendencies, and they want to fall in love, but as they live in the Oprah age they know they are wounded, unrealistic, depressed narcissists and they just want to make sure that you know that they know they are. Then, at least, they get brownie points for self-transformational skills and you don't end up suing them for emotional distress. This, then, sums up the dating scene in Hollywood.

This was Astrid's fault. I had heard so many of her inner monologues that I was no longer able to just switch off, and now my own would ricochet around my brain. I turned off the freeway and congratulated myself. Well done, Lucinda. Now you've really talked yourself into a great state about being single and over thirty ... just before meeting Al again. It's not enough that you're personally neurotic about love, you've now convinced yourself that the whole town is doomed and love can't thrive here. I idly wondered if Al was in therapy or a twelve-step group, or one of the reminders everyone here needed to practice their spirituality. Why the hell was I getting so depressed? Reaching for some chocolate I put it down to PMs; that, or I was picking up some weird, doom-ridden vibe I couldn't put my finger on. I debated looking at my daily astrology reading that I had texted on to my cell, but dismissed it as being too needy. Besides, I only got Leo and couldn't read Al's sign, sexy Scorpio, which I really wanted to be reading.

Driving over the disturbed Indian graves of Santa Monica, I came out in Malibu, the most expensive real estate in America. I drew up to a gorgeous, big-windowed house overlooking the sea. I knew I was going to walk into a dinner party with the super rich and super successful. Al had warned me. I sat in the car for a moment trying to convince myself of what I persuade my clients every day, that their value does not depend on their bank balance or latest film. But, perhaps being English, I was a much harder sell than my clients. The truth was I still felt humiliated that I had been replaced by a star in Al's movie and I felt inadequate. And as a career topic, somehow talking about being psychic made me feel embarrassed and upset, it was almost like masturbation; you just wanted to get on with it quietly, but having a spotlight put on it was just … indecent. Acting, I had the safety of a mask; there I was naked.

I rang the bell and was greeted by the biggest poodle I'd ever seen. He was like a small pony. Good. If the evening got too difficult, I'd hide in the corner and do a healing on Simeon the poodle. He had a swollen lump under his left leg, but I didn't want to worry his owner. I managed to pat him for a while and get a quick healing in. To my great relief and huge surprise, Ziers appeared.

'You again! Wherever I go you're there, party boy!' I exclaimed, hugging him. He looked completely unrecognisable from the last time I had seen him and had long red Rastafarian dreadlocks.

Ziers smiled delightedly. 'Is Jimminy with you?'

I almost had a moment of possessiveness; Jimminy was my name for him. Ziers was the only other person I'd met in a decade who had given him that nickname. Clearly, things were soul serious between my best friend and his new beau.

'Jim Jims is eating his second tub of pumpkin ice cream and watching telly. You'll find that out about him.'

'I hope so,' he said with vulnerability. I smiled at him. Good we could be friends. 'And lucky him …' said Ziers as he indicated the people in the next room. 'Welcome to the New Age famous crowd ...' And we both smiled, knowing we'd feel more comfortable at home with Jimminy, noses in tubs rather than here. I looked around the room. No Al.

'I wonder how Al knows these people,' I mused.

'He's the one Jimminy's told me about? The idiot director who replaced you in his film?'

Good old Jimminy, outraged on my behalf. I nodded.

Ziers smirked. 'Our hostess wants him here because she has written a book about renouncing the world, and despite the fact that she has a TV deal, she thinks that's beneath her and wants a movie to be made, starring her of course, about her renunciation of the commercial world. Go figure.'

Then the hostess came wafting up in her silk sari. She looked rather like a ghost, as she matched the white material and it flapped around her. I could never quite feel at peace with the sari as a Western fashion choice, unless you were Indian. Was that narrow minded of me? Or sensible? Or did I just not feel at peace with her and was blaming it on the innocent sari?

'Al's plane has been delayed but do come and meet everyone. Now Ziers tells me you're the most wonderful psychic!'

Oh God, here we go.

I smiled politely. Any moment now ...

'Now do let me know if you see anything for me later on, won't you?' She was like a magic snake, trying to hypnotise me with her New Age eyes. Where the hell was Al? I rounded the corner and was faced with a crowd of her friends, just sitting down for dinner. I was almost blinded by the crystals around everyone's necks. There were ten of us in all. Famous author introduced us in standard Hollywood style, with our résumés. Me, fabulous psychic, and Ziers, 'spiritual' hairdresser to the stars. A manager of New Age celeb writers. A TV-style guru, who specialised in manifestation altars, and yes, his new show had been picked up; a director who had won an Emmy for a ground-breaking documentary, with a rather desperate girlfriend who was the maker of the crystal charms everyone was wearing.

We sat down and I nervously started chatting to the guy next to me, I did not know, then, that conversations are in Hollywood rarely had purely for enjoyment. There's always a deal lurking. The renowned LA literary manager, pushing forty-five, fat and bald, the epitome of the desperate middle-aged male, asked me out of the corner of his mouth, 'D'ya have any friends I could meet? Female?' Then he gave it the New Age PR spin: 'I want to be willing to get my needs met.'

Oh dear. My fears coming true. Fake therapy-type talk. No fun.

But with a suitably earnest look, I said, 'And what qualities are you looking for in a woman?'

He licked his lips and pushed his peppered squid to one side.

'Qualities?' he squinted. This was clearly a concept.

'Under twenty-five, very fit, blonde and beautiful.'

It worried me that, despite the impressive list of writers he represented, and his renowned reputation for giving copious notes on scripts, his literary prowess was so wanting that 'under twenty-five' constituted a quality.

Then he winked at me. 'Only kidding,' he said, and I smiled with relief.

'She doesn't have to be blonde,' he said seriously. 'She could be a redhead.'

I caught Ziers's eye, who I knew was enjoying this absurd-ity, and rolled mine skywards.

'It's important, isn't it, to listen to our inner child's needs,' he said, as he eyed the women round the table.

In desperation, I turned to our sari-ed hostess. I wanted to ask her if we should worry about Al not being here, but didn't want to be the butt of the usual jokes, i.e., 'Well, you should know, right, you're psychic!' I told myself to stop worrying and chat to her. We engaged in a childish dog-sniffing competition. I got out of giving her a spontaneous love prediction by saying I didn't like to read under an eclipse. It would have been more honest to say I never read when I was bullied. She kept asking if she could take me off to her room for a quick private, and I was beginning to feel more and more like a prostitute, but luckily the eclipse got us off on astrology. You can quickly suss out if you're dealing with a New Age amateur when it comes to astrology, and she knew all the moves. Sun signs are for sissies; you go to moon signs and rising signs and then, if you're really going for it, Jupiter, Venus and Mars placements. At this point, you can move on to hot healers, groovy gurus and sexy saints. What distinguishes the women from the girls is how well, à la BBC newscaster, with grimaces and guttural sounds, they can do the full-on Indian pronouncement of the lineage of gurus. We were equally well versed in the New Age jargon until it came the question of satsang.

When I first heard the word 'satsang' a couple of years earlier, I innocently thought it meant you sat and sang. Luckily, I was not going to make that gaffe tonight among the New Age royalty of Hollywood. It means 'being in the presence of a saint'. Well, mere mortals have satsang with three thousand others, but the 'private satsang' is one up and often a privilege reserved over here for the famous with fortunes.

'I had a private audience with Sai Baba, and I witnessed a miracle!' she said, staring at me with spooky eyes. It was spiritual one-upmanship, a fine sport in Tinseltown among the eager-to-be-enlightened crowd.

There were gasps around the table at this point, as everyone was listening. She was making the point, of course, that she was very special, to have been granted this private audience.

'Oh yes, I was given a ring; of course he materialised it out of vibhuti.' She rubbed her fingers together, to symbolise the white ash that the guru played his magic trick with, and I couldn't help thinking it was the same gesture that is used the world over to symbolise making money. 'He told me I would be very famous.'

She carried on telling her tale, which seemed to revolve around the fact that this very important guru thought she was very important. Ziers, who had just been to see the same saint at the fashionable ashram, pulled aside his white Gucci shirt – where his renunciate sandalwood beads with a pendant of the same guru nestled – and whispered to me, 'Lucky you. She's ignoring me. Even though we have the same guru. But she doesn't pay attention to me. I used to do volunteer work there, I was the security guard at the ashram, so she looks down on me.' He whispered this out of the corner of his mouth.

'I thought the guru's message was that we're all equal,' I hissed.

'Everywhere but in Hollywood,' he replied, raising his eyebrow.

Famous author carried on about her guru. Just for fun, I tried telepathically reading the minds of the guests around the table. Ziers, I was pleased to see, was thinking of Jimminy. I didn't stare too long at his mind pictures as they turned X-rated. The manager was eyeing up the director's young, fit, blonde girlfriend. The director was doing storyboards in his head for his next picture, which definitely had nothing to do with famous author's self-serving renunciation film. The young girlfriend was in India at the guru's feet, being saved, and I was … feeling the absence of Al. We were all thinking about love. Strangely on the pulse, the great authoress pronounced, 'Everyone is searching for love. But we all know real love is love of Self. And the guru represents that. I am very blessed to have found that.'

'Do you think it's karmic?' asked the earnest crystal-maker girlfriend of the big director. He looked proud, like a dad, that despite being twenty years younger than him she could actually string a sentence together. 'All love is karma,' she said, rolling the 'r'.

'Last time I was on prime time I was asked that.' And that was when, although I still didn't know what she was famous for writing, I realised that the great authoress was seriously famous. It transpired that she wrote about finding true love for ever.

I glanced at her ring finger. She, of course, spotted me.

'I have been married – several times! Well, eleven. But I always say I never just dated someone, I had to marry!' Obviously had the PR spin down from Liz Taylor. 'The guru's blessed me!'

It was depressingly funny, really, how she was wrapped in her cashmere shawl in this idyllic house, espousing gurus who would, I suspect, have blanched at the waste. Lobsters that were largely uneaten littered the table and were being scraped into bins by the 'staff'. Everyone started talking about diets. And she was talking about how she loved the fact that her guru was intent on reaching the substrata of Asian culture, the untouch-ables, and yet I noticed that as she talked about this she blatantly ignored the Mexican servants who were removing her plate. The Mexicans are LA's very own version of the invisible workforce; they work for slave wages and usually have no immigration papers and no rights.

There was one of those pauses that, I suppose, inevitably follows the grand flurry of comments on carbohydrates and karma, and embarrassingly my cell phone went off with a very loud silly 1970s disco song that Jimminy had programmed for me. Ziers started laughing and I apologised saying I'd take it in case it was Al. I hurried to the loo, eager to have a break.

'Are you with Al?' Astrid hissed.

'No, he's late.'

I locked the bathroom door and sat down on the closed seat for a mini-break.

'That's not a good sign, according to *The Rules*.'

'Fuck *The Rules*!' I said, a little too harshly.

'How did you like Cindy and Bambi? Did the readings go well?'

'How did you know?'

'I sent them to you, you idiot.'

'You creep, why didn't you tell me they were your friends?'

'I don't know them that well, they just dance with me … they're in the second act. I just wanted to talk to you first … oh, and I have some news … I think I've got a job! That card you pulled was right! It's this producer I met here weirdly …'

I started to have an odd feeling in my stomach.

'Here; where?'

This was when I heard the Barry Manilow music in the background.

'Where are you, Astrid? I thought you'd quit the lap-dancing thing?'

'I had to pay the rent after shit face, I've been meaning to tell you, I just didn't want you to go all spiritual and judge me … Anyway, this producer's taking me out for a drink after the show.'

A picture flashed in my head. 'Brown hair, something in his house, in his cupboard …' This was reminding me of the police case I worked on.

'Last call for Sue. Last call for Sue.'

'Shit! That's me, I gotta go on.'

'Sue?'

'Stage name. I know, would you believe Astrid's actually my real name? See you tomorrow … gotta turn the cell off!'

And the line went dead.

Oh my fucking God. Astrid was Sue. The producer was the creep. She was the one who was in trouble. He was the stalker.

I walked back into the dining room in shock.

'I'm very sorry, I have to go. A friend's in real trouble.'

Several people got to their feet.

'Can we help? What is it? Is it an accident?'

'Not yet,' I said gravely.

'What a thrill,' said the director, voyeuristically, 'a psychic sleuth.'

'Do you need anything?' asked the director's girlfriend very genuinely.

'No, I just have to get to my friend before this … guy does.'

'Take my crystal for good luck,' she said thrusting it into my hands.

The fat manager walked up to me and gave me his card.

'If you ever want to turn this psychic stuff into a show, just call me.'

I felt sick to my stomach. If I had said my best friend had been run over, would the director have run out with his camera, with the manager trying to pitch a show on human road-kill.

I ran out of the door and bumped straight into Al.

God, he was beautiful. It really did hit me like being punched in the stomach, but I didn't have time ... Astrid was in trouble.

'Where are you going? I'm really sorry I'm late, I had to meet with these film investors and so I got the next plane ...'

'Don't worry. I have to go.'

A totally bewildered look crossed his face. I had the strangest feeling he was going to say, 'I love you.'

Or was it me? Was I going to say it?

Instead, I said, 'I have to go.'

He nodded and we both smiled, as if we knew the fact that we hadn't seen each other for four months and I was now running past him with no explanation was not that important. As if we knew it was just a tiny moment that would not dictate our destinies.

If I didn't get a move on, though, Astrid wouldn't have a destiny left.

Al yelled, 'Supper tomorrow?' Barely acknowledging him, I nodded yes and he lifted up his cell to indicate that he would call me. I ran to my car.

Where the fuck did Astrid work? Long Beach?

'Which way is Long Beach?' I yelled.

I realised the dinner party had gathered on the balcony to watch the drama.

'Take the 405 ...'

Fuck it. I was about to ruin my credibility with the New Age clan. I yelled, 'Is there a strip club there where they lap-dance?'

Horrified silence among the chanting-chakra crowd. Then the fat manager stepped forward.

'It's on Main Street. You can't miss it, red neon sign that says "titty bar".'

Al started laughing.

I would have done if Astrid weren't on my mind.

I pulled out to the poodle's howling, as if he knew I only had a short time to get there.

And get there I did, going at full pelt in the tiny bug, racing along the coast road with the sea spray salting the car and a couple of anxious tears doing the same thing to my face. Manager was right: it wasn't hard to find, the eleven-foot neon nipples being a nice clue. Threw the car in the lot and rushed around to the front.

Big burly bouncer. 'ID please, ma'am.'

'You gotta be kidding,' I said, at this point feeling 103 years old from worry. 'I need to see my friend ...'

'You the girlfriend?'

'Yes,' I said instinctively.

'Yeah, one of the girls was expecting her girl in from Australia.'

Thank God for ignorance. I was through the door. Spirit was on my side.

Shit, the show had just ended. Then I saw Bambi.

'Where's Astrid?' I yelled over the eerie red flicking lights.

'Astrid?' Then she saw it was me.

'Oh my God, what are you doing here?'

'Astrid – Sue?' I yelled, correcting myself.

'Oh, she came off stage, she went to have a drink with—'

'Did you warn her?'

'Well, she came off stage before we had a chance—'

'OK, OK where is she?' I said, looking around desperately at the half-naked women and men in suits.

Bambi came up and wanted to hug me, but the look in my eye stopped her. She stuttered, 'She's walking to his car with him ...'

'Where?' I yelled desperately. I had to calm down; I couldn't work psychically if I lost it.

'Where?' I said very calmly. But automatically I turned back towards the lot.

I could see Cindy at the bar, she was pointing me in the direction of the car park. I ran past the bouncers.

'Astrid!!!' I yelled. She was just getting into the man's car. She ducked in the seat.

Fuck, she probably thought someone was recognising her. 'Astrid?' I yelled.

One of the bouncers came out on to the lot. 'Your girlfriend leaving with a bloke?' But he was laughing.

I rushed over to the white Toyota. Banged on the window. Astrid's face peered out at me. She rolled the window down.

'Hey, what are you doing here?'

I gulped. Had to get her out of the car. Needed to get the bouncer's attention.

I started screaming, 'How can you leave me?'

The bouncer came over.

It worked. The guy got out of the car. I yanked Astrid out. She looked at me as if I was insane. So did he.

'What the fuck's your problem?' he said in a nasty tone.

The bouncer came up and grabbed me by the arm. Come on Lucinda. Come on Spirit. Come up with something.

Astrid was staring at me in a peculiar way. I stared at the guy.

'You've got a brother in New York. He's in a wheelchair.'

'So Sue's told you about me?' he said.

I needed more.

'You have an apartment in New York you haven't told anyone about. There are leather couches.'

I could see chains. Handcuffs. Videos. He showed them weird videos of chickens with their heads cut off. Then took photos of them. The girls he hurt.

'A video collection. Chickens, right?'

Turning to him, Astrid said, 'She's psychic, isn't that great? She used to work with the police. She's really good.'

That was the word I wanted her to say. Police. Then I dared him. I put my hand out. Shake my hand, you fucker.

He moved back. Got into the car.

'You know what, Sue? I'm not feeling so good, she's given me a headache. Let's do this tomorrow.'

Astrid looked at me angrily.

'Why the fuck are you being so protective of me? I don't need your help. Just because everyone else does ... I'm your friend and I'm fine.' I stepped in front of the car door.

'Don't get in the car, Astrid.'

And suddenly she knew. The way I had said it.

The bouncer grabbed my arm, tightened his grip and said, 'If your girlfriend is spoiling your date, Sue ...'

Astrid turned to them and said, 'No, my girlfriend's OK.'

The guy was in the car by now. She got it. The white Toyota pulled out of the lot.

'Is there anything we can say about him ...' she said, indicating the guy, 'to anyone ... can you prove ...?'

'No. Not yet.'

I sat down on the asphalt and hugged Astrid.

'Did I fuck up again?' she asked in a small voice.

'No, Astrid. You didn't get in the car.'

'How bad ... would it have ...'

'Um ... you don't want to know.'

'Bye bye bad?' she said in a flat voice.

'Not this time. He'll get caught sometime. Not with you. There's evidence in his cupboard ... He's a serial rapist.'

'Fucker!' said Astrid, her hand shaking violently. And suddenly she was standing in the parking lot, screaming, 'Fucker! Fucker!' And then, 'I hate this fucking town!'

Standing there, half-naked, with a rabbit coat on, screaming, 'I hate this fucking town!'

5
Love Guru

Astrid and I were on our fourth hot chocolate. Black eye make-up all the way down our faces. We talked about what had happened, what could've happened and what didn't happen. Every five minutes, she'd start crying and tell me how grateful she was that I had saved her. Every five minutes I kept telling her that Spirit had saved her and not me. I only wished I could rely on my psychic abilities to always help the ones I love. But it doesn't always work that way. Spirit have their own agenda and I had quit trying to figure it out. This time we were both lucky. She vowed she would never lap-dance again. I felt a huge, almost motherly relief when she said that and hugged her again. She handed in her notice over the phone. The outcome of the whole drama was great: even shit face was useful, as he knew one of the police chiefs, who had helped him in exchange for keeping quiet about various sex scandals, and the unofficial word was put out on the fake producer. I prayed Spirit had used Astrid and me to stop this man from doing any more harm. And I thanked whatever mysterious force had engineered her miraculous escape.

The California sun of a new day found us dozing off on the sofa. Our cappuccinos and second wind kicked in and we set off to celebrate the survival of our adventures at the Standard. Nothing like their eggs and pancakes to epitomise the American breakfast. I did my best to follow Astrid's old custard Beetle; as usual she almost killed someone as she wavered all over the road, jabbering into her cell phone.

We went into the hotel and straight to the restaurant. She sat down and said very calmly, 'I'm buying.'

'I don't think so,' I said, 'you're out of a job.'

'I don't think so,' she said, smiling, her voice almost singing. 'My agent called me in the car … The part I went up for yesterday morning, the part in the studio movie … I GOT IT!'

And she got up on the red leather chairs, shrieked with delight, and started jumping up and down. To my surprise, I started crying and shrieking too. She ordered a bottle of champagne and I called Jimminy, who in turn called Ziers. Soon we were all eating pancakes, drinking champagne and playing Astrid's favourite song over and over again on the jukebox. By the next hour the news had travelled the Hollywood grapevine. Big-star-tiny-body called. Most of the New Age crowd from the night before called to congratulate Astrid. Her cell was on fire. One of the waiters at the Standard had been in Astrid's acting class; he told his agent and then all the big agents, like sharks, wanted a piece of Astrid. Even Brick called.

'Which one should I go to?' she mouthed to me desperately.

'Tell then you'll call them back!' I said, smiling. So, Astrid told CAA, ICM, UTA, William Morris, Paradigm, Endeavor, she'd get back to them. It was a Hollywood dream come through and for what it was worth I was a part of it. My 'actress' self was a little shell-shocked, but honest joy for my friend won over. My turn would come in whatever shape and form. If Spirit could save Astrid, it would look after me.

The difficult calls also came: her present agent called, screaming that she knew Astrid would leave her now. Astrid promised she wouldn't, then called back one of the big agencies and set up a meeting. Then her present agent called again and Astrid worked out that she'd make a hundred grand in the next couple of months. I started being very sensible and told her to remember she had to pay taxes. She wrote a shopping list of all the very important things she hadn't been able to afford up to now and needed to buy. The first three things on the list were:

1. Cream-coloured convertible Beetle
2. Crème de la Mer face cream
3. HBO

Fearing that I was feeling left out, Astrid told all the well-wishers our wonderful tale from the night before. She made sure I was the star of the story. By the end of her PR bonanza, I had apparently driven to the titty bar without a map, 'hypnotised' the bouncers into letting me in with my extraordinary psychic powers, stopped the car with my Uri Geller like control over metal, and finally forced a confession out of the convicted rapist, telepathically, who had handed himself over to the police. Well, that was Astrid's version, and today Astrid was Hollywood and therefore that was the official Hollywood version. The waiter from Astrid's old acting class told everyone in the restaurant about the 'future star' sitting at one of the tables. And people came by, asking Astrid for her autograph already.

'You're going to have to come to the set and do readings for everyone; I mean, you're just brilliant! Will you do that?'

'Sure,' I said, smiling. Today she was the star-to-be, I was the psychic friend, and it was all right with me that day, that moment. Destiny is on speed-up mode in this town, from rags to riches as fast as instant coffee, you're almost dead one moment then made a star in an instant. And we celebrated that.

At about two in the afternoon, I reached the famous authoress from whose dinner party I had scarpered the night before. She was delighted to have been the launching pad for Astrid's remarkable tale of being saved by me (I again repeated that it was Spirit but she wasn't interested): I was the New Age star, and she insisted that I come over immediately. She said she wanted me to do some readings. Saying no to a celebrity is very difficult. They are used to being agreed with, and the very thought that I might even think about declining, when clearly this would be so good for my business, was, according to Astrid, a serious faux pas. 'If someone famous invites you to their home, go now. They'll be on to the next thing, tomorrow; today you're hot!' she said, somehow obliquely implying that if I didn't go, the authoress had the power to harm my business. Astrid had to embrace her new star schedule, and she kissed me goodbye as she rushed off to meet her new publicist and have her first session with her new private Pilates trainer, Sebastian – known as Sebastian sock-it-to-the-stars. I had to go and sock it to the New Age stars too, just as a spiritualist.

Arriving at the authoress's house I was surprised to see several vans outside, and groups of people kitted out in baseball caps, puffa jackets and sunglasses. Lights were also being dragged into the house. I made my way gingerly to the front door. It looked like *Extreme Makeovers* was being filmed. Harassed men in designer glasses moved potted plants and blacked out windows. The house was, for all intents and purposes, turned into a movie set. Propped on a chair was a black and white clapper board; on it I read, 'Amazing Women: The Love Guru. Episode Two.'

The Love Guru herself came out to greet me. She was in her usual uniform sari. Her outsides bespake peace – white sari, crystals, sparkly shoes – and this time I decided my prejudice against saris on wobbly white Western women was based on fashion sense, not prejudice. But her face was harassed.

'Ssshh, they're just filming my introduction. Do you want to come and see?' The question was rhetorical. This was a command; I meekly obeyed.

We looked over to the film set and I saw the hostess of the show, a perky, groomed blonde, take her gum out and stick it on to the hand of her Mexican assistant. Who was immediately shooed away by the 1st AD. The Love Guru was oblivious to any of this; she was transfixed by her own publicity. The hostess rolled her head around theatrically a couple of times then readjusted her silicone.

'Quiet on the set. And ... sound! Cameras rolling! ... And action!'

The blonde was on. 'We are here today with the woman we have all come to love and know as the Love Guru. She is the author of countless bestsellers including *Soulmates Forever*. Last week Hillary Clinton, next week Oprah Winfrey, and this week a day in the life of America's favourite Love Guru!'

'Cut!' yelled the director. The woman behind the camera started reloading.

'Wow, did they interview Hillary Clinton and Oprah?' I asked the Love Guru enthusiastically.

'No,' she said disparagingly. 'It's the pilot, so we just give them who they want.'

I idly thought of making a show reel with me beaming, saying, 'Last week I worked with Wim Wenders and next week Peter Weir and Ang Lee team up to work with me.' Call it a reality pilot and it pass it off as truth.

'Come on, let's sneak off before I'm on camera just so you have time to give me a quick reading!' She said it as though I was about to get a Christmas present. I walked through her house, which had the latest LA look: 'barefoot luxury'. Marble floors, wooden Buddhas, Diaphantique candles, and her obsession, her guru, in gigantic photographs. A Siamese kitten with a Sanskrit name frolicked under the Buddhas.

'What happened to the poodle?' I asked.

'He was too much trouble. I gave him away. Had a tumour.' She sallied on through her house. I was really beginning to dislike this woman.

Outside was the usual Hollywood luxury: an infinity pool and beyond-million-dollar views of the Pacific Ocean. The pool had never been swum in, and the sea was so poisoned that the last time I'd been there, a dying seal had washed up my feet and I had sat with him as he died in quiet agony on the beach. But if you didn't look too closely, my God it was beautiful. Then I realised what it was that disturbed me about this town. The sound of the city. Silent. An absence of joy. Children are rarely seen in LA and never heard. Those substrata noises of children yelling in playgrounds, extinct. It's like a sci-fi town at dusk, where the sets are perfect and pristine and everyone's gone home.

The Mexican assistant came up and shook my hand. 'Hi, I'm Hermelinda. Can I get you some water or tea?'

'I'd love some water, please.'

I noticed a little pendulum around her neck with the guru's smiling face on it. He seemed in touch with a bliss that was evading all of us.

'She introduced me to him,' said the assistant, referring to her boss, with a nervous smile. I wondered whether Hermelinda had gone to the guru because she had sensed his divine grace, or whether her boss had bullied her into it. Feeling suitably bullied myself, I plumped for the latter motivation.

'You're needed in fifteen,' said Hermelinda to her celebrity boss.

Then, rather peculiarly, a girl who was clearly the wardrobe assistant, safety pins on her shirt, gave me a quick once over and took a Polaroid.

'Cute look. Sorta rag-doll retro.'

Hmm ... so much for me blending in here with my clothes choices. Rag-doll retro, not laid-back boho with a quirky vintage feel, but more alarmingly the unmade-bed and out-of-the-fashion-loop look. Her pierced tongue glinted as she walked away. I was still feeling marginally awkward, not knowing what the real intention of the visit was. I remember she had said 'You don't mind reading for some people, do you?' And then out it came ...

'We'll do the reading in here,' said the Love Guru, smiling. She indicated her walk-in closet.

The closet was bigger than the living room that Jimminy and I shared. I wondered what wardrobe would call her personal style: kind of *Arabian Knights* meets Malibu, maybe. Unfortunately blousy sherbet-coloured numbers with matching turbans. I felt marginally better about what I was wearing. She closed the door and turned on the air-conditioning. Now I felt trapped and freezing. Her guru, the Indian master of mystery, looked on, ever implacably.

'One moment,' she said mysteriously. I had to put aside my feelings of judgement and be open. I was here for a reason. Doubtless it was a good one. Spirit was in charge. I kept saying this little mantra to silence the part of me that wanted to flee the house for no concrete reason. Just something was making me uncomfortable.

I perched on a red silk cushion and, when she emerged in what I could only imagine to be her reading outfit, a fuchsia sari, I couldn't help thinking uncharitably that her clothes alone would make a small fortune for those without clothes in India. But I thought this as I wrapped my own scarlet cashmere chanting shawl around me, so of course, I didn't say anything. There was some Indian music playing at that annoying level where you either want to turn it off or up, but 'my client', as she now was, swayed and sang along in anticipation so I lost my nerve and left it on; it buzzed like a drunken Indian bee.

Of course, because I was about to read for the Queen of Love, I was curious about her love life. So, I think, was she. I held her hand and turned over my tarot cards.

'The Lovers,' I said.

She looked pleased. But I sensed her smile did not match her inner turmoil.

'Can I hold your hand?' I asked.

She gave it to me willingly. A different story in her palm.

'You're crying all the time,' I said. 'You're not eating. You're obsessed!'

She nodded. Her eyes filled with tears and she quickly corrected me. 'I'm in love.'

'But,' I said, puzzled, 'he's married. And you're seeing him ...'

She nodded mournfully. 'But he's leaving his wife. He wants

to leave her, I know he does. No one must know we're having this affair,' she whispered.

I felt, I'm sure, how the Washington reporters must have felt when they nabbed Nixon. This was a national New Age scandal! This bestselling woman writer not only preached love, fidelity and truth to the masses, but also proclaimed herself as the know-it-all in the field of love and relationships. I mean, she was having an affair with a married man, for the love of all gurus! She knew, of course, that I realised the gravity of her situation, and with anxiety proceeded to justify herself:

'I know you're a spiritual person, so you'll understand, sometimes love is just destined. It's Spirit-driven and ...' Here it comes, I thought, the panacea for the inexplicable or morally outrageous, the clichéd platitude. 'This love is meant to be.'

I was gobsmacked.

She could tell I was not buying her karma of convenience, so she pulled New Age rank with, 'You know I understand the souls of men, because I've been married eleven times. So I have more experience than you of these things.'

I was glad I was not charging her for the reading because, at this point, it would have been a waste of her money. She was telling me what she wanted me to say. The truth was, she needed to talk to somebody about her obsession and be safe. A sort of Catholic confession. Or perhaps she wanted to justify her hypocritical behaviour by emphasising the magical aspect of her – to use one of her own terms – 'inappropriate' liaison.

'The problem is, my beloved, he just cuts off from me,' she said. 'He won't return my calls ... so I'm helping him not to be avoidant.' She scowled and slumped on her pouffe. I smelt a giant Californian sprat when she said 'avoidant'. I had a hunch she meant he didn't want to talk to her because he was the unwilling victim of her obsession.

'Last night I had to call him thirty-six times,' she said sadly.

Overwhelmed by her blaming him for her closet stalking behaviour, coupled with the reek of sandalwood incense, I was terrified I would throw up all over the guru's pictures, which would surely be an act of supreme inauspiciousness, so I fled to the loo. It was filled with her books. I opened one randomly, preaching the importance of trust in relationships. I sighed and prayed that the reason for me being witness to this insanity would become clear.

When I came back she took my hand and said, 'Darling, don't worry about me. I have been with the guru a long time. I know things.' She paused and nibbled annoyingly at the corner of an After Eight. Never trust anyone who doesn't finish a chocolate. It shows frightening powers of control, far greater than those needed for lesser gifts like fortune-telling. 'But tell me … I want to know what he's thinking right now,' she said. 'Does he really love me? Will he leave his wife? Anything about his child? I'm worried he'll always love his child more than me. He adores her …' She sounded full of rancour when she said that.

Well, full marks for honesty and more for blatant narcissism, I thought. I was contemplating how to turn this strange session back into a real reading when she was called back to the set.

I went to watch. I was fascinated to see what advice the Love Guru was going to give to her fans.

She sat serenely in the peach sari (frequent changes were clearly part of her make-up: gurus, husbands, saris …) as the hostess asked her a series of questions. Knowing her back-story, I found her answers so fabulously hypocritical that once again I was speechless.

The eager blonde addressed her professionally. The cameras were rolling. 'You list in *Soulmates Forever* several pointers for love success. Could you run over those for us?'

The costume girl's pierced tongue glinted in the light as she listened intently, as did the Love Guru's iridescent capped teeth.

'He needs to be single, of course. No married men, girls!' The Love Guru smiled serenely. The hostess nodded sycophantically.

Was it really worth my while listening to any more of this crap? I was so fascinated by her deceit that I stayed.

'He has to be the one who initiates the advances ...' I wondered where the thirty-six calls a night fitted into that.

'Avoid men who are recently divorced; too much baggage.'

But women who were giving Henry VIII a run for his money, i.e., her, no sweat.

I wanted to scream! This was ridiculous. How much I would have loved her if she had just burst into tears and told the fans, not her whole sob story, but at least how confusing and difficult love can be sometimes. How we fall in love at crazy times, with inappropriate people; how the people we love are married, or get sick, or die suddenly and cruelly; but not this anodyne list that fostered a sense of control over the one emotion we have no control over. However, this New Age fascism seemed to have taken the US by storm. Just like Astrid's favourite book *The Rules*. It was a foolproof way to kill love. Imagine it in other art forms: Picasso being given paint-by-number canvases ... 'Cut!' was shouted from the floor, interrupting my stormy inner monologue, and I became aware of 'Love Guru' wafting towards me.

'How did it go?' she asked me.

Thank God, her director came up to her and saved me from replying. 'I loved what you had to say!'

'Well, things must be progressing for you, honey, because

you've done all my seminars,' said the Love Guru patronisingly.

This woman runs seminars too, I thought; she makes Scientology look sane.

'But if you need a little psychic help you should speak to Lucinda. She wants to give you a reading ...'

'Do I?' Apparently. I smiled wanly.

Moments later I was back on the crimson silk psychic seat with the director.

I held her hand to feel the psychic energy ... and the director burst into tears.

Sobbing into her tissue she said, 'I haven't been touched for so long, you know ...' So much for the seminars. She didn't really want a reading, she wanted explanations.

'My life is such a contradiction ... I cast these huge movies, a lot of them are so violent ... and then by night I'm chanting Buddhist peace mantras. Every day, I wake up and say, "I am creating a like-minded community of peaceful artists," but I keep taking these jobs with ... well, men who would kill their grandmothers for a percentage point. And all of this would be bearable if I was with my soulmate.' She didn't really want my response, so she hurried on, 'You're young ... so you probably don't understand, but I'm fifty now, and there isn't a worse town to be a single, intelligent, fifty-year-old woman in. And I've done everything I can, I mean everything, to meet my soulmate.' Her frustration was building.

She almost screamed at me, 'I've done retreats, therapy, hypnotherapy, self-help books, and I still haven't met him! Why not? Where the fuck is God when you need help? How can you even believe in any of this when the world is in such a terrible state? If I just had someone to love ... what am I doing wrong?'

I put my hand on hers and psychically felt prison bars. I gave her the image. She looked stony-faced. Secretly I was questioning myself, wondering what Spirit meant. Had she been put in a cage by a weird man when she was a child? Did she feel imprisoned by her situation? Then I realised as it came in stronger and stronger ... man in prison. I gave her the next image. She looked shocked and furious all at the same time.

'I've been writing to this guy in prison and I know he's wrong for me; I just feel I can't say goodbye. I mean, he killed his wife ... but I know he's a new man ...'

The whole time that she had been doing courses and the Love Guru's useless seminars, claiming she was looking for her soulmate, she had been dating a murderer in prison. The One She Could Not Forget. She was resentful when I gently suggested that she would have to say goodbye in order to make room for a possible soulmate.

'But he's all I've got. It's easy for you to say, you're still young ... just wait till you get to my age. I won't say goodbye to him until something else comes along.' And she stormed out, crying.

Well, that went well then.

Almost immediately a face peeped around the closet door.

'I heard you were in here. Do you read men?'

'Sure,' I said, smiling. 'Sit down.'

'I'm Bill and I'm the producer, but I don't want to know about my career. Can you tell me about my cat?'

An image of a strange creature with white fuzzy fur and glassy blue eyes came into focus. Glassy from something weird. Tune in to the animal's thoughts ... The cat was pissed. In the American and the English sense. Drunk on something. And angry.

'There's something odd in his food ...'

'Oh yes, I give him Prozac to calm him down.'

How do you find words to react to that? Luckily, he went on.

'My girlfriend's very neurotic, you know. She's an actress.' He said 'actress' as though it were a viral disease. 'Used to have a career, but she's ... it's over for her. I just want her to settle down and have kids, and I gave her Prozac as well. She thinks it's the organic granola makes her feel good ...'

Now he had to be joking.

'Come on, I'm kidding!'

Thank God for that.

He also just wanted to be listened to.

'Anyway, she left me ... and the week after she left me she booked a huge role. Can you believe it? I wouldn't give her a part in any of my shows because she couldn't act, but now, I mean, she's a mega star!'

He told me her name. She was.

'We were together seven years. A couple of shitty pilots in Canada was all she did, and then she leaves me and becomes a mega star. What's that then? Karma? And she's married and has a baby. She's so rich now. And won't speak to me. I mean, the reason she left me was she saw me drugging the cat. And actually she saw me, well ... I wasn't joking about the granola. One morning, I'd just had enough of hearing her moan about not getting jobs, so I just moved the cat's bowl and put her cereal bowl next to it ... and popped the Prozac in and she caught me.' And without missing a beat he asked, 'What's in the cards for us? Are we getting back together or is she going to stay with her new husband?'

I took a long pause.

'Well, Bill ... the reason she left you was because you drugged her. And you drugged her cat. Her new husband is treating her a tad differently. So, Spirit is not saying anything. Sometimes Spirit responds with silence, but I sense that she's not coming back to you.'

'So it's fate?'

'Now if you want to call that fate, that's fate that you created.' I was exhausted by this insane afternoon.

He nodded.

'One more question. What sign are you?'

'I'm Leo.'

'Would you like to go on a date with me?'

'No, Bill. You see, I'm a Leo, and as a big cat ... that whole Prozac thing hits a nerve with me ...' Well, that had to be the best excuse I'd come up with in a long time.

Then the costume designer knocked on the door, she of the glinty tongue.

'You look great,' she said, looking at me. 'So, you're happy just to do a quick spot on the show for us. Can you sign this release form? And let's walk to the chair now.'

'Sorry, what am I doing?'

'We just want you to do a reading on television for the show?'

'Who am I reading?' I asked, once again exhibiting that pathetic British politeness at the most inappropriate moment. Why was 'no thank you' not in my vocabulary? I had a bad feeling about this, but went ahead because pathetically I was scared and intimidated. Funny, when I was in reading mode, helping others, Spirit came through for me, but as soon as I switched off, all that clarity and power disappeared. I turned the psychic switch on again, but my now I was sitting on the Love Guru's chair, the cameras were rolling, and a very pregnant Asian model was holding out her hand.

'What can you tell me about my child?'

Something was very fishy about this ... 'Umm ... give me a moment.'

There was going to be a child but not for four years. Oh God this was the last thing I needed; tell some poor girl she is going to lose her baby on national TV. Trust Spirit, Lucinda.

'There will be a child in four years ...'

'That's a long pregnancy, isn't it?' said the model. I heard the casting director laugh loudly.

'You've never been to hospital, ever ... you were born at home ... you've never had an accident ...' I was getting some messages.

'Wow, that's true actually ...' Great. She was giving me confirmation. I had to trust Spirit, it was bellowing in my ear. No child yet. No child for four years. Just say it.

'And there will be no child for four years.'

There was a round of applause. The model stood up and lifted up her shirt. She was wearing a fake pregnancy stomach.

Looking out over the cameras, I saw the director look really angry. With a sinking heart, I knew that she had set the whole thing up. She had been so furious that I had seen her jailbird boyfriend that she wanted to trick me, to try and disgrace me on TV.

The Love Guru was smiling fakely and saying, 'I told you she was great ...' But looking into her eyes I could see her soul was lying, and she too had been in on the whole thing. She didn't want me to know about her secret life as well, and so had created this fiasco. I suddenly felt wretched.

The model was apologising. 'I'm sorry, I didn't want to do it, but will you forgive me?'

I did; I wasn't even faintly annoyed with her. The casting director had disappeared and Love Guru was embracing me warmly. 'Well done ... This will get you lots of clients!'

I just wanted to get out as fast as I could. Despite the fact that some of the crew were taking my number for readings. As if I were American, I said I was 'feeling a little overwhelmed, and needed a moment to myself'. It being this side of the pond, they didn't think I was being self-indulgent; they thought I was taking care of myself, which in a way I suppose I was. I stepped out through the French doors and leant on a palm tree that was bowing over the infinity pool.

So much for being a helpful psychic. All I had done was discover everyone's secrets, and now, like in the good old days, I was being witch-hunted. I had been let into their inner circle, but they had to exact a price; they had to let me know that they were in charge. I felt I had been blackmailed to keep their secrets.'

I stared out across the silent, smog-ridden city. So this was why I had trained as a psychic, not to contact magical kingdoms and give hope, but to end up on a reality TV show, being tricked. And the worst part of it was that the crew applauded. What upset me about that so much, being applauded by the crew, being recognised for outwitting the tricksters? The part that upset me most was that it had nothing to do with the heart of being psychic. It reduced the skill to its lowest level. A party trick. It was about manipulation and cleverness, not soulfulness and healing. I looked through the windows and watched as the Love Guru continued her pontifications on love. It was as empty of honesty as Fox News. I sat down against the palm tree. I was so upset. I felt desperately alone and surrounded by completely untrustworthy people who were selling themselves as 'spiritual'; the Buddhist director, chanting for peace then violently scream- ing at me, the producer, so out of it he wanted to go on dates with me, having confessed to drugging his cat and girlfriend ... This was not a happy picture of humanity. I didn't want to see inside anyone else's psyche. I picked up my cell. Astrid would be too busy, I knew that; Jimminy was on his way to Vegas, wearing one of my frocks. Who else would understand? Without thinking any more, I called Al.

As I was waiting for him to answer, I knew I had to stop lying to him. I would turn into one of these women I'd been reading if I wasn't careful. Lying out of fear of falling in love. What a horrible way to have to learn a lesson. At least I had learnt it.

'Al?'

'Are we still on for dinner?' He sounded ... something under something ... vulnerable.

'Yes ... Ahh, at what time?' My voice was all shaky.

'Are you OK?'

'Yes.' But to my horror, I started sobbing.

'My God, what's wrong?

'I'm so sorry ...' I was crying uncontrollably. I even fell on to the grass. That always happened to me: I was fine, until someone asked me if I was OK. I collapsed.

'Has something happened?'

Still sobbing, I managed, 'Yes ... and no. I mean, nothing awful. Last night Astrid was almost raped – it was just awful – and she only just got away ... And I've just been tricked on this reality TV show ... and I'm not married ... I lied because I thought the Snake had given me the part because I was married ... I had a ring on at the audition but it was for the part ... because Kate was married ...'

'Well, you really are an actress, aren't you?' he sounded impressed. Then I realised he must be impressed at my duplicity.

'What do you mean?' I said defensively. 'I haven't pretended about anything else.'

'No, you misunderstood me. I meant, that's great you bothered to go to all that trouble.'

'Well, it doesn't matter, does it, because some star is going to do the part anyway ... but that's not what I wanted to talk to you about ...' I was crying again.

Al interrupted me. 'I'm really sorry about that. I wanted you, you were just the best ... The investors just had the final decision.'

I hid behind the tree; I did not want all the film people to see me crying.

'Please let's not talk about the part. I was calling because I just wanted you to know that I'm not married and I was pretending because I was scared.'

There was a pause on the cell.

'You know, I knew you weren't married,' he said gently.

'You mean you knew? How?'

'I asked Brick.' How could I have been so stupid? I felt humiliated.

'I thought it was cute that you were pretending. But I'm glad you told me the truth. Let's meet at Café des Artistes. At seven. You know what ... just come now.'

I felt happy for the first time that afternoon.

'Thank you. I'm sorry I'm such a wreck ... crying and ...'

'I love it that you cry. Too many hard women in this town ...'

'Wow ... that's a wounded opener from you,' I said, trying to regain my poise.

'I'll tell you my sad stories when you get there.'

'Well, I've got a couple more confessions to make ... something that might put you off me completely.' It was true. Lucinda the psychic. He didn't know that. I smiled. I could feel him smiling down the phone.

'Bye then. I'll bring a hanky.'

For a moment I felt as hypocritical as the Love Guru. On the one hand, I believe with all my heart that what I do helps people, yet I felt embarrassed to disclose it to someone who mattered to me. Was this duality part of the curse of my ancestors? Does understanding the language of Spirit scare love away? Something told me I would find out soon.

I walked back into the house feeling a lot better. All the pent-up emotion of the few weeks had erupted; strange that I had trusted Al enough. That was why I felt so on edge in this 'spiritual' house. I couldn't trust anyone. My Spirit sense that was telling me to get out. No surprise, the casting director was nowhere to be found. Love Guru was sugary sweet and hugged me goodbye. I knew in that deep way we do that she would only be in my life as long as she needed me, and then I would be dropped. Everything felt so temporary here; I needed the old country to reassure me.

I called Jimminy on the freeway.

'Your day?' he chirped. 'The pink Manolos are fab, by the way.'

'Well, after saving Astrid, we celebrated. She got drunk and did a striptease in the Standard at lunchtime, then I did a reality TV show where a nasty director set me up and tried to trick me by giving me a Lucy Liu lookalike with a fake stomach – she did that because I knew was she was dating a guy in jail who had topped his wife – and the Love Guru who preaches fidelity is fucking a married guy; and then I had a complete meltdown with Al and told him you weren't my husband ... because of course you're not. That was my day.'

'Excellent,' said Jimminy. 'Just another day in Hollywood.'

'It appears so.'

'So go and give yourself a happy ending with Herr director and don't get home too late. Astrid's booked you on the set of her show to come and do readings tomorrow. 6 a.m. call.'

'I promise. Jimminy?'

'Yes?'

'I don't know ... I forgot what I was going to say.'

'Good. You only do that when you're happy. I'm off, I've got money to gamble. Be back before bedtime ...'

It was late afternoon and I drove down Hollywood Boulevard. Past the Chinese Theater. A fake Marilyn in a white polyester dress, cheap white wig on, clutched a boy in braces to her silicone. Charlie Chaplin was having a fag behind the bus and Spiderman was taking a leak in the alleyway. Sex shops and sound studios were a blur as I raced to the hideaway café. I arrived first, and dashed to the loo to give myself new black eyes. I then sat at the table, aware that everyone else was wearing spaghetti strap tops in tropical fruit and flower colours, lime, lemon, fuchsia, and porno jeans, so low they had butt cleavage ... and I was in my usual Brit garb. Head-to-toe black.

Al was my twin. Black, but fun black. I felt him walk in; he was on his cell, trying to get some deal or other going. I had that physical reaction again, like the air being punched out of me, the attraction was so visceral. He looked beautiful as usual, dressed as if he were going to a Neapolitan wedding, wild and suited and black-haired. I looked like a funereal India-boho eccentric.

If we were a movie pitch, it'd be a hard sell as a combo: *The Godfather* meets *A Passage to India*. I wondered about our possible future as we sat at our table under the honeysuckle.

'So, confess away,' said Al, getting to the point. 'How bad is it ... you're a Republican? A vegan?'

I laughed. 'No, I'm psychic.'

'Well ... I like astrology, it's sort of fun.'

'It's a bit more that that, and anyway, I come from a long line of psychics and they've never found love, or been able to keep it. Basically, they're cursed.'

'Oh, that's OK,' said Al, opening the fizzy water, 'because I come from a long line of curse-breakers, and in my Italian village my mother was the official curse-breaker.'

'Really?' I said, eyes wide.

There was a snort from under his napkin. 'Of course not!'

I was staring at him.

'That's it then ... that's the confession ... there's not some ex you're still in love with?'

I shook my head.

'And the gay husband?'

'Is the gay best friend. Who lives with me.'

We sat together and picked at all the best Californian things: arugula and Parmesan salad, Portobello mushrooms, chocolate mousse. And we talked about all the important things you talk about when you want to mine someone's soul.

Favourite films. His: *The Godfather* (I'd been on to that earlier), *Network*, *Slave of Love* (he had to explain it was an obscure Russian classic, not weird porno) and Scorsese's *New York, New York*. Mine: *It's a Wonderful Life*, *Fearless* and *Wings of Desire* (all of which, he pointed out, had supernatural forces helping people).

Poets. His: dark and dangerous Dylan Thomas tying with Borges. Mine: Hafiz, 'Tonight the Subject is Love'.

Books (todays favourites): we were only allowed three each. Mine: *Santaram* (the Indian adventure story), *How To Be Good* (Nick Hornby) and *The Velveteen Rabbit*. His: *Women in Love*, *The Magic Mountain* and *The Rebellion of the Masses* (Ortega Gassett). Seriously left wing.

Books (life changing). Mine: *A Room of One's Own* and *The Artist's Way*. His: *As Bill Sees It*.

Websites: Mine: amma.org. His: moveon.org.

Heroes. Mine: Ghandhi. His: Che Guevara.

I listened and mused, 'So you're an existential depressed activist?'

He laughed and came back with, 'And you're a romantic optimistic hippy?'

We finished the soul excavation with bizarre obsessions. His: Alexander the Great's horse, Buccephalus. Mine: does the tarot deck have twenty-one cards or twenty-two? Favourite part of LA: Los Felix, both of us. Least favourite part: he said Santa Monica and I really wanted to kiss him. Of course, I restrained myself, which made me think of Astrid's favourite book, *The Rules*. He was a real man; he could talk like a girl. We discussed dating rules, and I told him about the Love Guru's ludicrous '5 Ss'. In order to be eligible as a good date you must be:

Sweet
Single
Solid job
Solvent
Sober

'How do you measure up?' I said teasingly.

'I'm grumpy, divorced – twice – directing, never solid, had a bankruptcy, and been an alcoholic. But I don't drink so I guess I get one out of five. What about you?'

'I'm melancholic and moody, single, but cursed, resolutely freelance, intermittently broke … but I don't drink. Interferes with meditation. So I get one out of five too!'

And that was when he leant over and whispered, 'We're made to be together,' and although we both fell about laughing, my soul was singing. But I wondered if Spirit wanted it that way. If he fitted the prediction. I fished …

'So you've been divorced twice …'

'Not great, is it? There we go,' and he broke his biscotti firmly.

I tried again. 'Did you have any other serious relationships … that were like marriages?' He needed to have *three* ex wives to fit the prophecy and Spirit often didn't clarify if it was a marriage as we thought of it, with legal papers, or a sort of soul contract. The truth was I wanted to see if I could make Al fit the prophecy. But he was a square peg. Not three marriages. Two. But we had three chocolate mousses. Maybe Spirit had got it wrong I thought hopefully. After three espressos, we sped our way through the tables. An arm suddenly grabbed Al's, the face on the end of the arm was line-free and fifty-five and fun.

'Al!' she shrieked. 'Ruth Liebowitz!'

'How are you?' said Al, attempting to keep moving. But, as ever, this was a work connection and that meant an up-to-date résumé.

'We had a great opening weekend with the last one.'

'I know,' said Al. '50 million, right?'

'Point five,' she corrected. 'And the project you were interested in got stuck at Universal in turnaround. We're in the middle of Jewish mafia celebrations,' she said, pointing to the table.

'Be careful, you can get sued for that sort of comment,' said Al.

'Well, not if I'm Jewish. Isn't he a *mensch*?' she said to me, winking.

I nodded.

'And what do you do? Don't tell me … an actress right?' Her inference implied that 'actress' was used almost as an insult here.

Al took a breath and at the same time he said, 'She's a wonderful actress.'

I said, 'I'm doing psychic readings at the moment.'

'Well, which is it? It can't be both?'

The table was listening. Before I could answer, she went on. 'I guess you can tell which part you're going to get before you audition for it then, right!'

'I don't always get that right,' I said, thinking of *How Did It Feel?* Al looked down, embarrassed.

'Give me your number … what's your name?'

'Get the psychic's number for me,' I heard one of the couture-clad women whisper.

'And can you speak without an accent?'

I just couldn't resist it. 'Do you mean without an American accent? Because to me I am speaking without an accent right now.'

'Feisty!' said Ruth. 'Good for you, Al, that's what you need, someone who can stand up to you.' She looked at me thought-fully. 'I may have something for you. Meet me next Thursday at one at Aroma. Can you do that? I really want to meet you; I know we're going to work together.'

Sure, I nodded.

'Give me a call next week. You must. And Al, you old … Come see me at Sony.'

'I will.'

'She's really interested in you,' said Al. 'She wouldn't set up a meeting like that if she wasn't. And she's a big shot.'

I decided not to tell Al what I had picked up psychically. First of all she wasn't Jewish, she was pretending to fit in. I knew because standing behind her chair was her Catholic spirit guide, St Anthony. Eventually she would come to her senses, stop lying and convert to Judaism formally. But that wasn't for a while. Also, she had no interest in meeting me; she was very Hollywood in that way, all mouth and no follow through. I didn't get into that though. I segued to, 'Interesting that they're called "shots" isn't it ... where does that come from?'

'I don't know ... something to do with people who've shot for their dreams ...'

'You Americans are so obsessed with your dreams and making it, I think it's called shot because you'd shoot people to get that. You die for your dreams over here, right? Isn't that what they say in all those screenwriting seminars over here? "Is you hero willing to die for his dreams ... die to get what he wants?" We don't get all worked up like that in England,' I said, laughing.

'Right, that's why your films are about trembly white-faced men standing in bow-windows, quivering. You did one of those didn't you? Wearing a corset?'

'I did.'

'I bet you looked sexy,' and he gave me a scorpio stare.

And that was my moment. The moment when I could have gone gooey and turned on and giggled. And I didn't. I felt deathly afraid that this lovely filmy friendship we were building was going to go awry, so I redirected the fizzy energy with a standard British cold-water cover-up.

'They made me want to throw up my lunch every time I squeezed my way into one.'

Good on him, he didn't try and push it.

'So you Brits …'

'Because all Brits are the same of course—'

'We're beyond that,' he said waving my comment away. That made me feel cosy. We had a mutual understanding.

He went on, 'You Brits don't have dreams you can own up to …'

I finished his sentence for him: 'Exactly, because we come from a culture where to succeed ostentatiously is … a little bit off. Here it's celebrated.'

'So you don't want to succeed?'

'I didn't say that. I want to be excellent at things, acting, doing psychic readings, writing, whatever, but the success bit … I mean Astrid wakes up every morning saying she's going to be a diva super-billionaire – I just can't get behind that as a life goal.'

'I'm not saying that,' said Al. 'The most important thing in the world right now is for me to get my film made. Ask any successful person, you have to be obsessed.'

'Scorpio, right?' I said, eyebrows raised. He laughed. But I wasn't laughing. Obsessions squeeze out love. Instead, I went philosophical on him. 'I just don't buy this whole Hollywood way of thinking.' Privately I thought to myself, Spirit runs the show. We just have to listen. I went on, talking about his show-biz life, trying to find out not just how he operated with showbiz people, but how he might operate with me.

'Look, if I'm being really rude, you could sound like one of those courses they do over here – applying sort of multi-level marketing thinking to the entertainment business. Make ten business calls every day. Have five meetings. Everyone you meet needs to know about your product. Everyone you meet could generate a sale.'

'That's Hollywood!' he said, shrugging.

'Is it? What about having the right meeting? Use your intuition, your gut, and take the meetings that are meaningful.' Al looked thoughtful for a moment.

'That sounds like you're God, like you know ...'

'No, I didn't mean it to sound like that.' And I didn't. On and on we talked. At the end of our drive, it was obvious to me that Al would almost do a Cotton Club and bump someone off if necessary to get his films made. As his movie, *How Did It Feel?*, was a sore point we steered clear of that, but it made me feel sad. Ambition isn't very sexy if your night-time reading is about renunciation and enlightenment as the way to inner happiness. Mind you, the Buddha didn't have Fred Segal on his doorstep. Rama Krishna didn't go to drama school. Saint Francis of Assisi didn't audition for a Hollywood movie. And none of them did psychic readings. The jury was divided. I was in love with his mind. I was in love with his sexiness, his look, his body. But I wasn't at all sure where his Spirit was.

As he dropped me off he said, 'I'll see you tomorrow then.'

I looked puzzled.

'Oh, Astrid's invited me to come to the set, where you're doing your readings. She said you wanted me to come.'

Astrid was going out of her way to do kind things for me; I had to tell her she owed me nothing. But she couldn't have picked a better thing to do.

'And I'd like to check you out as a psychic.' That I wasn't so sure about. But Al was still full of caffeine and on to his next thought, 'And listen, I debated telling you this all night, but I'm going to. I think the star that the producers are going after will say no. It's only a small art-house movie to her, and I made the Snake promise that if she doesn't go for it, the part's yours again.'

I wasn't sure how to respond to that. So I hugged him and said something grown up and pro, like, 'Thank you so much, I really appreciate it,' but I wasn't at all sure how I felt. I kissed him goodbye on the cheek. Because if I was waiting for my soulmate and trusted Spirits predictions, he was now an outside chance. He was not a writer, and had been divorced twice, not three times. Bummer.

Jimminy appeared at the doorway, wearing his red silk dressing-gown. He came out and shook Al's hand and said, smiling, 'I'm the gay husband and you're an idiot for not giving her the part in your film.'

Al looked down and said quietly, 'I did give her the part actually, but the producers ...' and to me he said, 'I feel like a broken record here.' I smiled back at him.

'Well, you should have changed the producers then,' said Jimminy with his chin held high, spooning little marshmallows off the top of his Irish coffee, which had nary a drop of coffee in it. He hiccoughed loudly, almost with pride, and then went inside.

'Sorry about that,' I said with a little face.

Al looked at Jimminy curiously. 'Don't be, it's his trip.'

'See you tomorrow.'

I went to bed that night curled up with Twiglet, reviewing the day. 'Twiglet, I'm worried about Jimminy: he seems a little too in love with the booze even by our English standards. And Al, I think, always puts his work first.' But Twiglet was sound asleep. I guess I was feeling that worst of feelings, loneliness after a day surrounded by people. Especially when it all looked so sparkly, fun, and successful; but the scales were falling from my English eyes. Hollywood up close was more tarnish than tinsel. I retreated to go and find respite in a greater wisdom than my small mind, to ask my Spirit whisperers for guidance. Like music, depending on your mood, you need different inputs. I was supermarket supernatural, had a lot of varieties when it came to deities, but tonight I summoned Ishtara, the Babylonian Venus, because she knew about Love; and my new friend, Lakshmi, the ideal Hollywood deity, Goddess of material prosperity and spiritual liberation; and to complete the Holy Trinity, I prayed to Green Tara, the Buddhist bodhisattra, Goddess of compassion in action. Sighing as I went into meditation, it struck me that this seemed to be my life's work. Trying to bring together disparate ideas in my different worlds. Perhaps I needed a trio of Goddess women, because, in my own life, I was looking for a major chord – love, work and money, just like in Scorsece's movie. I wanted to be in harmony. They never found it in his movie, *New York, New York*; but perhaps I'd find it here in Hollywood, Hollywood. Perhaps, *Hollywood, Hollywood* was my movie, with Al. Oh please, please give me a sign if he's the one ... And I fell asleep, knowing tomorrow I would be doing readings on a major film set with big stars ... and Al would be there. It was a pretty terrifying thought. I held Twiglet very tightly and we fell into a fitful, furry sleep.

6
On the Set

5.30 a.m. Woken by a dirty phone call. A man was heavy breathing, no ... it was Brick the agent on his Stairmaster.

'Audition today. 6 p.m. Sony. I'll fax the sides. She has an accent.'

'Any ... particular accent?'

'European.'

'Right. European. Any particular part of Europe?'

'Just look sexy, kid.'

Checked the sides. Great, I had to go to the movie set to do readings dressed as a James Bond girl-spy type. Miniskirt and boots. Russian. No time for dialect coach. I knew the solution: Rubin.

I drove to Griffith Park, where Rubin lived. Twiglet had met him first, as she was out for her morning walk. Rubin was an Armenian, thick-accented (close enough to Russian for the Hollywood ear), award-winning musician who had eschewed Hollywood prizes – money, house, job – and instead lived in an abandoned Pacbell van. He played his cello at dawn under the trees, walked all day, meditated at dusk, played some more

Tchaikovsky then went to sleep. Thoreau's dream. We struck up a friendship; although I think he was secretly resentful that I was vegetarian, because we only really bonded when I bought him a double pastrami with salami sarnie. That had sealed the friendship. And I admired him. I had once heard him fight with an obnoxious studio executive in the parking lot. The exec was new to the park and didn't know he was in Rubin's kingdom. He was in a rush and had parked lengthways in the lot, taking up four parking spaces. When he returned, making deals on his tiny cell, his show dog Weimaraner trotting to his obscene and obsessed staccato rhythm, it was Rubin who watched him get into his silver Hummer and who said, 'You are so poor, all you have is money.' And the people waiting to park, with their dogs cooped up in their cars, they all cheered.

Today, he seemed in a more melancholy mood.

'Lucinda, how arrre you todeh? The son is bootifoll, no?'

'It is, Rubin, it is.'

I got down to business. 'Will you help correct my accent for my audition? I have to do a Russian accent – I know you're Armenian ...'

He shrugged the world-weary shrug that most foreigners use when dealing with the average Hollywooder's inability to distinguish accents and histories.

'We talk first. For you. To hear accent. We catch up.'

We were sitting in the glade in Griffith Park, home of the famous observatory where James Dean knife-fought in *Rebel Without A Cause*. Every time I was with him I was torn between thinking Rubin was a rebel without a cause, or on his way to enlightenment.

'Do you like it here, living like this?'

'I love it. I pliy music all day, I always have enough to eat,

I recorded Bach's preludes and fugues in a church on Sunday. They paid me for my playing. What else is there that is that important, Lucinda?'

'Nothing really, Rubin,' I said, looking at the skinny model types with their iPods and rescue dogs striding up the mountain past us, towards the stars where they wanted to belong.

'Were you ever married?' I asked suddenly.

'She died.' He paused. 'You have time to hear?'

'Half an hour,' I said quietly.

'I always have time to talk and to hear,' he said with great pride.

'I was a doctor before, you know. Lot of people I helped. Came home one day, my wife and two children had been killed in a car accident. Drunk driver,' he said, holding up his whisky bottle. 'Drunk driver with his own fiancée next to him. He killed her. So, we all lost our women that day.'

Neither of us said anything for a moment. 'Two daughters,' he said, almost as if he were reading my mind. Wondering about the children.

'So, then you came here to America?'

'No. I danced for ten years.'

I looked at him, puzzled. 'You danced?'

He nodded. 'I danced to forget. Every day, I put on the roller-skates, and I danced, round and round in circles.' He was laughing. 'They thought I had gone mad, I did not speak for ten years in Russia. Then I came to America.'

'Why?'

'Just, one day, I danced my last dance for my children and wife. A day for every day of my daughters lives. I chose America, because in Russia they say we have the ideas, but no gas. In America, they have the gas, but no ideas. So I come here with my ideas.'

That was why I liked Rubin. He was a dishevelled poet mystic, one of the only people in the town who was in love with ideas for the sake of them, not to make money off them. But the price he paid was to be broke. I got out the peanut butter and jelly sandwich and gave it to him.

'No pastrami?' he said, disappointed. I shrugged, embarrassed. 'And don't ever try to trick me with that vegan soy shit.'

I started to laugh. That had been Jimminy's idea after one of our failed wholefood shopping expeditions. 'I won't.

'And what happened to your ideas here?' I asked.

'I still have my ideas. But I have run out of gas for a bit. So I am here to help for a little. Is good to help. Now show me your accent, and I hope it is not shit like sandwich.'

'It's not that bad,' I said, offended.

'Is shit sandwich today. Come on. Play!'

So I did. In my best Russian accent … as the dangerous spy-cum-terrorist in the hot new TV show. Off I went.

'I have come to America because I want freedom. In Russia I was starving, here I have been forced to join the gangs in Cadoga Park. I have to wear a short skirt and kiss thugs for a living, and you call this a life?'

'Accent good. Words lie. In Russia I was starving … Nice girl in miniskirt would be married to Internet millionaire making good. And the gangs are not in Cadoga Park …'

'I think it's something to do with where they can film,' I muttered, embarrassed.

'America wants us all to believe in money as God. I am more free than when I had contract with a studio. But no more about me. Accent very very good. You have ear. But why you do this shit? For money? Because it is lies about my country.'

And I couldn't find an answer. So I just shrugged.

'You are a truth-teller. This is not good for you, I think. But break leg. It is American opportunity and why you came here, no?'

'Yes,' I said uncertainly.

'Remember. In the end, you need something you can believe in your heart. Something your heart knows is real.'

My tummy rumbled. Breakfast was the real thing I needed right now. I didn't want to think about anything else, I was too anxious about the day.

I jumped up. 'I'll bring you something for supper from the set if you want.'

'Sure. Why not?'

Knowing I would see him later, I knew I'd left abruptly. He was forcing me to think. Why was I here in Hollywood? I had come here to act, and now I was going to a set to do psychic readings. The last thing I needed was an ego attack before having to be 'on' as a psychic. I was nervous enough of doing a good job without sabotaging the whole thing with doubts. I could do this.

I arrived at the set, got out of the car in my ridiculous outfit, and ran straight into the director of the movie. He was that famous, I knew who he was.

'I'm Lucinda, I've come here to do readings.' I shook his hand assertively. He looked at me suspiciously.

'You're the psychic? You don't look like a psychic, you look like an actress.'

Great.

'And you're a bit young, aren't you?'

Why is it that the Central Casting requirement for a psychic seems to be sixty, grey-haired, with slippers. This was so Hollywood: I didn't look like a psychic so I couldn't possibly be one. Before I could come up with a riposte he made it clear that he had way more important things to do than humour a clairvoyant, so he crossed his arms and said with a big fat I-run-the-joint grin, 'You need to sign in and go up to the set. I could tell you how to get there but you're the psychic, so you should know, right!'

I forced a polite grin. I have heard that line so many times it makes my third eye want to close up permanently. 'Thank you, I'll find it.'

I stalked off and, without thinking, absent-mindedly wandered into the hair and make-up truck where the actors congregate. Not a good start.

To my relief, I recognised the make-up woman, Miriam – she of the orange corn rows and pierced eyebrow – from a TV show we had shot together. I remembered that she had been shocked that I kept wiping off make-up, explaining that full-on pancake and eyeshadow were probably low on the priority list of an IRA terrorist. She had told me it was an American production. All the other terrorists had lip gloss. So much for Mike Leigh. Despite the brushes that she held in her mouth, she couldn't hide her look of concern.

'What are you playing?' she mumbled as she hurriedly flipped through her schedule. 'And if I put it on, don't wipe it off!' she laughed.

'Oh, I'm actually here doing readings,' I said apologetically.

'Readings? They're doing screenplay readings at the same time as the shoot?'

'No. Psychic readings. I'm a psychic as well … it's a long story.'

Casting aside her newspaper horoscope, she whispered, 'You know who loves that stuff?' and she whispered the name of one of the movie stars. I raised my decidedly unplucked eyebrows and Miriam noticed and pulled out a few stray hairs.

'She's lovely, you'll have no problems with her ... The director, on the other hand, he can't even remember my name. Weeks on the set, he still doesn't know it. Do you want me to take you to her now? I know she'd love it if you could do her first of all.'

Miriam shooed me to the star's trailer. Knocked a little code knock. The door opened.

I was staring at a very famous lipsticked mouth. It whispered to me, 'You know I'm a bit of a sceptic and I don't really believe in all this. But Astrid said you had saved a stripper from being raped and you tracked the stripper's stalker down telepathically or something? Anyway, I couldn't resist meeting you. Come in.'

I was so wowed by her genetic gifts that I just smiled adoringly. She had one of those faces that are beautiful more than pretty: a strong, brave face with prominent cheekbones and a 1940s glamour. The brunette with balls. She was in costume, wearing fabulous shoes, and had a gigantic fuck-off status-symbol bag lying inside the Winnebago that managed to be an extension of her – I recognised it from magazines and it gave off a sense of immense fun and serious style at the same time. She sat down and beckoned me to sit next to her. I smiled some more, a little inanely. She was probably quite used to people groping for words when they were in her orbit. I needed to get out of starstruck orbit and into psychic orbit. I explained that I was going to touch her hand and start the reading. She smoothed out her skirt, which was one of those rare jumble-sale look-alike Prada skirts, opened up her hand and laid it out flat on the blue Tibetan prayer bag. Laughing, with her outstretched palm towards the heavens, she playfully grimaced, 'It reminds me of Communion.' Then she obediently closed her eyes.

Instantly I could sense a spirit from a long time ago hovering in her aura.

'There's someone here ...'

I felt her not quite flinch, but psychically recoil, and I knew it was too soon to go into Spirit talk. So I just listened intently to see what message the Spirit had. This brought us both back down to earth.

'They want to talk about someone around your sister. David. He's close to her and she needs to be careful of him, and you might need to look after her.'

She stared straight ahead at the fake flames jumping up and down in the grate. The height of LA luxury: the fake summer fire.

'Hmm. That's funny. That's actually my sister's boyfriend, or ex. I'm not actually sure right now.'

'Ex I think,' I said slowly. She smiled, as if we knew one another quite well. And we did in that moment because I was chatting intimately about her family. The ego walls between us had suddenly dissolved: she was no longer the star and I was no longer a satellite in her orbit. We were on the same mission, after simple truths. Who to love, when to love, when to let go. She was trusting enough now to be helped and I was willing not to be intimidated by her status. Spirit had won over ego. We were ready to go deeper.

The Spirit who had waited patiently came forward again. He whispered me his name. 'Jodie,' I whispered, taking dictation.

Her long lashes fluttered like a horse that has lost his way. Her head cocked slightly.

'Tell me about Jodie ...' she said, with a look of absolute shock on her face.

'Young Spirit. Child.'

'Tell me more.'

'He was sick. He died because he was sick. And he's around you.'

'Is it all right that he's around me?' she asked, earnestly.

He nodded at me from Spirit, so I nodded at him. He was in fact smiling, having a fine old time. He reminded me of the curly haired boy in the Victorian painting *Bubbles*, by Millais, but with dark hair. He was giving me a clue.

'He was alive in Victorian times. He's very happy to help you.'

She was quiet, and then she turned to me. 'You know, I don't know if I believe in souls living on; I think I do, but I'm not sure. Several years ago, for a part, I read this biography, and in it there was a boy, the brother of this politician, and he died when he was a child, and his name was Jodie.' She took a deep breath. 'Well, whenever I have to do a heavy scene, have to really cry my eyes out, all I have to do is think of Jodie, and his life, how ill he was and how he died … and I'm just …'

Her eyes filled up with tears that were ready to fall down her face. She took another breath but, miraculously, the tears didn't fall; they seemed to return to her eyes, ready for another time. 'And I was worried,' she continued, 'because even though I don't believe in souls hovering around us, if they do look after us, then I was worried that I was perhaps keeping him here, when he wanted to … move on.'

She stared at the fire. 'Actually I find the whole thing a bit embarrassing and I have never told a single person his name.'

I just listened. And so did he.

Then she smiled a huge grin of relief. He had another tidbit for her.

'Also there's a part with fairies in it,' I said.

'How did you know that?' she asked.

'I just saw it,' I said.

'There is actually! Someone just called me up about this project ...'

She looked into the fire again, as if it had answers for her. Then she looked back at me. The whole afternoon was getting to her, I suspected. The unexpected heat and her secret muse friend Jodie introducing himself for the first time, in front of someone else.

'Perhaps there is life after death then – or something.'

'Perhaps there is,' I echoed.

We turned over some colourful cards, ran through house moves, love moves and TV-to-movie moves. It was all very encouraging, but as the fire was dying down, it was Jodie she was really happy about. She stood at the door and said quietly, 'I still don't know exactly if I believe in souls, but that was amazing. I didn't want to say goodbye to Jodie.'

'You don't have to,' I said. 'He's your secret acting coach.'

'He is, isn't he! My very own muse.'

'Just thank him.'

'Oh, I will,' she said firmly, as she wrapped her Pucci coat around her. 'I'll thank him at an awards ceremony.'

I suspected the thank-yous would be included in bedtime prayers, or yoga lessons. However, at an awards ceremony a year or two later, it gave me great joy to hear her thank her coach Jodie. She slipped his name in between the names of an agent and a producer. He loved it.

This was a great omen for the day – obviously it was going to be fun. I had been anxious for no good reason. Spirit was with me. I chirpily headed off to the set. I reached the top of the hill where the crew were setting up. We were in a house that overlooked a park and the sun was streaming through the windows. The first AD came running up to me, bellowing – they always seem to bellow to get everyone's attention – 'We're going to put you in here.' And he took me to a perfect spot, the study, where it was quiet and cosy and I could meditate.

I couldn't resist a quick peek at the set. It was magical: hours and hours of construction had made a whole new world. The actors were still in their caravans so I only saw the crew setting up the first shot. I noticed the director eyeing me again, so, out of fear, I scuttled back to my hole, managing to avoid the craft table, laden with chocolate and crisps. With my meagre little bowl of fruit I sat down at the desk and said my prayers. I asked that the readings be done for the highest good of all concerned. Then there was a knock at the door. Of course I was instantly taught a lesson. The person who I'd pegged as the bitter, annoyed witch-hater, who I swore was laughing at me, was first. It was the director of the movie.

The millionaire director sat down. Close up he looked like an ageing rocker with dying dreams. He had long dark hair and old dark jeans. But the jeans were designer. I picked up his hand and immediately knew that he was not here to talk about his career. I jumped in.

'You've just left someone you love. It's really over this time.'

He hung his head. 'That's true.'

Then I started psychically whizzing through his body, checking his health. Something was really not right.

I looked at him and he seemed to be sweating, although actually, as the early sunlight poured through the window, I could see that he was not.

'Your wife is very upset.'

He nodded. 'Am I cursed?' he asked sadly. This was the truth that had been hiding under the Hollywood bravado. I knew all about his fear.

I said gently, 'What's happened in your life so far is a result of the actions you have taken. You have created some "causes" that are not entirely beneficial and the "effects" have been devastating.'

'I'm a Buddhist,' he said thoughtfully. 'You're right on.'

That was good. They were giving me his religious terminology so that it made sense to him. I suddenly had an image of him at an orgy. It was bit early in the morning for the Bacchanalian images that were playing through my head; and he was very drunk in the pictures in my mind – not happy drunk or once-in-a-while, letting-it-all-go drunk, but blotto and nasty drunk.

'You've hurt your wife really badly,' I said slowly. They were being a bit strict with him, and I didn't want to sound like that awful American radio-programme therapist who shamed everyone and called it healing. But who was I to say? They knew better than I what he needed to hear and something got through to him. He bent over and burst into tears. Spirit told me why.

'You're actually very sick at the moment,' I said quietly, 'and you're keeping it a secret.'

'I have AIDS,' he said, sobbing. He was breathing deeply. 'I can't tell anyone. Not the insurance. Not my friends. I have to keep working. I have to make money for my family.'

Then, for some reason, a story Jimminy had told me about a friend of his who had died of AIDS popped into my head and I felt I had to tell him.

'My great friend was best friends with a star who got AIDS. In his case, he put it down to going to orgies.'

He was listening as if his life depended on what I said. He knew I knew this was not a random story, but specifically for him.

'Anyway, he found out that his wife was pregnant, and he made a promise to God. He promised that if his wife and baby-to-be were spared he would live with dignity and die nobly. To everyone's amazement, neither his wife nor his daughter were HIV positive.'

His eyes were locked with mine. He said, 'My wife left me and then found out she was pregnant by me.'

I looked long and hard at what Spirit were trying to tell me. They spared me from making a pronouncement about death, and infringing on God's domain. Instead they showed me his Achilles heel.

'They say you can't get sober. That's one of the problems,' I said.

'You won't tell the producer,' he made me promise. 'I need the money.' Then he stood up. 'You know what's so helpful. You're the first person who knows, who I've talked to about all this, and I feel so much better already. I don't want to know what will happen, I just wanted someone to understand. Thank you.'

I wrote down the name of an HIV support group. I had learnt to carry a list of groups for troubled clients. He was mildly scornful for a second. 'Do you think those support groups work?' he asked.

'I don't know,' I replied, 'but there have been some pretty conclusive studies done by doctors that show that talking can only help, especially to combat isolation.'

'Yeah, easiest city in the world to get isolated in here, isn't it?' He folded the paper into a very small square and pushed it into the depths of his pocket. 'Can Spirit take advantage of the fact I'm dying and say something very obvious, but because I'm dying you'll really listen?'

I nodded.

'Life is short. Think about what you would do if you had one year left to live, then do it.'

Then he gave me a strange little salute. And we just stood there and stared at one another. His eyes were so full of pain and love that I had to gulp to stop myself from crying. Eventually we looked away and he disappeared off to the set, to his pretend world. I knew what I'd do. I'd marry a man I loved and make a meaningful movie to leave behind. I disagreed with the old Hollywood notion, Lou Wasserman's: 'If you want to send a message, use Western Union.' Lou's days were over. It was the time for soul movies with messages. My cell interrupted my imaginings.

'Hey, Astrid! I'm here!'

'How is it?'

'Are you coming?'

'No, no ...' she sounded slightly defensive. 'I'm just really busy buying wardrobe for a *Vanity Fair* piece, rags-to-riches story.'

'Ahh, the life of a star,' I said with a silly sigh.

'I'm not a star, I'm a ... I don't know what I am. Does it sound really cheesy if I say I'm still me, and now everyone sees me as a star and I don't want you to fall into that trap?'

'Take it easy, Astrid, I was just letting you off the hook! Have fun!'

'Oh. OK. I thought you wanted something ...'

'Honestly, I'm fine ...' Somehow this was going down a weird track.

Astrid tried to right it.

'They're buying clothes for me at the Grove. It's great. Have you been there? You should go.' Oh God. The Grove. The open-air shopping mall.

'Fake Europe?' That was our nickname for it, mine and Jimminy's. We hated even the idea of it. Piped music and plastic cafés. It was like a set pretending to be a European square. I wanted to scream at the thought of it. Didn't people know it was normal to be able to walk around? They shouldn't have to pay to park and have a normal human experience.

'So I'll see you soon?' she said, sounding vulnerable. 'Oh, and by the way, I got a part on that new TV show. I'm a regular – it's a great role …' Then I heard someone wanting her attention – a stylist, a fan, someone was always going to want a piece of her from now on.

'Congratulations, that's great!' I said, but she was gone. I sighed. That was a weird conversation. Mercury must be retrograde, I rationalised. God, LA was really getting to me. The truth was I felt really unsettled. I contemplated calling her back but there was another knock at the door. I had to get back into the unconditional love mode, not worried about my friendship mode. It was the other movie star on the set, Lara Corano. I have to admit that as she came in I was once again momentarily dazzled. It is a very strange feeling, meeting the super-famous. Especially when someone has one particularly famous feature that you can't help but stare at. And there's the ridiculous sensation that the person is your friend because you've seen them in your living room so many times, on TV, but the screen evaporates and there they are, standing in front of you, and you can't help but stare. Also, all the tabloids have filled you in on the state of their love life and marriage, boyfriend and nail-polish choices, so it's, sometimes, hard to forget all that material stuff and stay clear-headed enough to read on a soul level.

She was very sweet but, at the same time, there was something a little off about her personality. And it was courageous of her to come and see me. Everyone knew a lot about her, but what I saw was not in the gossip magazines.

I took a deep breath and tuned in. 'You have two souls who are hovering behind you. They are babies' souls and I'm confused. I don't know whether you lost them from an abortion or a pregnancy.'

'It's both,' she said. 'I had an abortion years ago, and then I had an ectopic pregnancy.'

I nodded. 'You will have a baby. There's one trying to come through right now.'

'Really?' she said.

'Yes.'

'And it will happen?' She was repeating it to get security.

'It will,' I said.

I was touched that she was so open. She grabbed my hand. 'Is there anything I can do to help it happen?'

'You need to forgive yourself.'

I pushed the box of tissues towards her.

'I just think I'm being punished for the abortion,' she said, crying.

When had God been turned into a punishing right-wing deity? I wondered. I'd always pegged him as a liberal. But this was not the moment to get into a theological flurry; I needed to help. Watching her crying, I could literally see waves of energy around her body and I knew that if she continued to punish herself for having had an abortion, she would never ... heal something in her ... cysts ... ovarian cysts ...

'You have a cyst?'

'Am I going to die? A cyst? Is it toxic?'

'No, no, you need to see a doctor. Anything I tell you, check with a doctor, but I think you'll find it's a cyst.'

She suddenly sobbed uncontrollably and then, just as suddenly, the way someone who is paid millions to be in touch with their emotions can do, she stopped, and resurfaced in a millisecond.

'I've done IVF so many times, I was just beginning to give up hope. Am I doing something wrong? I'm not, am I?'

I shook my head.

'And I have a question about karma,' she said.

Once again I had one of those moments of DNA awe and distraction as I looked at her extraordinary face. I had to concentrate if I was going to see deeper than that.

'Do you think we are destined to have certain souls come to us as children, if they're adopted?'

'Well,' I said, 'I have two friends who both adopted orphans. One adopted a little boy from Hungary, the other a little girl from India. Both of them say they feel as if the children are their own children. They feel as if they have been reunited. So I do think that's possible, yes.'

She started to sob again.

'Does meditation work?' she said, through her tears. 'Do you think it will help me get pregnant?'

'Well, you know what the Dalai Lama says?'

'I love the Dalai Lama!'

Again Spirit was talking to me in her particular religious language.

'When he was asked what the most important thing we can do for our lives is, he replied, "Meditate, meditate, meditate."'

'I've been doing a special meditation for getting pregnant. I ate the root of a banana plant – I found it in one of the whole foods …' That didn't surprise me, after my expeditions there, with Jimminy.

'Then I sit with my back against my husband's, for thirty-one minutes every day – you have to do it for forty days – and I do the four-finger mudra and the four-tone chant. What do you think?'

To me it sounded curious – bats ... possible ... who knew? – but Spirit gave it a big fat indigo flash, a sure yes.

'I think you're supposed to be doing the forty-day Sadhanna.' This was a hip thing Astrid had done just before she got her big part at the hip Kundalini yoga centre, Golden Bridge.

'Exactly!' she said, excited.

'You're supposed to do it every day without missing a day, you know that.'

'NO! I thought I just had to do it for forty days. Oh, my husband'll kill me.' She paged her assistant: 'Get me a banana leaf root as soon as you can. What? Well, Fedex it to me, it's urgent!'

'And I do see a child. A little girl.'

At that moment there was a knock on the door. I think we both hoped that it would prove to be a divine intervention, or an angel singing choruses of hope, carrying in a baby for her, but it was the assistant, apologetically calling her to come to make-up.

'Oh, I almost forgot, I wanted to ask you about this script ... I mean, it's not that important, but if you have time ...'

'Sure.'

She pulled a script out of her bag and handed it to me. 'What do you think of it?'

I closed my eyes and held it. 'It's a great script. I'm being told that although it's an independent movie, it will be seen and it will get distribution. Fantastic part in it for you. This is a yes script. A must.'

'Oh good, because I really liked it, but you've decided me. And I love the title, don't you? *How Did It Feel?*'

I almost threw up. I was speechless. Al's movie.

'I've got several offers, but I'll say yes to this one now you're so enthusiastic.' And she walked up to me and kissed me full on the mouth. Then out she skipped.

Oh my God. The movie I had come over here for. She was going to play my part. I was gutted. Of course she was; she was a beautiful star and that was how the business went ... it was just that I had told her to do it! And Al had told me that if the star they'd given the script to said no – which she had been going to do before my stupid psychic reading – I could have done it! Why did Spirit tell me to do that? I needed a break.

I wandered around the set in conflict. I could clearly see that people found the readings helpful. Just little snippets of information that came from a difference space and time helped them in their lives. It's a good job, I thought. What I couldn't quite comprehend was what Spirit was trying to tell the actress part of me. On the one hand I didn't believe that acting was a distraction from my psychic work; if I hadn't been called to audition for the movie, all these helpful readings would never have happened. I knew they were connected. But why? Why was this happening to me? I wished I could hold my own hand and let Spirit come and help me, but it doesn't work like that.

Then a darker thought crossed my mind. Did Al give her the script himself, today? I wondered. Maybe he had just come to the set to see her and meet her – that's what indie directors did, found out where the star they wanted was shooting and then engineered a meeting – pretending he was coming to see me. Oh Christ. This was just unbearable. I went back to my reading room and waited for the next impossibly famous or beautiful person to come in wanting my help, just when my own life was in a complete mess.

'So are you going to make me cry as well? You've reduced the set to tears!'

Al sauntered in. Raising his eyebrows at the star's last words. I used the old trick of looking at him and pretending he was a child to sum up the unconditional love I needed to overcome an ego attack of low self-esteem.

'I thought you just came here to visit, not for a reading ...' I trailed off.

It was not easy to keep calm. I wanted to scream at him, 'Why are you giving my part away, you idiot!' I wanted to mix it all up: 'Don't you love me?' 'Why are you so cruel to me? Why? Why? Why?' I felt like a victim, which meant I thought I had no choice. Damn him. I had a choice. I was not going to show him my feelings, I was a professional psychic. He thought the psychic stuff was unreal. I'd prove him wrong. Just because he was a snake, I'd be spiritually superior. I summoned the other world to my aid. Although my faith in it was pretty shot after the last reading.

'Do you use cards?' he asked.

'Sometimes,' I replied. But I took his question as a sign that they might be a good idea with him.

'Shuffle them,' I said. He started shuffling. I suddenly realised I was speaking in short, sharp commands. I was really angry. I had to tune in to Spirit and fast. I used my favourite prayer for whenever I started desperately wanting something, or many things, as I did in this moment: 'Dear God, help me find in you what I'm looking for in him.' Love, acceptance, whatever it was. The feeling of human desperation started to lift slightly. I was just a psychic reading for a client.

As he shuffled the cards I began to sense several work projects connected with him. Shadowy pictures ... of what? *How Did It Feel?* with me playing the lead? – God this was tiring – I forced the picture out. Now my unconscious was trying to fuck with me. I took a deep breath.

'I wanted to talk about the scripts I have ...' he started.

He pulled out a pile of scripts from a satchel he'd brought in with him.

'I just need to touch them one by one, don't need to see the names.'

'Great. Here they are.' He indicated the pile.

I held the scripts, one at a time. 'No to the first two, yes to the third, no to the fourth and yes to the fifth.'

'Well, aren't you going to read them?' he said.

'I just did.'

'I mean read them properly.'

'I did read them. I read them psychically. You want details? First one has a legal problem, second ones the locations are a problem and the last one you'll find the option has run out anyway, so you can't do it.'

I was really wary of holding the other two, in case one of them was the dreaded *How Did It Feel?*. But I wasn't going to betray my psychic self and look at the name.

'This one you'll make with a partner. But you'll produce it as well.'

'Will I get the actress I want to play the lead?'

He was really pushing it now.

'Will you get the actress, the lead you want?' I repeated. Give it to Spirit, Lucinda. Hear their answer. Come on. 'Yes. You will ... And this last one I love. It's a commercial hit. I love it.

'You and half of Hollywood,' he said wryly. 'How weird, I feel like you're reading my mind. Can you stop, please?'

'Any time you want to stop is fine with me,' I said shortly. But he wasn't picking up on the snideness that had sneaked through my veneer of civility. He was impressed by the psychic show.

He leant back in his chair. 'How do you do that?' he said. 'I want to learn.' Then he asked, apparently randomly, 'Are you interested in quantum mechanics?'

'I've read some books about it,' I answered. Good. We could be heady now and move away from our hearts.

'So tell me, from a psychic's point of view, what you think of quantum mechanics?' He wasn't testing me, he was genuinely interested.

'From a psychic's point of view, and from a quantum mechanics point of view, we are all one big energy field, and the world is only perceived as it is because our brains tells us it is.'

'Are we on to ... this table isn't really here?' he said, his dark brown eyes penetrating mine.

'We are,' I said, 'so as far as scripts go. In a sense what matters is how you, the director, the perceiver, view it, because, as we all know, in Hollywood the writer doesn't really exist.'

He was laughing at my allusion to the fact that the writer, the creator, the god of the film, is always overlooked.

'In that case, if what really matters is my perception, why should I listen to what you say, in a quantum mechanics sort of way?'

'Because you and I are the same,' I replied, 'in that we are made of the same energy field, so in fact you're only listening to a reflection of yourself anyway.'

'So I too could have advanced mind-reading skills?' he asked.

'You could. You probably do. Because we all do. We all have the ability to be psychic.'

'Or is it just an advanced empathetic ability you have?' he said, staring right into my eyes.

'Both, if everything is everything,' I said mysteriously. He kept staring at me.

I moved back into professional mode. How funny that when I had first met him, I kept denying the attraction because I was the actress; now I was forced to deny it because I was in the role of the psychic. I tuned in again.

'You've been married several times,' I said.

'Is that a question, or a psychic hit?' he asked, toying with the cards.

'It's what I feel and see around you. In fact, although you told me last night you'd been married twice, you've been married three times.'

'How the fuck did you know that?' He was genuinely shocked.

'Because your dead wife is standing behind your chair, annoyed that you try to pretend she doesn't exist. Just because you married her when you were nineteen and she went mad and hung herself, she doesn't like not being mentioned.'

He stood up in the chair. 'I thought this was just ...'

'What? Some fake moving cards around ... some "you will meet a tall dark handsome stranger" thing ...?' I was clearly no longer in reading mode.

'Yes, frankly.'

'Well, it's not. It's serious work. People come here with serious questions about death and life and babies and who helps them in Spirit when they're running out of faith. But it helps to tell the truth. Why do you want a reading, Al? Do you want to know who is going to star in your film? Do you want me to tell you?'

'What are you talking about?'

'Nothing,' I said, realising I couldn't tell him about the star handing me the script. And also realising I was much more annoyed about the fact he had lied to me.

'Why did you lie about your first wife? I hate being lied to.'

'Your turn: why did you lie about a marriage that had never happened? Go on – your turn.'

I realised we were both standing up now.

'I asked first,' I said childishly.

'I lied about my first wife because a) I thought it would make me seem – I don't know – not serious about marriage,' and b) because I didn't think I'd date a girl who could *see* my dead first wife hovering behind my chair, giving my secrets away. Your turn: why did you lie about a marriage that had never happened? Your turn.

We both sounded like furious children.

'Because a) (I said 'a' in a really sarcastic tone – how dare he try to make everything seem logical when what was between us was far from logical) I really wanted to play the part in your stupid film and I thought that would make the difference to me getting the part. b) I was scared that I just had some silly crush on a director, and I didn't want to act on it, so I wanted to put you off by saying I was married. And c) no one wants to marry a girl who can see people's dead wives behind chairs anyway, so it was better to pretend to be married already. I wanted us to be professional and nothing more.'

He stared at me.

I stared back.

'Look,' said Al in a conciliatory fashion, 'I think this has all been a big misunderstanding ...'

'Really? It seems pretty clear to me. We both lied to one another ... that doesn't show a lot of respect, does it?'

'Because we were afraid ...'

'Look, I'm sorry, but I can't get into this. I have to do readings all day. You can sit outside with Lara and shoot the breeze, but I have to work and I can't afford to get upset, because then I won't be able to help anyone. I know, being American, it's an out-there idea to be helping other people's dreams rather than killing other people to make yours come true, but there you go.' I was so upset I was shaking. So was he.

'Fine, you sit here, like the Brits do, all stiff upper lip and not expressing what you feel, denying yourself what you really want, and go ahead, chat to the ghosts and help people uncover their secrets, while you're miserable inside.'

'Your arrogance is just typically American. You think you've got the corner on understanding feelings just because you yap about them all day. You have no idea what I'm feeling inside.'

'Really?' he said, and he was now standing really close to me.

'Yes,' I replied. Our eyes were locked together.

'Your time is up,' I said frostily. 'There are people waiting. I know that you come first, that's what you Americans call self-esteem – I hate to break it to you, but we call it being rude. So maybe, if you could borrow some English manners, you could please leave and let the others in.'

He moved away, eyeing me like a bird of prey. 'I'd be delighted, Miss Clare.' And he closed the door behind him.

I really wanted to shout out after him that I could see the film he wanted to do was going to be made by a soon-to-be Oscar-winning director, and that he should give up on it, but restrained myself.

There was a knock on the door. I really hoped it was Al, but it was the assistant, asking with a grimace if I wouldn't mind keeping going, as I was going to disturb their schedule other-wise. So in they all came. I squashed down all my personal feelings and threw myself into the afternoon. It was very depressing. If I was unhappy, they were chronically depressed.

Depressed but wondering if they ought to be, like a Prozac control group, because they had what everyone told them they needed to be happy. Most especially the Hollywood lifestyle. It was as if there was some magical solution that they all knew they had inside them but couldn't access. The second AD wanted to be the first AD. The first AD told me he was really a director. The photographer and the art director assured me they were also directors, and that they were just doing this job for the cash. The stand-in was thinking of producing something. Then visitors to the set came in. The director with a commercial picture wanted to make an art-house classic. The director with an art-house classic wanted to make money. The writer wanted to direct. The executive producer was getting ready to give up everything and retire. The assistant make-up woman wanted to go back to New York. Actually, 80 per cent of the people I read for said they wanted to move back east or live in Europe, or just somewhere else apart from LA. I have never been in a town where the badge of honour is to diss the town, and where there is a such a cross-class, cross-cultural sense of professional dissatisfaction. I wanted to jump up on my chair and scream. And all they could ask questions about were their careers.

What a relief to get out of there and go to the audition. I marched to get my cash. Took a cheque that paid for the month's rent, and wondered if it was worth it.

Oh no ... Lara had spotted me. She was looking pink-cheeked and perfect and I felt shabby, runny and exhausted.

'Just want to tell you the great news! I met the director on the set here, what a coincidence! He's delighted I'm doing the part. And guess what?'

'What part?' I asked, barely containing myself. I just wanted to get the fuck out of there. I'd had enough. But she was smiling wildly.

'I found out you're an actress too! Yes, you are!'

Oh God, I really wanted to hit her, she was so annoying.

'Marion in make-up said you're just great. There's a part in *How Did It Feel?* that you could play. It's the waitress – she has a great line and you get to keep your clothes on! I got you an audition!'

The smile froze on my face. I managed to make some kind of noise which could have been construed as gratitude, but in fact it was impotent rage. I walked out, my self-esteem in tatters, and drove towards evil Santa Monica, where today's audition was being held. I felt cheated, that was what it was. Some infantile part of me had thought that if I was just 'of service' then I would get the rewards … from Spirit, from Hollywood even. But clearly it had been a sham when I had 'dedicated my life' to Spirit after Steve got ill. It had been a bargain, not a choice. And I was beginning to feel the weight of that bargain. A terrible feeling of self-pity began to wash over me. A week before, sitting at the lights on Hollywood Boulevard, I had seen a girl close all of her windows and scream as loudly as she could. I couldn't hear her, I just saw the windows steam up. I wished I had the courage to be that girl, to be American enough – or fuck being American enough – just be brave enough to let rip. To be Liza Minnelli in *Cabaret* and scream at the top of my lungs until all the pain went away. The fact that I couldn't help the man with AIDS, that the star was going to do the part that I was in love with, and the man I was in love with was an unscrupulous liar. At least I knew that now. It was gutting to admit, but … but it was audition time … I was almost there. At least I could use all of that angst and despair and turn it into something, albeit a Bond type Russian floozy.

Maybe that was what all of this was about. I felt desperately lonely, out of touch with any Spirit guidance for my own pathetic life, and I was convinced that Spirit had brought me here to marry Al and make a dream movie. I was gutted. I was left with the consolation prize. I had to give to others what I couldn't give to myself: hope.

I showed up at the audition exhausted. Which, bizarrely, worked in my favour, because I had stopped thinking. I did my bit: tears in the right place; made everyone laugh at the right points; tried to ignore the fact that the girl who went in before was so beautiful I almost fancied her; came out of the room knowing I'd nailed it. Casting director gushed, director shook my hand.

By the time I was almost home, Brick called. 'Kid, you were great, they loved you ... said you were such a fantastic actress.'

Oh dear, I knew this speech, '... and they're going with a name. That's how it goes sometimes.' I managed a word of something or other and got off the phone sounding like a pro, but feeling like a complete and utter failure. This would never change. I was just exhausted with pretending: pretending to be resilient, pretending it was all OK. In American terms, I was unable to walk my talk. I had absolutely no faith and no trust, in my love life (a complete disaster), my dreams to make meaningful films (zero success), and that Spirit would be there for me. I could help everyone else, but not myself. How pathetic. Or worse, hypocritical. I was at a complete loss as to what to do.

I heard the cello as I walked through the park towards the van, Rubin's home. At least I hadn't forgotten his supper.

'Ahh! Now this is not shit, this is what I call proper food.'

He ate and then played for a bit. It was so beautiful just to listen to it.

'You know this. It is Richard Strauss. Fucking hard to play. But worth it.'

Tears started streaming down my face. This was pathetic. I hadn't changed since I was at school. All this Spirit stuff just made me cry.

Rubin stopped. 'Why crying?'

I shook my head.

'You tell me. You think because I have nothing you can't talk about things. No. I listen. I listen to lots of people.' Funny, he was just like me. The recipient of the troubled.

'It just sounds so ... spoilt when you ...'

'Don't rrromanticise me please. Is great insult. This life is ...'

'Shit?' I said, laughing and crying at same time.

'I need more words,' he said, acknowledging my statement.

'I listen now. And I don't want anything back, you understand? So, what it the pain in your heart?'

'I was on a set today ...'

'The audition was good?'

'It was great. No, I was on a film set ...'

'Now this is better, films better than TV. Art not ... bang-bang miniskirts. People trying to have dreams in films. Trying to buy bigger cars with TV. All about viewing figures, I know, girl producer talks to me about this.'

'I wasn't acting.'

'Pity.'

'I was doing readings.'

'Oh, talking to ghost thing. I know this. You told me this before. So what happened?'

'Well the man I am in love with … the man I thought was in love with me, he lied. He said he had been married twice, but he was married three times.'

'Is he rich? Or very handsome? Three wives not bad. You be fourth.'

'But he lied to me … and there's other things too.'

'Your problem, Lucinda, is life is not black and white. Either or. Psychic or actress. Liar or truth-teller. You have to learn to forgive. I forgive man who took my family away. You can forgive for this little lie. But you want it to mean something. All a sign. Every day I asked why that man kill my wife and children. What does it mean. But we are not God. We are not God. We have more power knowing that.'

I suddenly felt drained of all energy. But he went on:

'Before I came to America, eagle was my favourite bird. The American bird. All powerful, like president thinks he is. Now, the sparrow.'

'"Providence even in the fall of a sparrow,"' I said quietly.

'Exactly. Your job. Find the providence. Trust me, you may have to dance on roller-skates, but eventually you will find the providence. Very unhappy people here. And a few golden people. Director who has Oscar on his mantelpiece, he comes to park. We talk. He sends money to poor people all over the world. Lady, big in film … casting lady … she started … jobs for kids on streets. Find the good people here. They make dreams true and do good. Not either or, Lucinda.

'You need something real in your life. Another dog. Friend for Twiglet. I found dog with wound on neck, all blood round neck. Only puppy. You can help him?' And he took me to a hole of leaves where a small yellow dog was curled up in a ball. The puppy got up and sat on my foot. I could feel my heart again.

'This is the gods speaking. The dog has decided. You are his new owner. I call him Mishka, means "little bear" in Russian. When I found him he looked like little bear with much fur. Now ...' he muttered, 'is stupid name because he doesn't look like bear. However, could be good because name is like Baryshnikov, the dancer ...' I nodded. 'But he is most clumsy dog I have ever seen ... Name is Mishka. Enough thinking about what love means, what acting means, and talking to ghosts means; now Mishka needs you.'

It was true, his snout was poking at my ankle. Mishka and I drove home. I could tell we were going to be friends, Mishka and me. I wasn't quite sure how the Twig would take to her new sibling. Why was I worrying about what hadn't happened yet? Strange, Rubin was the only person I had met today who wasn't worrying about his future. Who was, he had told me, happy with where he was right now. And he had no money, a dubious home, no one to love. And I had been surrounded by some of the most envied in their profession who were miserable. Why was everyone so unhappy? They were making plenty of money, they were doing what they loved; what was wrong? The happiest person I had seen that day was Rubin, and he had a van to sleep in and a cello to play. I contemplated camping out with him in Griffith Park but knew Twiglet would be most disconcerted.

The house was dark and empty. I crept in with Mishka in my arms. Twiglet looked at me like a furious parent betrayed by her child. I put Mishka down for her to say hello. She took one look at him, then snatched the new plastic toy I had bought for him out of his mouth; and then very slowly, before I could stop her, she ate it, bite by bite and with a malicious look on her face. Then she peed on the blanket I had put down for him and stalked off. Mishka, although twice her size, started to tremble and sneaked off to a dark corner of the house, before peeing loudly and long on the carpet. I shoved them both out into the garden, furious. After madly scrubbing the carpet, I headed for the kitchen. If I could just have a delicious cup of tea, everything would be all right. I opened the fridge – Jimminy had finished all the milk. I ignored the howls of raging dogs from the garden and resolutely opened my post.

It was a card someone had sent me. I read the inside.

'Thank you so much for my reading. Everything you said came true. It must be so great to be psychic, to help you make your decisions about everything.' I sighed. Looked at the message on the outside of the card: 'Approach the present with your heart's consent. Make it a blessed event.' And I started to laugh. Soon I was laughing wildly. Then crying in big, messy, heaving sobs. What an awful day. 'Find the providence.' If Rubin – who had had everything taken away from him could – I could. As I stood there, from some far-off wounded recess of my heart: Al crossed my mind. He whirled around in my head. And from an equally deep but determined place I decided I was not going to call him. It was time for the angels to step in and help me. I was in the City of Angels; it was about time I behaved as if that were true.

Haunted by Love

The first thing I noticed about her was the gigantic crucifix hanging around her neck.

'I don't believe in ghosts.' That was her opener.

'Neither do I,' I replied.

She looked puzzled. 'Well then, how can you help me?'

'I don't believe in them. But I've experienced them.' I smiled. She liked that.

'But ...' she looked around as if the local priest was going to nab her, 'you know I shouldn't be here.'

The silver crucifix that hung heavy around her neck winked at me in the sunlight. Mary was an elderly American lady looking for answers that her church hadn't given her. They'd given her husband a burial and reassurances of everlasting life. She wanted more. She wanted proof of the afterlife. I was picking this up psychically as I looked at her. Her anguish and her despair were hovering just below her challenged beliefs.

She was right: she shouldn't be here, according to her church's precepts. But we were attempting a peace process. Her ancestors had burned me on pyres for heresy, and now she was in my garden, for some reason that she would not, dare not, reveal because the parameters of her religion prevented her from seeking help from me and my kind. Psychics.

'That's all I'm going to say,' she said firmly.

'That's fine. I don't want you to tell me any more.' She was taken aback; she expected me to probe for more information. I poured her a glass of water and she settled down under the big sun umbrella. She was being haunted. She called it haunted, I called it visited.

Pulling herself together, she added, 'I need to see if you can prove to me ...' she suddenly looked distraught, and finished with, 'just tell me something.'

I looked her in the eye. Under the circumstances I decided I'd avoid the tarot cards. Although to me they are glorious arche-types that reveal soul messages, to her they would be an absolute certainty that she was meddling in the forbidden occult. So it was to be just her and me. To my amusement we both had our eyes closed and we were both praying.

I blurted out, 'Bel Air!'

'That's where I live!'

Amazement but quiet amazement. This clearly wasn't the real reason she'd come, but she was reassured. I wasn't a char-latan. I knew she knew; her heart began to open.

'London.'

'I want to live there ...'

'Around Wimbledon ...' I saw a black dress pass by in Spirit as I said that.

'I love it there.' She smiled a big, soft, cake smile.

There it was again! The dress. Then a Spirit hand touching her hair. So near. Still no name. Nothing was clear, I was afraid she would lose interest and go back to that fearful place of judgement ... I looked more closely: it wasn't a dress, was it a robe? It was a man in a dress! A transvestite was haunting her? I looked at her. It couldn't be. I looked at him. Oh my God! It was a church man! And I had taken the Lord's name in vain in his presence. He was clearly a forgiving sort of Spirit, and on a much more pressing mission than policing my profanities. That was his voice I was hearing in my head: 'Profanities.'

She looked very scared suddenly, and was staring at me. 'He's here, isn't he?'

'There's a priest here.'

She looked terrified and turned around towards the gate. 'A priest in Spirit.'

Strangely, this was much less frightening to her. She smiled. 'I can feel him standing right behind me ...'

'He's touching ...' I started.

'My hair ...' she said, as her eyes welled up. 'I miss him so much. I don't know how I'm going to go on without him now he's dead.'

I smiled. Handed her a tissue. They were the living to me, the so-called 'dead'. Very much alive.

'David,' I whispered at last.

She gasped and tears streamed down her face. 'My husband ...' she said, letting out all the tears she had stored up in her loneliness. But now she was not alone.

'He's here. Now he's touching your ear. He's whispering to you. Squirrel ...'

'He used to call me that!'

'He still does.'

She couldn't stop smiling. 'He didn't believe in ghosts either, he was a priest,' she said, 'but he's here!'

Now she was actually laughing at the absurdity of it. Here

indeed he was, in his phantasmagorical form. He had defied his earthly religion too, to be with his heavenly soulmate who was still on earth. Love was triumphing.

He wanted to chat.

'He wants you to be involved in your church and he says they love your ringing.'

'Yes, I'm going to minister,' she said eagerly.

'Good, it makes you happy and you will help a lot of people. You'll go around clinics.'

'I want to help the dying ...' she looked suddenly thoughtful. Her brain was trying to digest all her church philosophies as they clashed with her experience here in a Hollywood garden. 'So the dying don't die ... there is everlasting life, isn't there?'

It wasn't really a question either for him or for me. More a soulful conclusion that she suddenly knew to be true.

I looked at the Spirit form that hovered behind her and read his thoughts to her: 'He loves you very much. He always will. And he knows you have faith.'

'I do,' she said simply.

Suddenly Al came into my mind. I didn't want to – no, I wouldn't think about him – I was going to concentrate on my work. I was with a client. Time to be British and get on with things. No personal, touchy-feely stuff. I'd belong to the Angelina Jolie girls-don't-cry school. Tough and uncompromising. Al was toast. Back to work. But my work was done. The soulmate husband was fading. The air was suddenly very, very still. It was an elderly American lady and me. Alone at the table. Our Spirit friend gone. Or 'the ghost' gone.

She clasped my hand. 'Well, thank goodness I didn't have an exorcism!' she laughed. 'My priest was worried about me but I knew it wasn't a demon! That's what some of the people were telling me to do ...'

I laughed too.

'I can't tell you how much you have helped me. God bless you.' And Mary picked up her bag to leave. And she was a Christian, I thought. A Christian who'd just spoken to a good old-fashioned witch. But we were both happy. No judgements, only love. Now that was practising religion for both of us.

She suddenly turned back to me and asked, 'Do you have someone to love, dear?'

I bit my lip to stop myself crying. So much for the Angelina Jolie school of emotions. I was defiantly more of the Halle Berry school: hopelessly emotional.

'I did yesterday,' I said, 'but we had a bit of a falling out ...'

'Well, I'm sure you'll make up, dear. I'll pray for you.'

As I watched her go, I thought it was a great pity that I was completely unable to believe in what I preached: belief in love. I went inside to check my phone messages – maybe Al had ... Nothing. What was I doing? Al was banished from my heart. I sat down at the table again for a moment, and seconds later felt a warm stream of pee on my foot. Twiglet saying good morning. And near Mishka's bed another of her offerings: a protest poo. She had followed me inside and was staring at the poo with great pride, letting us know how she felt about being ousted by Mishka: outraged. I knew all about how that felt, to feel rejected, so I sympathetically took her outside. This war between the puppies was exhausting; it had been going on for a fortnight now. I left Twiglet furiously landscaping the bougainvillea and sneaked back inside to love Mishka, who was still asleep, so relieved to at last have found a home. He was dreaming, his paws chasing some imaginary enemy, and I didn't want to wake him yet. Watching him sleep, I felt a lump in my throat. It was easy to love someone when they were asleep. Or dead. They were quiet and lost in deep psychic realms, not awake and fighting. And back it came: the thought of Al, and our fight. My instincts told me to leave him alone. Not to call him. But God, I felt lonely.

The front door opened and a very bedraggled Jimminy walked in, back from Vegas. I opened my mouth to talk to him but, looking at his stubble and red eyes, words were obviously not a welcome option. He had one word of explanation: 'Tequila.' Then he stumbled towards the bedroom. Eyeing Mishka he managed to mumble, 'Twiglet's grown a bit,' before collapsing on his bed. Then an envelope was tossed through the bedroom door, landing at my feet. I opened it to find it stuffed with hundred-dollar bills. Also inside was a note in his large, loopy, probably tequila-inspired handwriting.

'By the time you read this note I will be asleep and will not want to be disturbed for several days. Won big time on outsider, Outrageous Nelly. Thanks for the tip! Giving you a cut. For God's sake, go out of a town for a day or two on the winnings … this looked right up your alley.'

I noticed a rather stylish little leaflet advertising 'YOGA. Retreat! Replenish! 3-day getaway … and on the third day you will rise again, renewed!' I walked towards the door to return the wad of cash to its owner and then read,

' … and don't insult me by returning the money. You're not the only one with psychic powers round here – I know you, cut the burning martyr act and accept it please. Even spiritual people have fun sometimes, your bestest friend Jimminy.' PS – Ziers chucked me. Said I drink too much. I still love him. What to do?' Sadly, I sighed. I was in no shape to give him guidance.

Especially because I was just too close to Jimminy to see clearly. I only ever got murky hints, not nice bright clear messages. Always like that with people I loved.

I silently prayed that Jimminy would be happy again, and that one day I would be hideously rich so I could repay him in cash and kindnesses. Then I headed to my bedroom to pack for the luxury retreat. The perfect present. I pulled down my natty fuchsia weekend bag and piled in my skimpy yoga outfits. At least I was miserable so I'd get skinny enough to fit in them. There's got to be some advantage to a broken heart. Good. I could get out of town and lick my wounds in private. Now it was my time. I felt a bit selfish and Oprah-like thinking that, but then of course I would – I was English, and had been brought up be pathologically polite, which meant considering the feelings of others was paramount. Well, I'd taken that to a teensy-weensy bit of an extreme, some might say, encouraging a stranger to play the part I was in love with because it would be good for her career. Yes, of course it came from my psychic self, it wasn't conscious, but on some level I had known. That wasn't manners, that was sabotage. Sort of 1970s orgy-style sabotage: 'You like my husband, have him up against the new Formica, why don't you!' That, of course, was what I feared might happen next. Al was sexy and a flirt. The movie star was beautiful. Director and actress. Dot dot dot.

I headed for the Coco Pops in the kitchen, the solution to all problems. 'You'll get obscenely fat,' whispered my old friend, the enemy within. 'Don't care,' I whispered back. I poured a Daddy Bear portion. I'd work it all off with the endless yoga if the schedule of this retreat was anything to go by, I thought, examining the timetable on the back of the nifty leaflet: 4 a.m. until eleven at night every day. I wolfed down the trashy Coco

Pops, and left the incredibly expensive organic lamb and sweet potato dog food I had bought for the furries, with detailed instructions for Jimminy. Just as I was about to close the door and leave, I had a pang of guilt. Mishka and Twiglet. I couldn't leave them; they really needed me. I'd stay for them. Then I noticed they were nowhere to be seen – Christ, had Jimminy left the gate open in his drunken stupor? No, it was closed. Then I smiled. I had an instinct. Peeked into Jim Jim's room. The three of them – Mishka, Twiglet and him – were all piled up on his bed. Everyone was fine without me.

I drove up the coast and opened the windows. The salt of the sea stung my cheeks and I felt like crying. So I did. Alone at last, not having to look like the one with all the spiritual answers, I could fall to pieces. The relief of being able to have a good weep and to speed out of town at the same time. Nothing like it to get a new perspective on your life. Last time I had been speeding down the Pacific Coast Highway was to rescue Astrid from the stalker. When she was a stripper in a rabbit coat. Now she was a star in a Burberry trench. She had changed altitude with her fame; now that was a new perspective: I felt like I still was at the bottom of the mountain, while she was up there in the clouds with a better view of life. I knew that in spiritual terms that was crap, but Hollywood was run on a strict hierarchical system, and now we both had to overcome our feelings about her fame to stay friends. I took a deep soggy breath. Strange. I was single. Unemployed. Broke. And over thirty. A complete failure by Hollywood standards. And yet I began to feel happy.

Glancing up at the highway, I saw a picture of some action-figure actress and my brief moment of elation evaporated. I wondered angrily when actresses had become athletes. When had acting become more about beautiful biceps than a nifty nuance? I had come to Hollywood, like Astrid, to 'make it' as an actress. Why was that so important to me? I think that deep down I knew the reason: I was the redhead at school, with freckles, sticking-out teeth, and sticking-out ears. Movies and the women in them represented beauty, especially back then in grey old London. I remember, at drama school, wandering into a rainy cineplex in north London and watching *Pretty Woman*, set in LA, in which an outsider, a prostitute – tragically similar in the pecking order to an LA actress – triumphs and overcomes her past to get her happy-ever-after. Stuffing myself with popcorn while watching the movie, the palm trees, open-top cars, it had all looked so ... sunny and glamorous and possible, so much better than the Finchley Road or the pub at Swiss Cottage. I knew, in that moment, that I wanted to go and live in the film capital of the world and be the triumphant outsider. Ironically, here I was, cruising down the ocean road in California, and yet I had this oppressive sensation that I was further away from acting than I had ever been. I'd got the outsider bit, just not the triumphant bit. At drama school 'the art' was all we thought about, groups of us sat around in black, smoking for hours and talking about Meisner and Stanislavski. We were obsessed with acting, doing the greats, especially Chekhov. My problem was that I was a natural at Chekhov, but I wanted to be doing *Pretty Woman*, even though I looked nothing like Julia Roberts. And as a Chekhov girl I had moved to a town where the understanding of said playwright was slight, to put it mildly. I was in a town where the apocryphal tale went that one red-faced executive at a studio had actually got on the phone after reading *Uncle Vanya*, the great Chekhov masterpiece from the nineteenth century, and screeched, 'Get me his agent.' When he was told that Chekhov had been dead for over fifty years, he exclaimed, 'He's not dead! He's unavailable!' Ah, Chekhov and I, horribly misunderstood.

But people would remember Chekhov, I knew that, because he was brave and had a huge heart. I bet he had some dark times too, I reassured myself. Somehow we knew his life was not all dandy and cherry bowls, else he wouldn't have written like that. I must be brave and Russian and stalwart about my life. Defend my dreams like they defended Stalingrad.

Turning off the freeway into the green hills, the imaginary world and my place in it became less important, as I took in how beautiful the actual world, the countryside, was. The tall redwood trees reminded me that nature would triumph in the end, that it was a true and divine thing that would outlive us. There was an ancient wish in the tree to touch the gods in the sky, a worthy wish compared with the cult of biceps-building and screeching salesmen looking for six-figure deals. I drove through the arch of the hollowed-out tree trunk, something I had wanted to do since I was tiny. I whizzed through another ancient tree, God's centre, and rounded the corner sharply, almost running smack into the wooden door of the retreat. A reassuring gold 'Om' sign glinted in the early evening gloaming. The centre, originally an old hunting lodge, was almost crashed into by several other stressed-out girls. Getting out of our cars, we all looked like we were from Hollywood. Giveaways were the trendy film T-shirts and overpriced flip-flops. Were we all were retreating from failed love affairs or lost dreams? There's something about an ashram that isn't going to attract the jubilant. Solemnly, we all took off our shoes. Well, I guess this was more of the 'barefoot luxury'. Lots of burgundy toenails doing seva at a quasi-ashram. Rich people charged a fortune to stay somewhere beautiful, without the frills. Ashram penance.

As we checked in, I wondered what the price of enlightenment was. This was like the Starbucks of yoga. An exorbitant rate and no service; you do all the work. Carry your coffee to the table and pay five bucks for it. Here it was: hand over hundreds of dollars and make the lunch while you're at it, as vegetable chopping 'seva' (selfless service) was compulsory. And you shared rooms with strangers, to mimic the atmosphere of an ashram using enforced intimacy. And no talking was the rule. We were randomly paired off with room-mates and my bedfellow was a supermodel. We were each given a key and walked up to our expensive cells. She would make a greyhound look portly – the price of which I discovered on our first night together, sharing our room. She got up every hour, gulping what appeared to be some sort of diuretic weight-loss tonic which did indeed give her that figure, but which she paid for with sleep deprivation. She stayed up all night, slurping her magic potion and then doing mad stomach crunches on the hour. I knew because I was awake myself. Away from Hollywood I went into shock. I think it was the shock of having no one to occupy my mind except myself. I was so used to other people's futures renting my mind that, now they were gone, the experience was quite Zen. And all my possible invented futures that had occupied me since I had arrived in Hollywood – me as leading lady with love – were lost. And, as ever, in the early hours it was the mystic of the sixties who kept me sane: Mr Dylan humming: wail about having nothing to loooose (it's a long wail!). We were soul brothers, he and I. I was not alone. I hummed myself to sleep. For an hour. We were up at 4 a.m.

I was tired, but my room-mate looked positively cadaverous with exhaustion. We both stuck dutifully to the no-talking rule, but, mysteriously – to bond, I guess – she showed me her list of 'food intolerances' that an expensive Hollywood nutritionist had given her. Curiously her 'red' foods – i.e., the foods she must absolutely never eat for fear of weight gain or, God forbid, bloating – were papayas, lamb, lemons, lentils and avocados. I broke the rule of no-speaking and joked, 'Wow! So you can have chocolate croissant, coffee with whipped cream and French toast for breakfast but not a papaya!' She looked as sour as the lemons she had to forgo. I returned to the no-talking rule.

Luckily, we were immersed in meditation for five hours, then yoga for the next five, so we were sanctioned not to communicate at all. I always loved the mystery-school schedule. Most people hated it. I really couldn't see why. Getting up at dawn, meditating for hours, herbal tea break, yoga for hours, fruit-nibble break, chanting strange, magical, mystical mantras. Vegetarian feasts. It made much more sense to me than most of the 'real' world. I imagined myself getting old and disappearing up a mountain for a decade with these songs and my soul. Easier than everyday life in many ways. Just lost and abandoned to Spirit. I was finally beginning to unwind. A good night's sleep and I'd be off on my new life, the new, improved me. Stalwart and single. But that night I was trapped with the model again, who had, due to the daft diet, developed loud and unashamed flatulence. This, she assured me, was just the result of yogic spinal twists and was not caused by the ludicrous diet. I barely slept at all.

I left our room even earlier that the 4 a.m. wake-up call and wandered round the grounds of the old hunting lodge. I needed to be alone. I had decided to go all the way in daffiness, and do the whole California Essalen-type thing. Even though I secretly felt foolish ... I was going to hug the great redwood that had been flirting with me since I had got here, showing off its beauty and wisdom. I sneaked through the dew, checking no one could see me, and gave it a small, embarrassed embrace. I needn't have worried. Laying my head on its trunk, I could psychically feel I was not the first one to try and grab some of its benign wisdom. I could feel all sorts of lost dreams that had been left behind in its bark. Old boyfriends, loves that never were; many heads had been laid there that were too full of wishes to see the world in front of them. The giant redwood was still hugging me as I sensed someone looking at me. I spotted the yogi who was running the retreat, meditating under a oak tree, observing me in a playfully detached sort of way. He was leaning up against its bark. Even though he couldn't possibly have heard my bare feet on the wet, dewy lawn, he had felt me join one of his leafy teachers. Then he smiled at me. I realised it was the first time in a long while that someone had smiled at me without wanting some psychic guidance. A reading. A quick prophecy. A promise of a future. He closed his eyes and returned to the inner kingdom that was making him smile with such bliss. I liked him.

I sat through the formal dawn meditation, longing to lie down and have a glorious sleep. I wanted to forget Al, acting, all of it, and just sleep. I sneaked off for a snooze and was flat out snoring for several hours. I woke up in time to make the lunch I'd paid a pretty penny for. As I garroted carrots, imagining they were Al, the yogi's wife talked to us about the boundless compassion that yoga gives you. I ate lunch silently, ruminating on the differences between unconditional love and being a doormat. I felt obliged to forgive and forget Al, to rise above it all in some yogi-type, transcendent way, when in reality I felt angry, hurt and betrayed. It was very hard trying to marry a Western psychology (hate him, beat that cushion) with Eastern laissez-faire wisdom (love him, do a headstand). The yogi husband was clearly of the 'turn things on their head' school, as he could transcend whatever he wanted, most especially his age. He balanced on his forearms, in a scorpion stinging pose, while his toes covered his eyes. And he was seventy. A spit in the eye to the Hollywood horror of ageing. But his youthfulness came from Spirit and the trees, and it was free, not paid for in a Beverly Hills surgery.

I also discovered that afternoon that, in addition to his physical prowess, he was no psychic slouch. The supermodel had a question for him. She asked him how we could fulfil our desires using yoga as a tool. I half expected him to burst into wild Samadhi laughter at the shallowness of the question, but he was very kind and non-judgemental. To my surprise, he stared at me as he answered the question: 'Say for instance you really want to get married to a man you love, or you really want to star in a film you care about passionately, you would understand that if it is written in your destiny to have that it will come to you. If it is God's will, it will happen.' Throw a stone at a Hollywood ashram and you'll hit a girl in her thirties who wants to be married and star in a film. But still, I was impressed.

Impressed because he was a God's will kind of guy. A 'if it's yours it's coming to you' kind of guy. A guy who advised that we just need to be calm and be kind. I loved it. What a welcome change from LA. There was a different recipe for success there, it was 'do,' not 'be'. Do black magic feng shui; do a thousand millionaire affirmations a day; 'Just do it!' was the call to arms, because there it's all about what *you* do. *You* are the God who creates your world. *You* are in charge of your own success.

Phooee to God's will. *We* are God's will – look at our biceps and box office returns. It was the song in my head that gave me the clue to what I really felt about all of this, the Black Eyed Peas super-ballad asking where the Love was. Theirs was a peace song, a team effort, with the most important question: where is the love? Not the world as war zone meets luxury playground. 'How can I use yoga to get what I want?' That was her question. She'd actually hit the nail on the head. How can I take an ancient system, designed to dissolve desires, and rework it twenty-first-century Hollywood style, so I get to fulfil my desires and get exactly what I want? Because then I feel in control, and if I feel in control then I am not afraid. Afraid that people who we love die, that we will be left, that we suffer unrequited love, that our children get strange and terrible diseases, that wars happen in distant lands, that famines and tsunamis ravage us and that ultimately we have very little control. But the super-model wasn't buying it. She was in control. She was the cover girl for the American dream. She was determined to succeed on her great life quest, to be so thin she'd disappear. Not have to feel the terrible powerlessness of life. She redoubled her efforts that night with coffee colonics, adding explosive grunts to her already explosive farts. By midnight, she was pacing and farting like a hippo and I was hiding under the covers.

I drifted into an uneasy sleep, praying for a solution to this awful room-mate nightmare. The other world came to my aid, in the most surprising way. I felt someone standing over my bed, someone staring at me. I woke up to see a black man with a machete standing over me, staring at me. He was staring at me and he had a machete in his hand! This wasn't a dream … Help! I screamed a blood-curdling yell. The man disappeared. Vanished. Grappling with my logical mind I sat up, staring at the empty space in front of me. But I kept seeing his face in my mind's eye, staring at me.

'Oh my God, it was a ghost!' I shrieked. 'I saw a ghost!' I was actually sort of thrilled in a terrified way. Spirits I was used to, but this was a genuine ghost.

The supermodel, as ever, was more interested in her bowel movements than any minor event like a bloodthirsty ghost showing up. She was afraid and channelled it into a furious outburst. 'That was the first time I've slept in five days! What's wrong with you! There are no ghosts! You're delusional! You're mad!'

She began packing her bags in the moonlight; aromatic oils she had concocted for her sweet-smelling colonics spilled as she stuffed her nylon carry-alls with enema buckets. My yell and then her yelling had clearly woken up half the house, as the yogi's wife came in and asked if she and her husband could talk to us both.

She asked us to get dressed and come out into the garden so we didn't disturb everyone. She wanted us to talk to her husband, the quiet and mysterious yogi who had been meditating through the night. The yogi smiled at the supermodel, a smile she was not used to getting, I suspected, filled with kindness, not lust. And he looked at me in a knowing way. He asked me what had happened. What had frightened me. I told the truth. I explained that I had seen a man in our room. Or a ghost of a man. His wife asked me if he was holding anything. I nodded, puzzled that she seemed to know, and said, 'A machete.'

Under the moonlight the yogi relayed what they had all assumed to be an apocryphal tale of the place. A century or so before, a well-off white couple had owned the cabin, and they had owned a black slave. The young wife had married the rich elderly landowner to help her family. He was a violent drunk who beat her. She fell in love with their slave. They became lovers. The husband found out, and one night had burst into her room, the room we had been sleeping in, with a loaded shotgun. But the slave had been prepared. He killed the husband with a machete. Then he fled into the night at the urging of his lover, who did not want him to stay in case he got caught and killed.

'And what happened to her? Did he ever come back? The man she loved?'

'No,' said the yogi. 'That was the man she was destined to be with. But only for a short time. That is why he haunts her now; he is still trying to find her.'

WOW. So The One You Can't Forget could even come at you from the grave.

'Why?' I said, with a sort of buried desperation and urgency that surprised me. 'Was it her karma to suffer?'

Again he looked at me. 'You can change your karma through prayer.' Looking at the supermodel he said, 'You can pray for God's help, you don't have to do it all by yourself.'

Walking back the supermodel and I started to chat. We were both deeply affected by the love story.

'Do you have a boyfriend?' she asked me.

'No. I did. Sort of. What about you?'

'No, I'm too strange. My habits. Do you think they're odd?'

'Well, they are a little. But at least you don't see ghosts. Trust me, that can be a real dampener ... Especially if you see your boyfriend's dead wife, who he pretended not to have.'

And she laughed. 'That's true? Very funny,' she said, still laughing. 'But at least you had a boyfriend. I have no one. I sit in my room and cry. Go out to clubs and everyone's too intimidated to ask me out. They are scared of fame. Men are scared of a lot of things,' she went on, 'especially tears.'

'And what are you scared of?'

'I'm scared of never finding my soulmate.'

So I sat down, and taught her the soulmate exercise. Very simple. Just imagining that there was someone there who would love her exactly as she was. She loved it. Felt him. Felt him hug her.

'Thank you,' she said. 'That was my karma-changing prayer.'

When we got back to our room, neither of us were afraid any more. And I had a brainwave. I gave her a number: shit face. Astrid's old boyfriend. They were ideal: he was as successful as she was, they both had peculiar scatological obsessions, they were both plain peculiar. She promised me she would call him. I, meanwhile, had to call Al. But I wasn't going to use a phone. I'd call him telepathically. And then pray.

I walked back to my tree in the dawn darkness, and as I felt the wet grass touching my feet I wondered if I could touch Al's soul, if he could hear my prayers. I mean, there had been all those studies of patients in hospital who fared better when people prayed for them, so why should it not work for us? In a rare moment of divine inspiration, brought on by the presence of the selfless yogi, the supermodel and the spectre, I sat and prayed under the redwood tree. I prayed for Al's peace of mind. I prayed for my own. I prayed for understanding, clarity and right action. I prayed he would find happiness and I prayed he would be reunited with his whoever his soulmate was (I got a bit twitchy at that one; I wanted to explain to the silent senders of the prayer that it was me me me, but I resisted), and finally I prayed that whoever played the film part was the one who was meant to, by divine right. A tremendous weight lifted from me. Walking back to the haunted room, I somehow knew I wouldn't be bothered by the ghost any more. We both slept soundly that night and ate a proper breakfast together the following morning. We parted with big hugs. I had had such a great time, I went to thank the yogi's wife. She was packing up boxes and boxes of clothes.

'What are you doing?'

'We're sending clothes to the poor. Almost all of the money we make from the course goes to the poor. We tried before to ask for charity or donations, but no one gave us anything so now we charge for the course, and then use the money to do this. It works.'

I felt the size of a small pea. I was so unused to meeting genuine people, having lived in LA for several months by now, that I couldn't quite fathom that my cynicism might be quite unfounded. I thought they were just greedy New Agers trying to make a fast buck, selling happiness. But this woman was some sort of Mother Theresa type, so I handed her the last of my cut of Jimminy's winnings. And I left feeling genuinely light, inside and out. Was it LA that was making me this distrustful? I was so used to seeing spiritual only on the outside, I was shocked when I realised there was an inner integrity.

LA, my new home town, looked like a ghost city. The streets were deserted. There are some things you just don't do in some cities: ask a waiter for ketchup in a Parisian restaurant; wear a bhindhi in Kashmir; wear a one-piece in Rio; or walk in LA. I rebelled.

Parked on Robertson, just shy of Beverly Hills. I was walking through 'the heart' of LA, although, significantly, there is no heart of LA. I tried to stop myself, but I couldn't help comparing it with London. I remembered my time there and all the good things about it: Marmite, buses, faces full of lines and character with funny teeth and outrageous noses. I had a wave of home-sickness and remembered how I loved walking through the heart of London, walking in and out of galleries and libraries and parks. There, in the streets, I never thought so much about what I looked like; I thought about what I was looking at: ancient buildings, bizarre Dickensian shops, clothes that didn't look like they did here – endless pyjamas, lingerie tops with sweat pants. There we wore proper shoes that covered your toenails, and had long Doctor Who woolly scarves and ridiculous bowler hats and dandy suits. Here I felt as if I were an overweight heffalump condemned to wearing flip-flops. I mean, what sort of a grip could you have on the land if you wore flip-flops?

I walked past the lunchtime crowd at the Ivy and saw the typical Hollywood sight. The same face over and over again, like Andy Warhol wallpaper. And cloned bodies, all with gigantic bosoms and stick legs. It was really disturbing. What on earth was I doing trying to make this my home?

I was hungry and wandered into an American chain super-market – not my beloved Whole Foods. You can move from gloomy to suicidal pretty swiftly in a place like this. The food was vast, bland and tasteless. It reflected LA perfectly. So injected and morphed that it had lost any sense of style or indi-viduality. I picked up what claimed to be a tomato; it was plastic and dead. And I remembered my favourite childhood smell, of tomatoes off the vine in the greenhouse at home, so full up and sweet that I would sneak in at night as if I were stealing chocolates. I even missed English food: leeks in white sauce, mashed potato and blackberry and apple. Maybe this was just hunger, maybe it was low blood sugar. I walked into a hip café. I sat at the wooden table, the only thing that seemed vaguely real. No wonder everyone spent all their time on cell phones, it was too painful to see this reality and not at least laugh about it with someone. I think Al would have laughed at this. He had a great sense of humour. Fucked-up values but a great sense of humour. But I wasn't speaking to him.

'So the special today,' said the waitress, 'is scrambled eggs without the eggs, but with tofu, and the toast is either sourdough multigrain wheat-free or gluten-free, and in your coffee – decaf's our speciality – there's non-fat or semi-skimmed or soy milk ...' She went on. This was funny when I first got here ... not any more: macrobiotic beans, vegan toast, something ... and on and on she went ... and idly I read her future, looking at her. She was an actress. She had dreams, she'd get a couple of parts, then she'd want to do a one-woman show so that someone would sit up and take notice, but no one would, because she was good but not great, funny but not hysterical, pretty but not a stunner. Back home was a guy who loved her, but he couldn't heal her with the recogntion she desperately craved, so she had come here, to be a star. And that wasn't her destiny. She couldn't understand it. She was thirty-nine now, and still waiting tables, but far, far worse, she was still waiting for her life, waiting for this town to say she counted. And all she was counting was the years that had gone by.

'Boiled eggs with soldiers, please.'

The girl then did what anorexics often do and urged me on with gay abandon. 'Treat yourself, why don't you!' she said.

I'd obviously made her day by eating egg yolks. I watched her as I walked out. She was me somewhere, lost and chasing after dreams. At least, I thought to myself, I am not living in delusion any more. The yogi in the trees had cleared that up in a way. Where was Jimminy when I needed wisdom?

Jimminy was on his way out of the door of our home.

'Darling, we're having a doggy day. Haircut, blow-dry and manicure for the pooches. You put them in a washing machine, it's the latest thing. They're still not the best of friends, but I'm trying! Dying to chat. Later!' And I watched my little two- and four-footed family leave. I felt so restless. I was supposed to be calm and yoga-ed out – I speed-dialled Astrid. Urth Café in ten minutes. Perfect.

Astrid was already at our usual haunt, on Melrose, with Big-star-tiny-body.

As I arrived at the café entrance, five overweight men with cameras were stalking the joint. I used their lenses as compasses to find her. Astrid raised her eyebrows to me and grouched, 'Fucking paparazzi! They're always around her! And I left my American Spirits in the car.'

'I thought you'd given up smoking,' I said, as she dodged down the stairs.

'I had ... until this morning,' she said grinning. I was so happy to see her. As she walked to her car the paparazzi started chasing her. She fled back to the safety of the café, where, in LA, due to the high quota of celebs, press cameras are banned.

'They came after me,' she said, bewilderment on her face.

'Of course they did, Astrid. You're playing the lead in a national TV show now.'

She raised her eyebrows again. 'Lucky me ...'

We sat inside, even though it was boiling hot, because of the cameras. Was it that important not to have your photo taken? I wondered. Astrid had wanted this for years. Fame. She had woken up wishing for it. Now she was hiding from it. She ordered the usual bizarre LA food, as long as I would pick off her plate.

Then Big-star-tiny-body came in from the bathroom. She

had a baseball cap and sunglasses on. Jesus, if I thought the supermodel was skinny, Big-star-tiny-body was Belsen-thin.

'How's Piglet?' she asked attentively.

'She's amazing,' I said gratefully. 'And it's Twiglet.'

Astrid was staring out of the window. 'I feel like killing them sometimes,' she said, still obsessed with the paparazzi. She turned to Big-star-almost-extinct-body. 'How do you cope with them?'

The skinny star said very calmly, 'I have a guy who deals with anyone who bothers me. You know, fans, stalkers, blackmail. All of that stuff.'

There was something about the way she said 'deals with them' that was sinister.

Astrid clocked it as well. Big-star-tiny-body went on: 'Yeah, there was a guy who was trying to blackmail me ... you know, nude photos when I first got here. So my guy found him and dealt with him.'

I practically choked on my vegan sausage.

'As in ... ?' asked Astrid.

'As in ... dealt with him.' And her tiny, perfectly manicured hands made a thin slit across her throat. I was actually dumbfounded. Luckily her $50,000 dollar cell phone (made of platinum with jewels in it) rang and she disappeared, mouthing 'publicist'.

'Whoa!' said Astrid. 'Did we just hear that?'

'I think we did,' I said, still not quite able to take in the concept that people killed to maintain their stardom. Literally killed people.

'I think I'm disassociating,' said Astrid. 'That's what my therapist says we do when something's too weird or painful to deal with.'

'We psychics call it having an out-of-body experience.'

'Yours sounds more fun,' said Astrid.

'Most things are more fun than therapy,' I said, stirring my cappuccino.

'Fuck, that's heavy,' said Astrid, then she picked up the *Hollywood Reporter* that was lying on the next-door chair and flicked to the TV ratings. 'Oh well, let's read about the business,' she said with irony, perfectly aware of her avoidance. But whatever she was reading seemed to be upsetting her even more.

'What is it? Your show's ratings aren't good?' I asked, spooning my foam into a big heart on the top of my cappuccino.

'What makes you say that?' she said, with a very slight edge that you would only detect if you knew her very well indeed.

'Nothing … I just felt you were upset about something. I assumed it was your new TV show.'

She paused. 'No, it's not the show … it's Al's movie … Did you know that Lara is playing your part? What a trippy coincidence. You gave her a reading, didn't you?'

I nodded.

'Look, it's here.' And Astrid showed me a picture of Al with his arm around the girl. They were both smiling; all teeth, like soulmate sharks.

'Yes, I did know.'

'Did he tell you that he was going to give her the part? Having promised it was yours for the *second* time? I fucking well hope so.'

'Not exactly. But I sort of knew,' I said, smushing the heart on top of the coffee.

'What a creep! That's bad.'

I took a deep breath. As Astrid wasn't in love with him and high off a yoga retreat, this was a rational response, really.

'Well, it wasn't all that great anyway, was it?' said Astrid. She seemed to want to pick on me. She carried on. 'Why do you care so much about this film with Al? It's only a film.'

Fuck it. I'd be uncool and tell her the truth. 'Because if I died and I'd made a film like that, a profound film like that one, I'd feel proud of myself. I'd die happy.'

Astrid was listening very intently. So I ploughed on.

'Look, I can sum up my life as an actress so far: I've worn corsets endlessly, blow-dried my hair and cried buckets about imaginary problems with imaginary men. Sort of like my real life, and the compensations have been a résumé and a paycheque. Which is great on a material level. But on a soul level, I think … it hasn't really been … well … very profound. And this film …' I felt like I was trying to talk about a secret lover, it made me tongue-tied and emotional. 'It's just … this film … well, anything I say about it isn't as good as the film itself, but … it's about two sisters, who don't get on. They can't get on … because of a secret … and in the end … what happens … it's like life, it's dark and sexy and people make mistakes … But in the end, it just made me cry and cry … and you know …' I trailed off. She probably didn't know why I loved it. That's why I wanted to do it. So I wouldn't have to explain anything. It would be out in the world and would speak for itself.

For some reason Astrid seemed really upset.

'So you must think my show is just superficial and stupid?'

How did she get there? Did everything relate back to her? This was the problem with therapy. But I was a spiritual person who could transcend my petty feelings. I took a deep breath.

'Well, it's a sci-fi series – and it's great – and you're obviously supposed to be doing it …' I felt like I was defending something I hadn't attacked.

'But basically you think it's crap.' I could see a guy with a poodle at the next-door table trying to listen in.

'I didn't say it was crap,' I said, lowering my voice.

'No, but your project with Al is deep and meaningful,' she said 'meaningful' in bitter inverted commas.

'Astrid, calm down. First of all, I'm not even doing Al's film whereas you are working, making money, and it's great ... I'm sorry, how did you become the victim?' That really annoyed her.

'You don't think I deserve this, do you? You can't understand why someone as fucked up as me, a small-town stripper with great tits, gets the gigs? Not a proper actress like you!'

I had had enough of this rubbish. I was upset anyway thinking about Al. 'Of course I can understand it, this is Hollywood ...' This time I sounded bitter.

'Your problem is you're so fucking British you just won't admit that you want the same vulgar things Americans want, like money and fame and success! I saw you looking at my new Beetle, you love it!'

'I'd get a hybrid if I was going to get a new car,' I said snootily.

'Get them both! You're not in England now, you're not saving the world in India, you're in the USA, for God's sake! You're in Hollywood! You're so busy helping everyone else with their dreams, what about yours? What's happened to your dreams?' Poodle man was really earwigging which irritated me. So much for the fucking retreat teaching me to be unconditionally loving – right now I wanted to strangle poodle man!

I lowered my voice to a furious hiss. 'I don't want to talk about this ... I don't want to think about this right now. I don't want to think about the movie and Al.'

'Oh, and stop going on about Al. That's a dream you don't

need! He's obviously not for you, is he? He breaks every one of *The Rules*,' she said it with such self-righteousness it made me furious. I was livid! That stupid fucking book she lived her life by. Didn't she realise there were no rules? Where were we, at school?

'Whereas your boyfriends? They're just great!' I yelled. 'Shit face, for instance? I mean, he literally wanted to crap all over you? Could that be a sign that he may not be the one? Or the stalker producer? You were only interested in him because you thought he could get you a part, and after all he only had a criminal record as a rapist! And I'm not even going to get into Brad Pitt's gardener! Brad Pitt's gardener, for God's sake!'

Poodle man moved tables.

'I'm dealing with all of that in therapy,' she said, her voice cold, but I had really upset her.

'Well then, stop getting at me!'

'Because you're so busy being the spiritual one, helping everyone else, it's really irritating. You don't smoke, you don't drink, you don't eat animals … what do you do? You're so busy being good and trying to get it right. Why don't you go after what you want? We used to be really close, and now …'

'Now what, Astrid? What? I'm still the same … You're the one whose life has changed. You've just got everything you've ever wanted. What is the fucking problem?' I felt so frustrated.

'I don't know,' she said … and suddenly she looked liked she was going to break into pieces. She looked like a child who has been betrayed so badly they are never going to trust the world again. 'I don't know – I mean, all the people who never gave me the time of day want to be my friends now … I just feel … why are they treating me differently? I'm the same person.'

'Because they believe the lie,' I said with great calmness. 'They believe you are different because you're successful; you must have some magic stardust on you and they want to be near you so it rubs off on them. And you're still Astrid, just famous Astrid.'

'It's terrible!' she said, sobbing.

'I feel so sorry for you how you're making fifteen thousand an episode ...' I started laughing.

'You fucking cow!' said Astrid, now laughing.

'You pay a therapist to be nice and understanding to you. I'm your friend. I can tell you the truth.'

This set her off on more tears. Real tears. Not drama-queen or diva tears. This was serious. 'The truth is I'm upset because my sister – when you started talking about your film and it's about sisters – that freaked me out ... it's a sign – I'm not imagining it – you see my sister's come to stay in my apartment – and now there's a ghost!'

'What!' I shrieked. 'Why on earth didn't you tell me that to begin with!'

'It seemed too weird ...'

'Astrid, it's me you're talking to! This is normal life to me. But come on, let's go there now!'

'I'll run out and get the car – I'll pick you up in three minutes.'

Big-star-ridiculous-body came out. She smelt of sick. For some idiotic reason, I just blurted it out. 'You've just been sick.'

She looked horrified. As if I'd discovered her doing cocaine or watching porn. 'No!' she lied.

There was actually a piece of regurgitated food on her shoulder. I indicated it embarrassedly. Then I was so ashamed of having outed her, I tried to cover up. 'The fish was a bit off, I think.'

'I don't eat fish,' she said very self-righteously. 'I don't eat anything that has a mother!' She was standing there, trembling, and I felt so embarrassed but all I could think of was, do eggs have mothers?

'I have to go,' she said, gathering up her $50,000 jewelled phone packed with celeb numbers. She picked the piece of give away food off her designer top and stormed out. What was wrong with everyone over here? What was wrong with us all?

Astrid beeped the horn of her new convertible bug. It was cream with a black roof. Guinness on wheels Jimminy called it. I was about to tell her about my perculiar moment with Big-star-tiny-body, but Astrid was sobbing.

'My sister thinks it really might be a ghost, as things "Have moved by themselves".'

'What's your sister like?'

'She's jealous of me. I'm the one that got away. And after our mom died … well, it was hard.'

'What does the therapist think of all this?' I asked, genuinely curious.

'We were doing fine, but we reached a bit of a sticky point when I started with the poltergeist …'

'What did he say?'

'He asked me if I had a history of mental illness.'

'What did you say?'

'I said clearly, or else I would never have decided to be an actress.'

'Did he laugh?'

'They don't laugh much, do they? They think jokes are getting away from the pain, don't they? Anyway, to be honest, I got kind of freaked out and told him I needed help from a psychic, because he ended up saying I "might be a borderline personality who needed psychiatric help". I told him being a borderline personality was great for acting, but he wasn't impressed. That's why I wasn't seeing so much of you ... I wondered if he was right. Not that you're loony, but maybe my sister's been imagining it all?' 'Maybe,' I said doubtfully.

We arrived at the flat, which had changed little since I had camped out on the Ikea sofa, except it was freezing cold. As I walked towards the bedroom I felt queasy. To my intense relief, and slight disappointment as a psychic sleuth, there were no moving objects; it was just bitingly cold.

'That picture moved last night,' she said, pointing to a photograph.

'Who is it?' I asked.

'My mother,' she said, shivering. I looked at an old sepia photograph of a woman with dark hair and darker eyes. Sad poet's eyes.

'When did this start?' I asked professionally.

'Two weeks ago.'

'Did anything else happen two weeks ago?'

'Well, that was when my sister Joan arrived to stay.'

'Joan? How come you were Astrid but she got Joan?'

'My mom was over her hippy phase and into her spirit phase. She watched that beautiful old film about Joan of Arc. Anyway, Joan's here if you want to meet her.'

I smiled and said, 'Can I?'

Astrid stopped me by the door and whispered frantically, 'Be warned: she's a little hostile. And she won't talk about the poltergeist because she doesn't believe in all this.'

'But she saw it move, right?'

'Yes,' said Astrid, making a face.

I walked into the kitchen but could hardly see from one side to the other because of the dense clouds of smoke. For a moment I thought it must be the work of the poltergeist, but then a thin, bony hand and a beady nose appeared. This thing was definitely human.

'So you're the fucking psychic,' it growled.

'Among other things.' I smiled. It clearly wasn't going too well. I thought I'd start again. In a very friendly, love-bombing way I said, 'Hi, how are you?' but realised it had come out sounding rather more children's TV presenter than I had intended.

She picked up on this and, in a I'm-the-adult-in-the-room tone, announced, 'I'm Astrid's sister, Joan.' There was a pause as she sized me up. 'So what exactly do you do? Chat to the dead?'

I hesitated, 'Umm ...'

She cut me off. 'Oh, don't be embarrassed – I'm sure you make a packet.' This was going to be hard work.

'What do you do?' I asked, feebly changing the subject.

'Shouldn't you know, being a psychic and all that?'

I'd stepped right into that one. She suddenly laughed in the way the wounded and vitriolic often do, I thought smugly to myself. That was it! I would feel sorry for her. Sadly, she was without a spiritual path. Poor thing.

'I'm only kidding ...' She dismantled my arrogance with a surprisingly charming smile. I smiled back at her. Maybe I could like her. ' ... but it is all crap, isn't it?'

God, she had me again.

'It's like astrology, isn't it? I mean, it just doesn't make sense.'

I was about to embark on a discussion equivalent to a chat about racism with a National Front Nazi who had a broken bottle in his hand. She wanted a fight, not a conversion. I was Cordelia looking at Lear, trying not to be bullied into explaining the invisible answers we have in our hearts to life's mysteries.

I realised I had not replied and Joan was heating up. Smoke came out of her nostrils like a small dangerous dragon. Astrid came to the rescue.

'Joan's a journalist,' she said. 'She works for the *National Enquirer*.'

Well, that explains a hell of a lot, I thought.

As if on cue, she started to interview me: 'When did you first know you were psychic?'

I was startled to see a flash of blue light around her head as she asked me the question. I decided to keep that very quiet. I imagined myself attempting to give her details of a dead family member trying to connect with her. I'd be annihilated.

'Hello?' she said, in a Radio 2 fake-American-disc-jockey kind of way. 'Anyone at home?'

My heart skipped a beat at the frightening thought that I might go into some sort of trance with hostile Joan. 'I'm sorry. What were you saying?'

She huffed, 'Your great powers from beyond – when were you aware of your gift?' She lifted her voice and it cut the room with its irony. Then she launched into what was clearly a well-rehearsed monologue: 'They make the star signs up. I know because I used to ring up one of the top magazine editors and we'd make up sexy ones for our boyfriends and she would print them, and then we'd read them to our guys and make them do what we wanted!' This was clearly her trump card and she sat back in triumph.

I briefly wondered why she thought two lazy journalists making up lies for the gutter press somehow negated 2,000 years of star-gazing, but I let it go. I stared at her and observed that her red-lipsticked mouth was opening and closing and I suppose sound was coming out, but I couldn't hear a word. It was as if I had been struck deaf. In the silence I heard the clear, precise word 'violet' float into my big, empty, echoey mind. Around and around it went, repeated like a chant. I was mesmerised. As if hypnotised, I opened my mouth and out it came into the world as vulnerable as a newborn. 'Violet,' I announced.

Whatever part of the monologue Joan was about to get to, we will never know. She just opened and closed her mouth and stared at me as if I had just announced that her mother had died. In fact I was telling her the opposite: her mother was alive.

'I have a message from your mother. She says to tell you "Violet" and you will understand.'

Joan's stringy body, in her neat black miniskirt and tights, doubled up like a tiny teatime sandwich. When she eventually lifted her head, uncontrollable tears were cascading down her face. She let out a muffled noise that sounded like a hurt animal. She couldn't speak. She gestured to her sister to speak for her.

Astrid turned to me and quietly explained why 'Violet' was the 'open sesame' to her sister's heart. 'My mom moved to England and lived in Yorkshire. She moved there after Dad left. Wanted to be alone. Far away from anyone else.'

My mind joined her in one of those small, grey Brontë cottages – so desolate and beautiful.

'One day, she was walking back from a friend's house, a couple of miles away on the moor, when she had a heart attack. She fell on the grass and she never got up. She died all alone. Well, it took a while before they found the body because she was a loner and spent a lot of time by herself. Her friend Maggie found her.' She paused for a long time.

'Well, after the funeral, Maggie went for a long walk. She

took the path they would walk together, the path where she found the body, and there on the spot where she died was this big clump of violets. They had just sort of sprung up, strong and alone on the moors, just like Mom.' In a very quiet voice she went on, 'Violets were my mom's favourite flowers. She loved them. Not a lot of them grow in Yorkshire, as I'm sure you know.' She smiled softly to her sister. 'And Joan and I would joke that if she could hear us, if she were still ...' she groped for the word, 'around, then ... well, actually we asked her, you know, in our prayers, to let us know.'

'I think she just let you know.'

Joan nodded tearfully. But the most significant change was about to happen.

'Does she have anything else to say?'

'She wants you two to be friends. You've been fighting.' By their silence I knew she was right. 'And she's standing here with your youngest sister ... who is in Spirit. She died in Hawaii ... she's showing me water ... she drowned.'

Astrid looked at me and said, 'I never told you that. I've never told anyone that.' She was staring in shock. I'd never seen her so pale.

Joan was sobbing again.

'Your mother said that's why she moved to England, she needed to get away and she's sorry for leaving you.'

Joan was now like a small child. She asked me, 'Where is she? Can she hear me? Can you see her?'

'She's here in the room. She says she needed to make the pictures move to get your attention. You're not to worry about her. She's in a beautiful place, and she's wearing the red dress she got married in and dancing! She loved dancing. She's dancing with your sister. They are looking out for you both.'

'But I don't believe in any of this, I write about it to show how false and gullible people are. How can this be happening?'

'Does Sadie have anything to say to us?' said Astrid. Sadie was their dead sister.

'She knows she was meant to go at that moment, and she is with a young baby ...'

Astrid looked at Joan. I knew this was a family secret.

'Joan, you had a child at seventeen, and then afterwards, everyone in your family pretended that it had never happened. They never talked about it again, and that's why you became so angry. You had to give up your baby for adoption, and a year later the baby you never knew died. Well, Sadie wants you to know, she is with your daughter now.'

I almost considered stopping the reading because Joan, unlike the Los Angelenos, had never had therapy or done acting classes, and so she was crying from a place of unhealed hurt that was overwhelming her. Three of her closest relatives were all in the room with her in spirit: her mother, her sister and her daughter. Astrid was similarly awestruck. Their mother gave the final message.

'Astrid, I know a terrible thing happened to you ...' and again I saw the images I had seen on the first day I met Astrid. I recognised them, images of Astrid being hurt and violated.

'... Please talk about it, I was wrong not to talk. There are so many things you realise in Spirit that you forget when you are down here. Talk about it, tell your story, and tell it as often as you need, then one day you won't need to tell that story any more, and you will remember that you have a hidden wholeness. Don't be afraid to remember that. I was so afraid I thought we'd break from pain, but lean into your pain, and then lean out into the world.' The three of them were looking at the three of us. A grandmother, an infant and a young child, all in Spirit. The missing links for Astrid and Joan, where they had come from and where they were going; the first time the whole family had been together and told the truth. And finally the greatest truth. 'You're not to worry about us, we are all right. We are a family for ever.' And then they faded.

After a long silence, Astrid wanted to lighten the mood. She said, 'Pity there wasn't a will or something,' to make Joan laugh, but Joan didn't.

'But it was better than that, really wasn't it?' said Joan seriously. 'It was better than getting money; it was getting ... our family back.'

Joan was almost in a trance from shock and continued to tell the truth. 'I came to LA because I wanted to get money off you, Astrid. And I thought you just wanted money,' she said to me. I shook my head no.

Astrid replied, 'I know you did ... and I can give you some ...'

'I don't want that. I never did. I just want us to be friends.'

Astrid disappeared into the kitchen and, with a forced levity that belied the nervous anticipation of her sister's reply, said, 'Do you want to stay for a while, then? It might be fun. You can write from here, can't you?'

'Sure,' said Joan. And it was the first time she smiled.

As Astrid came back into the room I looked at them both from a psychic, energetic point of view. Their auras were blushing like pink roses. The colour of the heart. The colour of unconditional love. I knew it was time to leave.

Astrid flung her arms around me. 'What have I done to deserve you?'

'You probably fed the poor and helped the lepers in your last life and so this time round you get looked after.'

'Do you think?' she said, contemplating it.

'I'm making it up!' I said, laughing.

'But you weren't making up that other stuff, were you?'

I was serious. I put my hand on her arm. 'No, I couldn't have ...'

'We have a pretty fucked-up family, don't we?'

'No more than the average star on the E! channel.'

And that was it. We hugged and I left them together. As I walked out a light breeze blew through the apartment, almost as if the Spirits were saying goodbye.

I walked back to Le Pain Quotidien and felt a lightness of being. Everything was OK. My world made sense again. Astrid's family in Spirit were there for her; all they had to do was accept their past ... was that the message? It was more than that; it was in my heart, but I couldn't quite articulate it, even to myself. Still, I felt at peace, and I knew the two sisters did too. Then I got into my car and idly turned on the news. No peace here. I was now living in a country which was at war, and you didn't have to be psychic to know it was a pre-emptive strike and we were being lied to. I felt so angry and sad. The only weapons of mass destruction were the US warmongers. The psychics were on to all of this a long time ago, I mused. What was it Nostradamus had said, the American great seer had announced that 'at the beginning of the twenty-first century, the most powerful nation in the world will be run by the village idiot'. I had come to Hollywood because it was a tribe of great film actors, artists, dreamers and truth-tellers; I had come to escape something – my past maybe, the stifling class system of England – for the freedom of America, and now I felt like I was in prison again. Maybe it was time to leave.

Back home – in the canine trenches at my Hollywood Hills home – Mishka and Twiglet, despite their fashionable haircuts and flashy new collars, had reached an uneasy truce. They lay across the room from one another, eyeing each other's snouts intently. The news was on at home and Jimminy was passed out, with a bottle of whisky rolling around on the carpet.

Then I saw a postcard from Al on the table. He must have dropped it off by hand:

'We're at war. Embarrassed to be an American. Embarrassed to be me. So sorry I hurt you. Want to be at peace with you. Love.'

Funny. Sometimes when the world changes, we imitate it. My life, along with my adopted country, was about to go into a distinctly dark patch. A certain lovelessness was afoot. I scribbled on the card, 'return to sender'. I didn't want to get hurt. It was that simple. I knew my heart could be broken by this man, and I wanted to be safe.

the Dark Side

'Is this Lucinda Clare?'

'Yes, it is.'

The voice sounded very formal. 'This is Milton Grossekaese, from Grossekaese, Mittelkaese, Kleinekaese.'

I sat up in bed, shoving aside the wreckage from the night before – a papaya skin, so I didn't eat chocolate, and then a chocolate wrapper on top of it, as I'd ended up eating both.

'I'm sorry, what is this about?'

'I represent Lara Corano, the actress, and I am advising you that she is filing a law suit against you.'

'I'm sorry?'

He carried on officiously. 'Where were you exactly two weeks ago at 4 p.m.?'

'Two weeks ago? I have no idea. I have to look at my appointment book.' But I did know. It had been 14 days since I had seen Al.

'According to my client's recollection, you were at—'

'Yes, I was on a film set.'

'And you gave my client a psychic consultation?'

'Yes, I did.' Christ, where was this going?

'Apparently you kissed her goodbye.'

'I'm sorry?' I moved the sleeping Twiglet off my legs so I could concentrate.

'According to her statement, you leant forward, held her hands and kissed her.'

'I probably did. I mean I might have done, we're European, we do that – the *Mayflower* was full of our party poopers ...'

'I am warning you that she is filing a law suit for sexual harassment.'

I started to laugh. Was this someone playing a trick on me? This was really ridiculous. But he hadn't finished.

'And what are your qualifications for being a psychic?'

I restrained myself from using Diana's phrase, 'It was written in my destiny' – probably not a great line with a lawyer. He was into records, just not the Akashic ones.

'It's not like being a lawyer, we don't have exams.'

'So it's built on personal reputation.'

'Well, if you want to look at it that way, yes.'

'Well, I'd be careful of your reputation if I were you. I'd think about what happened. I'll contact your lawyer when we decide to pursue this.'

And Milton Grossekaese of Grossekaese, Mittelkaese, Kleinekaese put the phone down.

Sexual harassment? I thought she was going to call because she hadn't liked the reading or was suing because her future hadn't manifested itself, but sexual harassment? Absurd. I was in so much shock after the whole weirdness with the script of *How Did It Feel?* ... but I knew I hadn't pounced on her, for God's sake – I seemed to remember she had lunged at me, come to think of it! What the hell was wrong with her?

I called Astrid to get the LA behaviour translated.

'Get a lawyer.'

'A lawyer? I don't need a lawyer, for God's sake!'

'Everyone has one here.'

'I know – I used to watch *LA Law*. Do you think I could get one that looks like Blair Underwood? I wouldn't mind being accused of sexually harassing him ... but this girl – it's ridiculous!'

'Of course it is,' said Astrid, 'but get a lawyer. Trust me. I needed one. I'll give you the address of mine.'

I caved in and called Astrid's lawyer, Rico Mentira. Made an appointment. Showed up in an office that would have housed several immigrant families, but it was just him and his cigar.

'Let's start with a few basic facts. Are you a citizen?'

'I'm not.'

'You have a visa?'

'Sure. I applied for an extension,' I said proudly. In one of my few organised moments I'd got that all sorted out.

He put his fountain pen down. 'You did what?'

'I applied for an extension. So I could stay longer. Legally.'

'That might be a problem. Hang on a moment, let me check something.' And he went into his computer. The smoke from his cigar calmed me down. It reminded me of gentlemen's clubs where tradition was preserved. I felt reassured. I'd be fine.

'Are you aware that you are now on a list?'

'A list? What kind of list?' The absurdity continued.

'Anyone who applies for an extension is now viewed as suspicious, and you have exactly twenty-one days left to stay in the country.'

'What?!'

'There is only one way of solving this. You have to prove you are an extraordinary alien.'

'Are you a Scientologist?' I said, concerned.

'I beg your pardon, Miss Clare?' Clearly no sense of humour. And the only person in Hollywood who didn't know that the basic tenet of Scientology is that we are all descended from aliens.

'You are not a resident alien, are you?'

'I don't think I am.' The green card had the fantastically sci-fi name 'resident alien'.

'Then you have a serious problem here. The only way you can stay is to get an H1 visa that proves you are an extraordinary alien. Unless you can prove that—'

'But what about the harassment suit, won't that count against me?'

'You have a bigger problem than some spurious suit. I know Milton Grossekaese. He's made a lot of money off people who are new over here. Most people just don't want the scandal so they backhand him twenty grand or so and he goes away. He encourages his client to file because he's on the clock – and everyone knows Lara's a bit la la. My daughter dated her trainer, she's not all there – this isn't the first time I've dealt with one of her neuroses that her lawyer sees as a cash opportunity ...'

'So it's a sort of sophisticated blackmail.'

He nodded. 'But, I repeat, you have a bigger problem than that. You need to stay in the country, and you need to get a visa to prove you're an extraordinary alien. Exceptional in your field. A special person.'

'I have to prove I'm special?'

'Yes. What do you do?'

'I'm an actress and I write.' Wasn't going to mention the psychic stuff right now.

'Oh, not great. I've got a lot of Brits trying to get in on that. Anything else you can think of?'

'I do psychic readings,' I said lamely.

Strangely, he didn't laugh. 'Well, how good are you?'

'I don't know how good I am. I just do it.'

'Why?' he said curiously. 'Why do you do it?'

I was in a lawyer's office so I gave a lawyerly answer.

'It pays the bills,' I said simply.

'You make a living at it?'

'I do.'

'So you're a professional psychic? We might be able to get you in on that. But you have to have meet the criteria. Press cuttings. TV appearances. Paranormal expertise. Ever done haunted houses? I could find you one. Some of my biggest wins have been law suits against ghosts.'

'What?'

'Oh sure. Tenant buys a house. Owner doesn't disclose it's haunted. Law suit. Big money. There's one house comes up again and again. Ozzie and Harriet Nelson's house.' I looked blank.

'You don't know Ozzie and Harriet Nelson? America's sweethearts of the 1950s. The ideal family. They had their own show …'

'Like Lucille Ball and Ricky?'

'Sort of, yeah. Anyhow, I can get you in there to prove your expertise. If you come out without a heart attack!'

'They're scary ghosts?'

'Well, put it like this: that house has been sold many, many times in very few years. Beautiful house – famous when Ozzie and Harriet were alive, notorious now they're dead – although apparently they still live there!'

He stood up to indicate the meeting was coming to a close. 'And get some letters from respectable professionals – lawyers, law enforcement, you know, respectable people.'

'No, I've managed to avoid respectable people ...'

'And get some publicity.'

'I've managed to avoid that too.'

'Well, if you want to stay in America, you'd better stop avoiding and get your act together.'

'But I don't want everyone to know I'm a psychic – it's embarrassing. I mean, I'm an actor and writer ...'

'That's not my problem. I suggest you deal with that with your therapist. You applied for an extension to your visa—'

'Yes. Because I thought it was the honest thing to do.' I was getting frustrated.

'And you realise now that it is standard for the government to deny it, not to give it to you. So, I repeat, if you want to stay in America, you'd better get the press and paperwork to prove yourself as a psychic.'

'I did a TV pilot ...'

'Great. Can you get letters from movie-star clients?' He was joking.

I wasn't. 'My clients prefer to remain anonymous.'

'Well, it's up to you. You'd better get cracking, as you guys say. You've got a week. I can help you, but you've got to help yourself.'

I went for a walk to try and sort out the noise in my head. Fuck it, fuck the rules. I lived by the rules of Spirit. I was not going to be defeated by this. Did I even really want to stay in this absurd place? Well, I could go back to England and be a miserable theatre actress yearning for a bigger life. And that awful weather. And everyone smoked and drank like Jimminy and I'd live on fried eggs. I didn't feel so nostalgic now if there was no choice about whether to go back. Fuck it – I was going to have to do this. FUCK!

I headed up to the big houses north of Sunset. The LA architecture was as absurd and make-believe as all of our dreams. I wandered around, wondering what the next right thing to do was. Soon I was lost. In every way. How the hell was I going to get everything the lawyer needed to get the wretched visa? Just then a police car came out of nowhere and drew up next to me. Great I'd get directions. But it wasn't an English bobby; it was a Wild West kind of guy with a gun.

'Ma'am. Where are you going?' He glanced around at the multi-million-dollar homes I was jay-walking around.

'Um ...' I said, in my best over-enunciated Queen's English, 'I was going for a walk.'

'Where to?'

'Well, not to anywhere in particular, actually.' Too true.

This stumped him.

'Just walking,' he said, and he chewed over my words as if I'd said I was contemplating abseiling down Barney's, the Harvey Nichols of Beverly Hills.

Then he actually said, 'You're not from these parts.'

This was so out of a movie, I wondered if everyone referenced movie talk as reality. Probably because of my dire situation, I found it hysterically funny. I stepped back towards some bizarre billionaire's topiary, a bush shaped like a bear, grinning wildly at me, mad as this city, this ridiculous so-called life I was in. I had to pull myself together.

'No, I'm from Ireland,' I said. I used the other half of my nationality as a shallow ticket to bond with the police officer whose last name I could see from his badge was McCloughlin. It didn't work.

'Step away from the bush!' he commanded. Then I stupidly started smirking. He didn't like that. He was in the business of control. Then I saw his gun and, ludicrously, that made the whole thing even funnier. We were playing out cops and robbers. I started laughing. Then I had one of those moments where your life has become so absurd that you sort of grind to a halt and leave your body, in the hope you can press rewind and try again. But I couldn't stop giggling.

'Are you intoxicated?' he asked me suspiciously.

Was it the Irish reference that had given him licence to stereotype me? I idly wondered if I could make my fortune by suing him for racial discrimination – that would be an LA win, an LA story. I could see him going for his walkie-talkie.

'Do you have an ID card on you?'

Shit. If he looked at that he'd go into the data bank, and there I'd be with all of the other suspect characters who weren't Republican. Help. Lakshmi, Ishtara, help!

'Hey, wait a minute. I recognise you!' he said, squinting at me. 'You were in that TV pilot. My wife's a producer. You were great! You were the psychic! You guessed the girl wasn't pregnant! We loved it! You showed them! Good job!' Apparently my threat to national security had been wiped out by my slender TV moment ousting a fake fat girl.

Oh my God, I had an idea. Maybe this was my chance to get help. 'You really liked it?'

'We thought it was great. We need more of you. Give us a call if you need anything.'

That was my cue. Stop being English, ask for what you want and fuck the manners. 'I do need help. I need some letters for my visa ... green card, visa thing ... letters from respectable people to say that I'm good at what I do. I've helped the police in England.' It was a pretty pathetic request, but at least I made it.

'Well, you were good in the show … that was you, right? I mean I know most of those reality shows are shit and they make all that stuff up …'

'No, no it was real.'

Just then his walkie-talkie went off.

'Wait a moment, ma'am.' He looked at m, sizing me up.

'If you come down to the station with me … Do you have any qualifications at all? I could write a letter … but … any qualifications at all?'

'I have a degree from drama school.'

'You can get a degree in acting? Who knew. I thought you just had to be pretty.'

'Well …' I was stumped at that.

Then he suddenly perked up. 'I tell you what, you help one of the guys down at the station with his audition, and then do a psychic reading – then they'll know you're for real and we can give you an official letter from the LAPD. Girls like you deserve to be helped.'

'No problem,' I said, mildly terrified that I was going to go into an American police station.

'There's a whacko guy down there you might be able to help us with … we're getting nowhere. Maybe you can read him?'

'That's fine,' I said.

'Great. Wait till I tell my wife about this! She'll freak! So you want some fun? We'll put the sirens on …'

I sat in the back of the police car. It had very hard plastic seats and a sinister grid I gripped onto as I tossed from side to side. In cop time we arrived at the Hollywood police station.

We walked in. 'Hey buddy!' said McCloughlin to his pal with a matching gun and uniform.

McCloughlin disappeared downstairs to get clearance for me to be there and I observed police work, Hollywood style. This was like some post-modern joke. I couldn't believe the conversations I was overhearing. On the TV cop shows they talked about real crime, gangs, drugs, rape, larceny. But here the Hollywood cops were talking about movies.

A big, bulky, ginger-haired cop with a beard was complaining loudly: 'I'm not doing the security on that screening, fuck the free passes ... *Fahrenheit 9/11*'s a crap movie!'

His pal was with him. 'I agree. Why stand out there and freeze my arse off for some fat fuck? I mean no one's even pretty in the movie. Why should I protect Michael Moore when he doesn't want us to be protected? Know what I'm saying? I don't want to do nothing for that Moore motherfucker. I'm an American!'

A third cop joined the intense huddle. 'Hey, man, it's a good movie! My boy's in the army, he went to see it, and now he's leaving and gonna be a cop like me. I'm telling ya, there's something in that movie.' They walked out of the station, still arguing.

A skinny journalist with cheap Ray-Bans was on his own mission, pleading with the black receptionist behind the grill. 'Come on, who got arrested? I need the copy ... Was it Robert Downey Jr? Paris Hilton get drunk? You can tell me, baby.'

'I'm not saying anything, Warren,' said the receptionist, and she tapped her four-inch curly gold nails to show she was in charge here. Warren knew he'd lost today's battle and slunk out to commit his crimes: reputation murder by flashbulb.

I had a hunch that it was McCloughlin's buddy who sauntered in, Dave, the fab fireman. I was impressed. He was six foot, hunky and saved lives for a living. But he really wanted to be an actor. Go figure, as Astrid would say.

He took out some crumpled-up audition sides for a top TV show. 'McCloughlin said you can help me?' He sat down and suddenly he launched into his audition for the part of – surprise surprise – the hunky fireman. He finished. I nodded thoughtfully.

'That was great. Great ... just one small thing. You only have to read *your* lines, not the other person's as well.'

He stared at me and whooped. 'Hey, that's great. Great feed-back.' Then he looked at me again, 'Hey, I recognise you. You were in *Law and Order* ... you were a terrorist.'

I felt the whole place go still. Heads swizzled to stare at me.

'Yeah, it was *New York Undercover*. I played a terrorist, from the IRA, and I did a *Law and Order* too.' The addiction to fiction was so high here that I really punched that one home. I was in *Law and Order*, so I expected justice. Didn't want to end up in a cell with no trial – that would be even worse than being booted out of the country.

'You were scary. Good job.' That was really a great compliment. A real US cop – well, almost a cop, fireman Dave – thought I was scary.

McCloughlin came in and overheard us. 'She's not as scary as the nut-job downstairs. We got no details on him. If you can find out anything, do a reading, you'll be helping us.'

'She's doing a psychic reading on him,' said McCloughlin to fireman Dave, with pride in his voice.

'Like in *Medium*, the show?'

'Like in *Medium*.'

'Cool. You up for it?' said McCloughlin.

I took a deep breath and said, 'Sure thing,' as though it was all part of my everyday life to saunter into the LAPD and do a reading for a lunatic that even the police were nervous about. 'No problem.' McCloughlin took me down to the cell and fireman Dave went for his audition. I sympathised. I felt like I was auditioning for my pass into the country via my performance with the guy.

The first surprise was how good-looking he was. I then reminded myself that Ted Bundy had been a looker too. He looked at me, and I then realised that, by some bizarre coincidence, I'd done a cheerful reading for his twin sister, Cassie, a couple of months earlier. Where I saw a lot of success and sizzle for his sweet music and I urged her to bring her evil twin.

The evil twin was the double of his sister. Both of them were stunningly good looking. It's a very strange thing to be confronted by someone who you know is both troubled and dangerous and to feel as if God cheated by making him so beautiful. An extreme example of the outsides not matching the inside. Symmetrical and perfect, straight out of a Marc Jacobs campaign – edgy, dirty and dark outsides, but inside, beyond grunge, beyond lost-artist gloom; deep-down dangerous despair turned to hatred of the world. Couldn't hold a mirror up to his soul, too painful for him, so I was the one holding the mirror. Funny, I remembered his twin really well; he'd shown me a photo of them both together as children. Such a sad photograph: the sweet twin, the sane twin, was standing looking at his brother, and the one in front of me, was leaping in the air like a cross between Tim O'Leary and Johnny Rotten, mad, drugged, but strangely brilliant. I had to find that part of him and connect with it.

First step in the reading is usually to hold the hand. I turned to McCloughlin. 'We're cool.' So he left us alone in the room. We were under observation, but alone.

I felt an instantaneous horror at the idea of holding his hand, and a terrible primal need for the cop to come back. I calmed myself down. I would not get hurt. Being professional, I began.

'I've come here to help and to give you a psychic reading.'

He looked up at me and I could tell he liked that. 'A prophet. I'm a prophet of my times too. Tell me the news.'

OK. Definitely a bit off, but I had to go beyond that. The police were not going to leave me in a room with someone who would actually hurt me. Then I noticed we were being observed through a window, like in the TV shows. As if I were a psychiatrist. Which in a way I was, a psychiatrist of the soul.

'I'm going to say a prayer before we start, so if you can just close your eyes.'

I contemplated all the movies I had seen where the victim thinks she is perfectly safe and suddenly the prisoner lunges forward with a concealed penknife, or wire from his mattress, and does away with the idiot who thought they were safe because they were in a police station. I was locked in a room with a mad man. And all to get a piece of paper. He twitched next to me.

'God help me,' I whispered silently as my hand approached his. For the first time ever I debated not touching a client's hand – the energy field was so violently disturbed it felt like pins and needles, and he had that strange smell of metal that I associate with mental illness. That was a clue. I touched his hand.

He was very, very quiet. Then, like a small mouse with a big bomb, he whispered, 'I have fantasies.' He looked at me, to give him permission to continue. I was momentarily dumbstruck.

'I'm going to New York and I'm going to kill people. With a

gun. I think God is in me and the Devil is in them.' He looked at me, desperately searching for salvation. He looked like a very tiny lost child on a raft that had long ago left civilisation.

'Right,' I said. Then out of my mouth popped, 'You're a very talented man. Wonderful artist.' My God, why was Spirit giving him this? I was reading Hitler and talking about his paintings. This was screwy.

'You know about my paintings?' He was incredulous.

'They're very beautiful,' I said softly.

He wanted to go with the beauty but he couldn't. 'But the darkness ...' He stared at me. He really stared at me.

I cleared my throat. 'Well, you can cure that.' That came from Spirit.

Suddenly he gripped my hand exceedingly hard. He was having none of it.

'Oh Jesus, help me,' I prayed.

'I want to get on a plane and go and kill people,' he muttered urgently, 'and you have to help me.'

An Indian symbol glinted around his neck. I took the hint. 'Speak to him in his language,' urged the Spirit whisper.

I eyeballed him. 'That would be very bad karma. For life-times,' I said sternly.

'Have I been here before?' he asked. 'What was I? Did I know happiness?'

His eyes were huge and dark and I couldn't help feeling shocked, again, at the contrast between the physical beauty and the psychic damage. LA was getting to me. I was being conned by appearances again. I reminded myself that we were sitting in a jail.

'Oh, God,' I prayed. 'Help me to find more love than fear.'

Love kicked in. 'You can't do that,' I said firmly. 'You can't go to New York. That would be damnation for your soul and you have a beautiful soul. You've been lost since your girlfriend left you.'

His eyes filled with tears. He looked at me in awe. I went on, 'Spirit sees your beautiful paintings ... you go every week to the art store in Los Felix, your dedication is noticed ... and they know you're lonely ... now Annie's gone. Your brother's been your only friend. But you must hear Spirit, these thoughts of killing people aren't real. They're a manifestation of your mind. Your mind needs healing.'

'Am I sick?'

'Yes, you are. You need help. You can't kill demons outside you. They are in your head. And before you go there ...'

He smiled. He had gone there.

'You can't kill yourself because it would be a sin.'

'It would?'

I nodded.

'What about Annie? Will she come back?'

Now there was only desperate, unrequited love in his eyes.

'No. Annie's gone. She's with someone else now.'

'I know,' he nodded.

'But Annie wants you to be well too. You need drugs. You need a psychiatrist. You are not going to go on your divine mission.'

'That's what they say! They call it my divine mission!' He was ecstatic, no longer alone. 'No. This is the dark side. This is the other side.'

Suddenly he was no longer the dark force. He was a frail, cracked vessel that the dark side had taken over. I could feel he'd made holes in his energy field, through his drug use – marijuana, harmless for some, but in his case he'd let the bogeyman in.

'Stop the pot-smoking.'

'I'll stop the pot-smoking,' he said meekly. 'But God is angry with us and God wants me to kill the sinners ...' He was back to the massacre idea again.

'God will cry if you kill his children.'

'But New York is bad. It's bad, isn't it? We need the elimination. The cleansing of sinners.'

I gripped his hand tightly. This was my last chance. 'You're trying to cleanse your own psyche. And you can do it. You can do it with help. But the other direction brings hell.'

His mouth went into a little 'o'. Then, sadly, he sighed and switched back to his only salvation. 'Will anyone ever see my paintings? Hollywood's not very kind to me.' No wonder I'd thought of Hitler. Never underestimate the fury of the unrecognised artist. 'They will.'

I stopped. He was exhausted. He was sweating profusely. But all of a sudden his energy field was much calmer.

'Do you have the name of a doctor? I don't want to hear the voices telling me what to do any more. That's why Annie left.'

We were back in the obsessive loop: it was death or love.

'That's why Annie left,' he repeated; it was his negative mantra. Then he gripped my hand even tighter. 'You're marvellous. I'd do anything for you!'

A lump of pure white fear came into my throat: I imagined a possible future being stalked by this man. I could see him on my doorstep, in his designer jeans with flowers in his hand, day after day, pretty as a commercial until you looked into his eyes.

'Now I want you to make me a promise.'

'I will,' he said in an ominous tone.

'When you leave here, you are not going to buy the Uzi. The one in the magazine clipping ...'

' ... the one that will carry out the cleansing of the demons.' He finished my sentence.

We were staring at each other now. Suddenly I felt myself psychically transported into the complicated runway system of his brain. I could feel neurons firing and cells pulsating and a tremendous heat. It was as if his brain were literally frying.

'Well now, we're going to take you to a nice man who is going to kill the demons for you. That's the only killing we're going to do. You're going to see the doctor in Beverly Hills. You have a chemical imbalance. You are going to take your medication.' I have no medical training, but out of nowhere the solution came to me: 'You need lithium.'

'So there are no demons to kill?'

I shook my head. 'And then you are going to live a happy life, with a new girlfriend and a big dog and your art. That's the life Spirit wants you to lead.'

'OK,' he said simply. He stared at me from his lifetime of pain. 'I promise.' He sighed.

'Now can you tell me your name. The police say they need to know your name so they can help you.'

'Robert,' he said. 'My name is Robert ... I'm psychic too. When I come here ... to this place in my head ... I ...' he pointed up to his third eye, 'I can see things too. You don't have to be a good person to be psychic, you know. When the demons stop chattering then I can hear the angels talking to me.'

This was the moment when I could have stopped him. My reading was done. But something in me told me to stay and listen. He looked at me intently. 'You love someone. But you have had a fight. You blame him. But it is you. You are more scared of love than you are of me, and I am mad. Think about that. And if you want America to be your home, it can be. But you have to be braver. You have chattering demons too, they just don't take over like they do with me. Good luck. And send my love to John the Baptist. Baptisms in pools, that's how it happens over here.'

He was on a winning roll until the John the Baptist comment.

'And they need your next of kin and your address,' I said, very professionally.

He wrote it on a scrap of paper.

'You're scared of madness, aren't you? I can see in your eyes that you would never come here.' He pointed to his heart. 'Be mad for love, mad for life ...' He put his hand on mine and I could feel volts of strange, seductive energy shooting through him.

'And we need your brother's telephone number,' I said, removing my hand.

'I've got your number,' he said. 'You're scared of love.' He leant forward. 'I know I'm in no fit state, but just listen to the angels more than the demons, that's the thing.'

And he leant back. Good. No wire in my thigh or penknife in my chest, but just a very real pain in my heart.

'And the reason I talked to you and not the police is that you're full of love. I can see it hidden behind your eyes.'

I wanted to burst into tears and hug him. I knew he was right, I could feel the fear that stopped me from being brave. I could sit in a cell and feel love, because it was by accident; it sneaked up on me when I least expected it, in a reading. But outside the cell, I didn't need bars because I had my very own soul bars. I really wished I could hug him, show him how much his words meant to me.

'Yeah, I want to hug you too, but I don't think it's cool.'

I burst into laughter. 'You're good,' I said.

'You too,' he replied.

And then we shook hands. Two seers. Both of us mad in our own ways. We left each other to our soul madness that only Spirit could help, but for today we were Spirit.

'Thank you Robert, for helping me.'

I walked out and leant against the wall opposite a cell filled with prostitutes. All staring at me.

McCloughlin closed the cell door behind him and said, 'Any luck?' I handed him the paper and we walked upstairs.

'Try that number,'. McCloughlin gave it to a young rookie, who eyed me curiously and went off to try the number. 'He said it's his brother. And I think your guy's mentally ill, manic depressive, and he can get well. In my humble opinion, he needs a psychiatrist.'

'What made him talk to you?'

'I think he liked me holding his hand.' I knew it was more than that, some strange soul connection, but I'd be the one locked up if I said that.

The cop took that on the obvious level, 'Creep. Yeah, we always used to do that to girls we fancied when we were kids, hold their hands and pretend to read their palms. I didn't realise you could really do it though!'

'I think he's into psychics, likes that stuff.'

'Yeah, a lot of whack jobs do,' said McCloughlin grimly.

The younger cop came back with a piece of paper. 'Hey, good job, lady with the voodoo. It is his sister and she's coming round to pick him up.'

McCloughlin was impressed. 'You've earned yourself a letter from the LAPD.'

I shook hands. No hugging, I'd learnt my lesson there. They handed me a letter for the immigration lawyer. I gave my address and was escorted by the police to my car. I was so grateful to have a little time to myself. I felt very shaken up … that a mad man in a cell could read me psychically ... and accurately ... underneath all my spiritual guise of being a psychic. He was right – I was scared of love. Astrid's therapist would have put it down to childhood alienation, being psychic and misunderstood, the trauma of Steve almost dying, but there was no solution there – more awareness, more knowledge, but no change. There he was, Robert, mad as a hatter, but superpsychic, psychic enough to help me through. 'You have to be braver' – those were his words to me, and there was the irony: each of us was in our little cell, able to help the other but not ourselves. Perhaps that was the real curse of being psychic.

I felt so happy to be home. Greeted by two blurred bundles of unconditional love, Mishka and Twiglet. As I hugged them and felt their complete and utter devotion, their willingness to love fully and freely just because they were alive, I felt emotional again. Somehow I wanted to tell Al what had happened, but I wasn't going to call him. Was I? No. Not today. I wanted him to miss me. It was childish but true. Love was with me anyway, I had my best friend here with me, looking after me. Full on domestic bliss was in operation. Jimminy was boiling the kettle and making Marmite sandwiches. With the intuition of a friend he knew I'd had a tough day.

'Teatime,' he said cheerfully, wearing my pink apron with roses on it. I felt so relieved to be back home with him and the dogs that I didn't want to get into my dire visa drama and the *Silence of the Lambs* encounter. I needed a tiny respite.

'We're like an old married couple, aren't we?' I said, kissing him on the cheek.

'I'm not sure about the old bit, darling ...'

'Jimminy,' I said, tucking my legs underneath me, 'do you think I'm scared of love?'

'You'd be an idiot not to be.'

I watched him pouring the water into the good old-fashioned brown English teapot, and thinly spreading Marmite on the toast. Exactly as I liked it. True friendship. Watching him closely I also knew he still hadn't opened up about Ziers and the break-up.

'What do you think I should do about it?'

'That's obvious. Be brave.'

The phone rang. Jimminy pounced on it; I could see he wanted it to be Ziers.

'Who? I think you have the wrong number, as I assure you she doesn't have a lawyer—'

I grabbed the phone, giving Jimminy an 'I'll explain later' look. He cut the Swiss roll into slices, eyeing me curiously.

Rico Mentira was talking, on the clock I was sure. 'You need to become ordained. As a minister. Preferably Christian. You need some spiritual qualifications on paper.'

'You really must be joking now ...' Once again I forgot he was paid to be both brief and humourless.

'It takes three minutes on the Internet.'

'Wow. The people who went to seminary for four years must feel a bit miffed by that.'

'I'll email you the site.'

'Then we need to find a famous Christian to vouch for you.'

'Right, because the famous get through to God quicker?'

'No, Lucinda, because the famous are God over here. They're the ones who've got the clout. And Christians have a hotline to the White House. They can help you. I mean, there's a director I know in town – you know him, what's his name, won an Oscar – he speaks to Bush every day. They discuss the content of his films.'

'I'm sure Bush's comments are very enlightening,' I said flatly.

'I voted for Bush.'

'I thought the British papers gave an interesting response,' I said snippily.

'Which was?' Amazing. Even the bright lawyers over here were insular and only read the US papers, which would explain why he had voted for Bush in the first place.

'How could 50 million people be so dumb?'

He laughed. At least he laughed. 'If you want to stay in the country, you'd better keep quiet about your leftist tendencies.'

'I'm not leftist,' I said, 'I'm a spiritualist.'

'Isn't that what Jesus was?'

'He was until the Christians got hold of him. Now he's become a bigot.'

'Get a move on with those priest papers and we'll make the US your home. And you have an appointment at the haunted house tomorrow night, at seven.'

'But it'll be dark!' I shrieked with ill-disguised terror.

'Isn't that when they come out? My client will look after you, he lives there. Let me know how it goes. A letter from him would keep you in the country. He's a big contributor to the President.'

'Yippee!' I said. But there was not much yippiness about it. Which of course went unnoticed by Rico Mentira.

I went online. Was it really worth doing this to stay in the country? My God. It was unbelievable! He was right. The website offered, as advertised, a free three-minute online ordination!

The bonus, in cheery letters next to the icon of the flying dove, was that I would receive a 'pop-up instant credential'.

Three minutes after that, I could make weddings, funerals, and even purchase some other services, including absolution of sins and granting of penury indulgences. My new business. Now, because 'the business of starting a ministry can be confusing', I could buy the acclaimed 'ministry in a box'. What on earth did I have to believe in order to be a part of this? I had to agree to promote the freedom of religion and do that which is right. Which I got to define. My God, there could be some real nutcases out there who were legally ordained as ministers. But, for thirty-five dollars, I could be a doctor of metaphysics. Best of all, I decided, was the real don't-miss item. A pentagon and brooms badge, hideous beyond imagination, with 'clergy' written in grim red italics. At the end the little side bar jingled, and 'The Lord Loves a Joyful Giver' flashed with an icon of a basket overflowing with money. Oh my God. To what lengths had I stooped? I pressed send for my instant ordination. My only comfort was the message at the bottom of the page: 'Whether or not it is clear to you, no doubt the universe is unfolding exactly as it should.'

Well, now I had one more piece of paper for my petition. Maybe I could marry the dogs. Practice. And give them a nice gold certificate that came out of the ministry box. Although technically they were siblings, even if both adopted, so that would be incest. Not the right way for a priest to go, encouraging sexual abuse, although maybe I was right on line if I was up to that. I had better not meddle with any of it. I would put the piece of paper away and it would be a secret. No one need know, except the immigration lawyer. I locked it in my drawer and went to Jimminy for tea, which was still hot.

Despite the Swiss roll, Marmite and steaming tea I had lost my appetite.

'Cough up,' said Jimminy. 'Lawyer? Not parking tickets?'

I told him about the visa problem, the LAPD, reading the disturbed twin, and then I couldn't resist inviting him to be the first to join me in my new ministry, as I was now ordained. He shrieked at that, and partly to egg him on I then told him about the ludicrous trip to the haunted house. But Jimminy looked devastated. As though it was Christmas and he hadn't been invited. It was the Ozzie and Harriet Nelson house? His voice went high and squeaky.

'It's not fair! I'd love to go and you don't even want to!'

Now I thought about it, what was wrong with having him come? Safety in numbers. We were on.

The next morning I awoke in a cold sweat. What the hell was I thinking? Haunted houses were deadly serious. I needed psychic advice.

'Diana ...'

'The haunted house, that's why you're, calling right?' She didn't bother waiting for my reply as she didn't need to. I laughed.

'Well, darling, here are the basics. You will be working in Code A.' Thank God for Diana. 'We can all operate on different brain frequencies, depending on our level of consciousness ...' Once again we were two spiritualists grappling with science. 'Beta is the so-called "normal" frequency the brain functions on. Over 13 cycles per second. Beta is basically "Anxious" and "Stressed".'

Perfect for Hollywood, I thought. The heartbeat of the city.

Diana continued. 'Then there is Alpha, which is "unstressed

consciousness" or "efficient waking state". It runs at 8 to 12.5 cycles per second. Then there is Code A, 7.83 cycles per second. Now that is what the earth resonates at, 7.83 cycles per second. It's what we psychics like to call the "cosmic clock". Then we have Theta, the dreaming-trancework-meditation state, running at 4 to 7 cycles. Finally there is Delta, or the deep-sleep state, running at 1 to 3 cycles. The one you need to work in is Code A. On no account are you to slip into a meditative state, as nasty entities can attach themselves to you. Or have a drink, ditto.'

'Tell me more about Code A,' I said, intensely.

'It is the state that you do readings in. It is the only state to be in in a haunted house. It is also the state animals are in naturally. If you come out of that state and go into the normal reactive, emotional state, you could be in danger in the house.'

'Should I say a mantra or meditate?' I asked enthusiastically, looking for added divine protection.

'Absolutely not,' said Diana sternly. 'That would put you in the Theta state. You must stay very awake and very aware and survey all around you psychically. Most importantly, locate the portals. The portals are the supernatural hallways if you want, the thresholds the ghosts come and go through. You will need to locate them – often there's more than one portal. Be especially alert around them.

'Look for the most significant spots. Find out about the people who live there, or used to live there; ask if they are male or female, and ask for any information. By that, of course, I mean ask Spirit; don't Google the haunted site or ask anyone there for details. You must give the owner the information. And finally, trust that you can do it. Trust. Talk to the ghosts. Ask them how they feel.'

'Ask the ghosts how they feel?' I echoed, nervously. 'And

what if they respond by throwing things around the place, like in the movies?'

She replied very seriously, 'Well, darling ... sometimes that connects to certain objects that you may see lying around. The flat in Finland that I just did had an archaeological collection that should not have been removed from its original site, and once that was taken out of the flat and restored to its rightful home, there were no more flying masks. Sometimes one spirit may be trying to get your attention. But you'll know about that if they're poltergeists.'

'Jolly good,' I said with ill-disguised terror, having visions of airborne Emmys knocking me on the head.

'You will also need to ask the right person to go with you.'

I felt really chuffed. I'd done that already. Jim Jims the brave.

'One acts as the medium and the other as the gatekeeper. And on no account, I repeat, on no account should either of you have any alcohol before going into the house.'

I wondered if that was why Diana had pushed the alcohol comment home. Jimminy was a normal Brit, he had a beer every day.

'And finally, always respect the house owner – they might like the ghosts being there. Remember that. Trust your instincts. Do your best. Remember, it's all about being of service. There's an African prime minister on the other line. Good luck, darling, let me know!' Click.

Dusk came round very fast. I got dressed up in my prettiest 1950s-type dress. I wanted to show the ghost I respected them and their era.

'You're scared,' said Jimminy, unable to cover up his own excitement.

'I'm not,' I lied.

'You are.' He narrowed his eyes.

I caved. 'Scared is a rational response.'

'No, it's not. Most people don't believe in ghosts, so … scared is an irrational response.'

'You don't believe in ghosts?'

'No,' said Jimminy, 'but if you talk to them, don't tell them I'm an unbeliever. I don't want to piss them off.'

'I'll see you there then?'

'See you there.'

As Jimminy walked away, I thought about the way I was feeling. Was I scared? Of what? Scared the owner of the house would find me ineffective, then report it to the lawyer, who would report to the government and then they'd kick me out of the country for being a crap psychic. That wasn't it. Of the ghosts? That they would feed off my fear and haunt me or possess me – or annihilate me? No. I wasn't even afraid of that. What was it? I kissed Mishka and Twiglet, asking their little souls to send good canine protective vibes, and set off to visit the most terrifying haunted house in Hollywood. Walking out the door I knew, somehow, I had to become unafraid. Kill this nameless fear. I had to come from such a powerful place, such a place of truth inside that I would shine a psychic light on their attacks and be safe and unharmed. The only way I knew to do that was to be Love in action. If I could do this, I could do anything.

The house looked perfectly normal from the outside. Shuttered, beautifully painted, mowed lawn. Innocent. Like a teenager before she turns into a vampire. As I approached I did one last check of my fear level. Mistake. My mind wouldn't play – it shut the door with a bang and a 'Keep Out' sign was there, strong and forbidding. These kinds of fears can't be solved by the mind, they are primal: the fear that wakes you up with the nightmare of the man about to kill you; the fear that the chair in the corner has turned into a predator; the fear that you will one day die and will never have done what you came to earth to do – you are running out of time, and there's no cavalry on the horizon, and you realise you are the cavalry and you don't even know how to saddle a horse, you're so spent and faithless. That was what I needed: faith that I wouldn't fail in the house. This went way beyond proving myself as a psychic so I could stay in America; this was what I had always feared, to be given a doorway to your dreams and then just not quite be up to it – not failure, the glorious failure that all the greatest people have achieved, near death, bankruptcies, debaucheries, drugs overdoses and miraculous recoveries; no, mine would be a quiet, humiliating mediocre failure of … she's not quite up to it. So, armed with this great consciousness and awareness but no relief or respite from it – nothing that made me feel better – I walked towards the house. I paused, like a child playing grandmother's footsteps, expecting it to come to life and pounce on me.

I took few more steps towards the house. Truly deceiving, like most dangerous things, it didn't have fangs and claws … It looked normal. Like the murdering paedophile who lives undisturbed in the neighbourhood, the guy who everyone said seemed like such a nice guy, who kept himself to himself. Well, there's a reason why people who keep to themselves are often way-off or whacko: they don't have anyone around them to rub off of or smile at them – not that a friendly smile would necessarily alter a paedophile's destiny, or indeed the house. My mind was again racing ahead of me, as if trying to protect my soul.

Now I was facing the main entrance, the gateway. How ironic: the shining white colonial-style house, home of America's favourite Norman Rockwell happy household of yore, white picket fences et al, perfect green lawns, photogenic trees … and underneath a nest of poltergeists and despair. I stood at the big iron gate. Funny how Americans were so ostensibly welcoming but loved to keep you out of their homes. Welcome, welcome, and then buzzers and security cameras and videos systems to scare you away. Don't make a false move, you're being watched. Not that cameras and security buzzers were going to keep our ghosts or poltergeists out – they loved electromagnetic stuff.

I was ready – I really was. I rang the bell. The gate opened slowly and I walked in. The yellow brick road that led me to the front door. I was in Code A. I was the witness, the observer. But my innermost psychic instinct was on red alert. I knew there was something inside this house that I had never encountered before.

I stood at the doorway and I felt a hand stroke my neck – like a new lover, it sent shivers up me. I turned around. Of course there was no one there. I was not imagining it, there was no breeze; it was a very distinct sensation. An energetic force was playing with me. Then my hair was ruffled, as if by a lover. Strangely, it wasn't frightening. It was fascinating and intriguing and mysterious. And I wasn't scared at all. I was surprised. I thought they would be violent, malicious or angry ghosts. Not seductive. But just because I wasn't scared – in fact, to my surprise I was sort of bizarrely aroused – it didn't mean that I would ignore the danger signals my psyche was sending me.

The door opened – almost by itself, I thought at first. It was Jimminy. He looked red-eyed and exhausted. 'I got here first because I was so excited – he thought I was the psychic first of all …'

'Who?' I blurted immediately.

'You know who. Why didn't you tell me who it was? How did you wangle that? Anyway, he's been the only surprise so far, but it does feel very spooky ...' And Jiinminy walked me to the living room. Which should have be called the dead room, as it was full of them. I could feel them all gathered around, hungry ghosts watching from Spirit. And why wouldn't they?

The star of the room was lounging on the sofa. Playing with a Blackberry. No doubt texting dirty messages to groupies if his smirk was anything to go by. And frankly, if I were one of the groupies to the rock star-movie king sitting on the sofa, I'd have gone up to his hotel room and let him do whatever he wanted with me. He had that fatal kiss-me charisma, mixed by the mischievous gods. And my own personal favourite, that intoxicating gypsy cocktail of black hair and black eyes. Even on the sofa he looked like he belonged on a gigantic stage with several thousand people chanting his name. Rock stars are usually out as sex symbols in my world – too much boy energy, skinny-legged trousers and long hair – but he was different. Apart from the ink hair and eyes, he had hands that you could paint, and his leanness wasn't vain – it came from anguish and soul torture and anything else that keeps you up all night: cocaine, chicks, conversations ... I could feel I was going overboard about him, but it was an animal, chemical reaction. And the house just felt ... well almost like a lascivious lust pad – the energy of the other world, the ghosts, who were all seducers, wanting to be in their bodies again, physical again, and touching up us mortals was their thrill. Having checked out the rock star's muscles I checked out his aura too: it was as big and bold as the sun. It was then that I noticed that Jimminy, my supposed Rock of Gibraltar in the enterprise, was afraid. His aura had shrunk to a miniature mushroom shape. In the showdown between spectres and humanoids, the stud on the sofa and I constituted the team. Jimminy was not looking good.

The rock star got up to say hello. I instantly knew that at some point tonight I ought to mention I was in love with someone, and in the same instant knew I wouldn't. A hand, the same invisible hand that had stroked my head earlier, now stroked my neck, almost to calm me down. My only physical reaction was to breathe more quickly, but it was a physical shock more than anything. I'd always known spirits were around – now I was just feeling them, and I'd never come across sexual ones. It was so strange I couldn't help but blurt out what was happening because it was so outlandish …

'I can feel a hand on my neck, stroking me.'

Jimminy looked shocked, intrigued, and as if he was about to faint.

'Oh, they do that,' said the rock star, as if he were discussing his private planes, normal to him but very out-there to the rest of us.

'They do what?' I asked.

'They seduce all the beautiful women that come in here.' And he smiled a sort of high-wattage smile that crackled as much as the high energy in the room. And of course the 'beautiful' comment gave me an added tingle.

Jimminy was still computing and catching up. He blurted out, 'Who's stroking her neck?'

'They are,' he said. 'The succubuses. I looked them up when it first happened to me and there they were, in some occult dictionary. Succubuses are ghosts that seduce you. They don't come out for everyone. Some people get the rappers.'

'Singing ghosts?' said Jimminy.

'No,' said the rock star, laughing, 'they rap on doors or floors.'

'Why?'

'To scare you, of course. Although who knows? It could be some sort of spectral Morse code.'

He had a sense of humour about it all. Which was obviously the right attitude. I relaxed slightly and let go of my Code A witnessing stance. All of a sudden I felt … great. I looked around. It was a beautiful house really, full of bright-blue sparkly lights – that was always a good sign. There were sexy spirits but they meant no harm really. They weren't going to hurt me: they were my friends, I was their therapist; I cared about how they felt. There was no reason to be afraid, except – Diana had warned me to stay in Code A …

'Did they give you any signs?' said Jimminy, interrupting my thought process. He was talking to the rock star.

'Do you want a sign?' he replied. Jimminy nodded, with a silly smile on his face.

'Well, this one usually works. They like this one. Turn your cell phone off.'

Jimminy did.

'Count to three.'

'One … two …' Jimminy took a deep breath, 'two and a half … and three.' Nothing.

'Do you want a drink?' said the rock star, casually. Jimminy nodded.

Rock star moved to the bar, and before he finished unscrewing the top of the Jack Daniel's …

Jimminy's cell phone began to ring. He dropped the phone. 'Bloody hell, I mean, for fuck's sake!'

'You might need a double,' said the rock star nonchalantly,

clearly pleased that the poltergeists had played along with him. 'The electricity is screwy all over this house because they play with it every day.' As if to prove his point, one of the lamps flashed. Luckily Jimminy was still examining his phone in disbelief, so he missed that one.

'This room, by the way,' he said, now seeming to be on best host behaviour, perhaps to calm Jimminy down, 'is where Ozzie and Harriet used to film their episodes. They drop by all the time now, move the chess pieces, the drinks, even ring the bell sometimes when I'm in the shower, so I know they're on their way. And the phone trick is one of their favourites.'

Jimminy walked to the bar in a daze. The rock star handed him what looked like a beaker of Jack Daniel's, then walked purposefully in my direction. He smiled – the sort of smile that has a sneer in it somewhere, a brazen, seductive sneer, and slightly sympathetic – as if he felt sorry for me because he knew he was going to get what he wanted. And I could hear one of his songs in my head as he sauntered towards me. It was a song about staying up all night and sex, that seventies kind of song, and somewhere in his soul, and certainly in his swagger, he was still singing it. Somehow it managed to be panther sexy.

'I need to take you upstairs alone,' he said, almost whispering as he brushed past me.

'Do you want me to do this part first?' I said, in my full-on psychic professional mode. Loud enough for Jimminy to hear.

'You "do" whatever you want to do ...'

Confusing. I thought I had been invited here to locate the ghosts and verify their existences, with names and evidence. But he was behaving as if I was just a girl he liked. Perhaps he didn't take this work seriously. I mean, when I had offered to 'do' the house, he had turned it into a sexual innuendo. I became very businesslike.

'I want to find the entrance points.'

'Go ahead. Tell me where the entrance points are.'

Again, he said 'entrance points' as though they were human, sexual, available and he was about to enter them. Well, I had fallen into that one. That was a stupid choice of words. I psychically protected myself with white light, and instinctively walked to the corner of the room. It was icy cold and thick with energy, like a room in which you feel the remnants of a terrible fight or a great sadness. In my mind's eye I could sense – almost like a Spirit staircase – a black hole, where the faded celebrities could come back and visit to relive their former glory.

'Do you feel them anywhere in particular?' he asked, watching me intently from beneath his suave façade.

'I do. This corner here is one of the portals.' I was rather proud that I had made use of Diana's lesson.

'You're right. That's what all the parapsychologists say, they use machines and pick out that spot.'

Interesting. He'd already had parapsychologists here, so he didn't need me to help him. I really was just being tested to see if I was any good, then he'd tell his pal the lawyer and I'd get my papers. But ... it didn't quite make sense. Stars like him rarely did something secretive and altruistic. Altruistic, yes. Secretive and altruistic, no. I quizzed him.

'Why did you have parapsychologists here before?'

'Well, it's a legal issue. In LA, before you buy a house, if it has a ... supernatural file, which this one does, a good real estate agent or, in my case, lawyer will advise you to do it, along with earthquake and foundation checks. I don't own the house, I was just thinking of buying it, but I mean, it has been sold so many times that I wanted to check ...'

'What conclusion did they come to?' asked Jimminy, who had been politely listening all along.

'That – surprise, surprise – the place is haunted. They didn't believe me first of all, the psychic team; they thought I was a sixties casualty, an old acid-head rocker or something – tripping out, having hallucinations. But there were too many reports in the end, especially from all the past owners. It's one of the highest scorers in terms of psychic energy in the country now. And whoever or whatever can make the phone ring with no power is dialling from up there ...' He pointed upwards.

'I'm pretty sure you'll find they're making calls from the other place,' said Jimminy, tilting his head downwards. The thought of it caused him to help himself to yet another whisky.

I turned back and looked at the rock star as he was leaning against the pillar. Because I was standing on a small step, just above him, he took advantage of how he leant – I knew he wanted me to see his skin underneath his shirt, from his collarbone all the way down to the tufts of gentle hair at the top of his leather trousers. There are probably about three men who can wear leather trousers and not look gay or like a member of Duran Duran – a Spanish bullfighter, maybe; some crazed and beautiful young thing like James Dean; and him. I knew he knew he was beautiful, and I could feel he was fascinated by me – I was equally fascinated by him. I admired him, not for all the gold records, but for all the soul that had made him a songwriter. I loved poets, they were almost mystics, hanging on to this world with as slender a grip on reality as I had. He was staring at me from across the room – and then I distinctly felt a hand brush my breast. I looked astonished, felt turned on and outraged. I gulped and tried to think how to reprimand an invisible pass. But the real truth was I didn't want to.

He laughed. As if he knew I was secretly as thrilled and fascinated as he was by all the invisible naughtiness the ghosts were getting up to. And then the thought came to my mind: is he controlling them? Is he the one designing this whole seduction? Is he using his own charisma, like a black magician, to get the ghosts to do his bidding ...

'Are they feeling you up?' He interrupted my thoughts.

'Yes,' I said, totally confused and suddenly afraid.

'Well, they would. As I said, they do that to beautiful women.' And he headed to the bar again. Poured himself a Scotch on the rocks and lit another cigarette. This was not the LA I was used to; this was more like my parents' London in the seventies scene, everyone drinking and smoking up a storm.

'You sure you don't want one?'

'No,' I said, very firmly, remembering Diana's instructions, although the thought of it was very tempting. Just to take the edge off the fear.

'You're sure it's them who moved the glasses or the chess pieces, no one you know playing a trick on you?' said Jimminy hopefully. All he had wanted was to have some ghostly experience, and now that something inexplicable had happened to him, he wanted to rationalise it away.

'They're the ones who play tricks on me – and I'm sure you'll see some more tonight ...' and the Rock Star walked towards the archway leading to the rest of the house. Jimminy, a little alcohol braver, wanted to follow ...

'I prefer to take people up one at a time,' he said with the firmness of a Roman procurator. Jimminy moved to the side and I followed the rock star in silence.

'You'll be fine down here.' Jimminy looked extremely doubtful and headed back for the bar.

As we walked through the study, my psychic sensors went back into high alert. I felt spirit hands almost undress me! This was so ludicrous and strange and unexpected. I expected bumps and bangs and raps and even disembodied voices, or floating figures down the stairs. Not a sort of sexual assault that felt tantric and perfect. Rock star looked at me, and ran his finger down my arm, 'Goose bumps. They really like you ...'

Rounding the corner to the large spiral staircase in the centre of the house, he continued to lead the way.

I turned back to look at Jimminy, who appeared to have lost consciousness and was lying down on the sofa – I'm sure Diana had said something about no alcohol, but maybe that was just for me. It was hard to remember anything very much except where I was right now: I felt floaty and out of it, like I was in an opium den. I followed the rock star's stellar figure up the stairs. Get a grip. Go to Code A. The trouble with Code A was that it wasn't very sexy. It felt very removed, cold almost. But I reluctantly altered my mental state and became businesslike. Thank God I did.

He looked at me and watched carefully as I walked up the stairs. I got to the seventh step, before I started spinning and thought I was going to pass out.

'What the—'

My legs started to buckle; the blue spirit lights were flashing like police lights, almost blinding me. I hung on and remained conscious, then I felt the presence of hundreds of people, all invisible, pushing towards me. My Code A shield was like a rope at a packed nightclub – if I'd not been in that psychic bouncer state, rebuffing them, I would have been used as the conduit, the bridge, the messenger ...

'Get off that step. I'm afraid I was testing you – I should

have told you always to skip that step. Most people pass out completely if I don't warn them.'

'That's the main portal,' I said, walking up the remainder of the staircase.

'Exactly.'

Thanks for telling me about the swooning step, I thought. But then, he was here to test me as a psychic, so fair enough.

'Every person has a different experience in here. But tell me what you psychically pick up about the portal.'

I reached the landing and took a deep breath. Staying in Code A, I gave my report: 'The main portal is on the seventh step. It's like a railway station platform for spirits. I felt there were many of them lining up to get into your house. The energy was unhappy, many of them suicides. You can tell by their energy – they went over very suddenly ... and are starlet suicides.' I tuned in some more. 'Dead girls who had come here to Hollywood, when they were alive, with a dream to make it. Now they are being drawn here ... to the Hollywood mansion ... the ideal they had never managed to live in their lifetimes ... because even in death they are obsessed with what could have been. They are hanging on to the idea of fame, and at least now they get to live in the big mansion ... and be special and impor-tant ... even if it's as ghosts.'

I had the feeling the rock star was encouraging them almost. I told him, 'You have groupie ghosts. They want to hang with the famous, including you. And of course they are always flirt-ing and they have sex with everyone you bring in here. They want all of that ... and they like you, because you don't cramp their style. You even enjoy them.'

'You don't say,' he said darkly. 'And what about this floor?'

I scanned the place. I was already being shown pictures.

'There was a piano – in that room … And a black dog was in the home. And a child's room was up there.'

To me I was reading off a laundry list, taking dictation, doing my job – but the sex-symbol singer went wide-eyed.

'You're good. Yes to all of them. You're good at your job. You don't need to prove yourself any more to me. We can stop that part now.'

I wondered what the next part was. God, I wish I didn't fancy him so much; it was so chemical, the attraction, I felt so powerless over it. And he knew it. You don't get to be a sex symbol like that without understanding women a lot.

'Why do you stay here with the ghosts?' I asked as we walked through the corridors.

His eyes glazed over and went hard. 'I guess it's just an extreme example of a dysfunctional relationship. I've been divorced three times, so I'm not great at commitment; I don't want to leave something else right now. I want something to be stable, so I don't want to leave.'

'Don't you think that's dangerous?'

'Do you?'

'I do.'

'Yet you're here. With me. Alone.' He faced me. It would have been so easy to kiss him. But out of my mouth came:

'Like Maria.'

Now he went white. 'How did you know about her?'

'I didn't know … I heard it whispered to me.' It was true. And whoever had whispered it was a different kind of spirit than most of them in the house. She had managed to get her name to me. And it certainly had an effect on the beautiful rock star.

'She was my girl. But I know you already knew that.'

'I didn't, actually.' But I did now.

'Come on, let me show you the rest of the house.'

He was behaving now as if we were in a perfectly normal house, just having a tour. Didn't want to talk about the ex.

I stumbled into the bathroom, almost as if I had been pushed in there. It was dark and I fumbled for the light switch. Pushed something, but nothing happened. Well, this is what poltergeists do. I turned to leave, and the light went on. But there was a rational explanation this time. The rock star had come in behind me and turned it on. What had I pushed?

'You pressed the steam-shower button; look, it's next to the light switch.'

But I wasn't looking in that direction. I was looking at the glass on the shower door, which by now was filled with steam. Then – possibly the strangest thing that has ever happened to me in my waking life – standing side by side, we watched, very slowly, as an invisible finger started to write in the steam. Letters. M. Then A. Then R. Three letters were written in the steam: MAR, they were writing 'MARIA'. This filled me with such a profound sense of shock that I completely disassociated, and instead of shrieking and fleeing I went into arch-psychic mode, and analysed the moment: 'Ah yes, ghost handwriting on glass in steam shower ...' He went into a version of that too ... the old wolf who's seen one poltergeist has seen them all – it's just a supernatural text from a friend. However, neither of us had noticed Jimmiiny who had woken up and, clearly not wanting to be left alone near the portal, come upstairs to find us. He had also seen the ghostly handwriting of the letters and had the only logical reaction ...

'Fucking hell!' he said.

'Did you see that?! Fucking hell!' he was shouting.

I nodded to calm him down.

'Are you crazy? Something just wrote without a pen!' He was delirious with fear. 'Let's get the fuck out of here! ... You can't stay here.' He grabbed me.

But the rock star grabbed me by the wrist too, in a very intimate, sexual, pin-your-wrists-down kind of gesture, and suddenly there was no way I was leaving.

'You go, Jimminy, I have to stay and work.'

I was the husband working late at the office. He was the wife. The rock star was the secretary. The husband left. And I wasn't thinking of working. In fact, after that shock ... I wasn't capable of thinking at all. I needed looking after. Rock star picked up on that.

'You need to rest,' he said, walking me to the bedroom. We were on a break. Good. I needed a little break.

'Come to the bedroom,' he said, with an inference that I suspected I might be imagining. What was Maria trying to say? I wondered. Too tired to do that. After the rest I would open up psychically again. And I let him take me to his bedroom.

'Let's lie down and talk about this.'

It seemed the most natural thing to do. Yes, we needed to just talk. Bond. Communicate. Behave normally. The ghosts would leave us alone then. With my psychic Code A stare I was bothering them. I wanted a rest. And he and I had a real soul connection. Perhaps this was love? Instant, karmic ... maybe we had been together in past lives ... maybe I was scared of true love and sexual connection ... He lay on his stomach and took out his cigarettes. This was surreal. I was lying on a bed with a stud rock star, with poltergeists all around us, watching us silently, not bothering us now as we weren't bothering them ...

and I knew he wanted to have with sex with me. I didn't need to be psychic to feel that ... and I was just as attracted to him ...

'When's your birthday?' I asked.

'Does that help your psychic read on me?'

I nodded. I was lying. I had a crush and I wanted to know his sign.

'January 28th.' Strange coincidence: the same as Steve's. This was getting very possible.

'And you?'

'August 21st.'

He smiled. 'A lion. I love lions.'

Around us the blue lights twinkled. Spirits were sparkling with excitement. But they were not the only ones who were: I knew if I gave him the hint I'd be pinned under the black silk sheets with a great Hollywood seduction tale to tell. I had been wrong, and Diana was from a different generation – this having to stay in psychic mode when ... sex and Spirit were twins ... sex and Spirit didn't live in separate realms – that's why the saints had intense orgasmic experiences before they saw God. I was really ready to do something brave and outrageous and fun ... why not this fling? Then like a flash it hit me. Married three times. He wrote ... songs. Maybe he was the one in the prediction! ... He lit another Marlboro. The smell reminded me of Steve. I glanced at his bedside table. Somehow it felt like lying on this luxurious bed was the only place in the world to be. My eye caught a book, a beautiful book that I had just finished reading. Another sign. He noticed me noticing.

'I've just optioned that. We're making a movie of it ...'

'I love that book.' It was about tantric mastery.

'You could play a part in it. I can talk to our lawyer – he said you were a great actress – I just need to get your help and I think we could work all of this out.' In the 'work it out' there was a sexual promise and it was a wild, guilt-free, orgy-of-two kind of connection. He was the tall dark stranger – and he wanted … what did he want?

'Why did you ask me here? What kind of help do you need?'

There was a crackly pause, and he lit another cigarette. It was so quiet and the air was so filled with sexual tension that the lighter flaring up sounded like a field catching fire. I was breathing faster, and this time it wasn't the ghosts.

He sat up. Propped himself on one elbow. Looked serious and sultry at the same time. Under the bedroom eyes, he was Svengali determined.

'I am under psychic attack. From the dark side. Not from this house. From a black magician. A woman. She's a psychic con artist, a friend of my ex-girlfriend, Maria, or used to be …'

'This black magician put a curse on me – I thought that stuff was bullshit, but I assure you it's not. My two favourite race-horses were both killed in freak accidents, one hit by lightning, the other by a falling tree … almost like a warning to me. Then I came to this house, because after Maria died …'

'She's dead?' Now I felt sorry for him, as a woman. But as a psychic, I now knew I could get to the bottom of all this weirdness. Maria was trying to communicate something, writing her name in the steam so we wouldn't forget her …

'My daughter was an A student up to that point, went out on the streets, addicted to crack – the black magician put a curse on her too, which is unforgivable. That's what enraged me, so I knew I had to deal with her – to stop her – especially after she hurt my daughter.'

I was listening. He went on.

'So … there's a Santeria practioner I saw …'

'Santeria?'

'Voodoo disguised as Catholicism. Saints but animal sacrifices. There's a hot Santeria place in Puerto Rico where a lot of A-listers go – some for Oscars, some for spells to get parts; you remove curses and enemies so you can get what you want. I wanted to deal with the black magician. I sacrificed the chickens, but I failed to do the last part of the spell – bury the chicken in a graveyard. So I think it almost worked in reversing the curse – almost – but not quite.'

He lit another cigarette. I was trying to take in the fact that clearly very famous actors were prepared to kill animals and daub themselves in blood for a little gold statue.

'Worked but not quite, meaning?'

'I got back to LA and the black magician was in a coma – mysteriously, no prior illnesses. She almost died, but didn't. She's still in hospital. Now if I'd buried the chicken as the Santeria guy told me to …'

'She'd have died.'

'Exactly.'

'And I'm not going back there, especially to tell the voodoo priest I didn't do what he told me to do.'

'Did you ask him for anything else?'

'To win the bidding war on the book I optioned, and to get a couple of parts. I got everything I wanted.'

'And now?'

'I got really into all of this. I started reading ancient tantric texts – I mean, you obviously skip the bits about child sacrifice, that's black tantra …'

'Right—'

'Well, you ask me why you're here. In order to fight this

curse, I need to be in top psychic form. The tantra gives several options. One is to find a teacher, a powerful psychic, so I can fight the evil. And in return I can help you. I just need to harness this power. And of course the best place to gain psychic strength is in a house full of spirits that even a novice like me can see.'

'And how exactly am I supposed to help you with the psychic power?'

'Tantrically.'

He stared at me. Why was he so fucking attractive? I could feel the heat of him lying near me on the bed. Everything he proposed I liked. Power to fight evil sounded like a real need to me. I was used to my mind being blown in readings, only this was disturbing to me on a soul level, this was an unexpected assault on my lower chakras and they were loving every minute of it, becoming softer and easier by the millisecond. I had a feeling he could almost read my mind, because he lightly segued to specifics.

'I read in one of the texts that if you were to make love in this house, you'd be changed for ever, on the molecular level. I mean, lovemaking changes you anyway, but this would really revitalise you. And depending on the psychic level of the lover, when you penetrate her she will give you her psychic power.'

He spoke using 'you' in the general sense, but I knew it was a test and an offer. He stared at me, and like animals a moment passed between us that was pheromonal, hormonal and savage. Why not fuck a rock star in a haunted house? Claim my psychic rejuvenation package with an orgasm with a superstar. Yes. Life is short. Yes. Although I didn't want it to look like he'd won me over that easily.

'But the man in the Tantra book – he sounds almost like a vampire,' I said, 'sucking the woman's energy to use it for his life.' We both knew we were talking about the possibility of each other.

'But look how happy the women were who became vampires themselves …'

I challenged him, 'I thought they were condemned to live in the shadows for eternity until someone drove a stake through their heart.'

'Women vampires were the first symbols of sexual liberation – no longer condemned to be the good girls but finally to succumb to sex and power and seduce men themselves.' He lay on his back at this point. And he let his hand rest lightly between his legs. It was a proper come-on. Then he turned and casually propped himself up on his elbows, and we lay with about half an inch between our groins. He opened his mouth slightly, then moved his mouth right next to mine. He stayed there. Both of us were panting like animals on heat … our lips were almost touching when …

I HEARD THE SOUND OF BONES CRACKING.

What the fuck was that? I pushed him away. He didn't seem to mind. He thought I was playing a game with him to make things more interesting. What the hell was that noise? Whatever it was, it wasn't good. He hadn't seemed to hear anything. I stayed still for a long moment, frozen. So did he. Nothing. A false alarm. I looked at him and he was looking back at me. And suddenly I thought of Al. A picture of him flashed across my mind. I couldn't do this. I got off the bed and he watched me with fuck-me eyes. I had to get away … God the house was like a sauna now … I rushed down the stairs, avoiding the seventh step, and eventually I was outside on the perfectly manicured lawn and next to the swimming pool. I put my feet in it. And then, crazily, like a love-drunk fan who had heated up too much,

I knew I had to get in that water as fast as I could to cool down – something was urging me to go in – so fully clothed I dived into the pool. The water was an icy reality baptism. Strangely, it was the only thing in the house that was not sexually charged. I swam underwater. But as I surfaced, I had a terrible pain in my head. Very bad pain. I swam. I saw the rock star screaming at me from the side of the pool.

'Get out! Get out of the pool!'

I must have managed to pull myself up to the edge.

'What the fuck are you doing? It's not safe!' he was screaming. 'Why are you in the pool? Don't you know what happened?'

'A woman dived in at night. She was drunk, and the pool was empty. She hit her head, she was in a coma … and then she died. You shouldn't be in there … it's bad luck. How could you be so crazy?'

I stayed in the pool. My unconscious knew exactly why I had dived in. He was lying. Bad luck? That was feeble. Something was going on – and I had to learn the truth. As if on cue, my mind's eye was shattered with images again. And I heard the name Maria again. But I saw the headlights of a car, a body flying through the air. More bones breaking. Pulverising. A heart beating slowly to keep alive. Great deal of pain. A man on the asphalt … lying on the road … WHO THE HELL WAS DYING? AND WHO WAS TELLING ME ABOUT IT?

I stepped out of the water. Awake.

'How could you be so crazy?!' he shouted.

'I have to go.' – I didn't know where yet. I was so cold my teeth were chattering and I was shaking.

He kept staring at the pool, as if he were in a trance. Then out it came. Suddenly I knew. She told me. 'It was Maria who died in the pool wasn't it?'

He didn't say anything; he looked horrified.

'She's trying to tell you something ...'

'What? What?!' He was screaming, trying to stop me from hearing her. 'It was her fault, she wasn't looking where she was going. Tell her to leave me alone! Leave me alone!' He was down on his knees, screaming ... and then back came the random psychic flashes again: another man on his knees, screaming ... in agony ... lying in a pool of blood ... he was dying ... Then I felt Maria again ... in Spirit ... tell him ... please tell him ... I was high and he couldn't have saved me ... he couldn't have saved me ... he wasn't looking at me ... he was in the corner injecting himself ... and then I had dived in ... She was trying to tell me something else ... Tell him I forgive him ... I forgive him.

'She forgives you. Maria forgives you ...' That was it. She had been trying to contact him to tell him that, not to frighten him; she had been trying to make love to him again, to touch him ... and suddenly he realised it too.

He fell on the ground, sobbing. 'Why didn't I see her? Why didn't I just—' and he let out a howl of anguish.

'Stop torturing yourself ... you have to forgive ...'

I wanted to help him, to tell him more about Maria's forgiveness, but I was pushed away from the pool by a bigger force than compassion. It was Maria who had been giving me these pictures ... the other man ... I had to find out.

I tried to wake Jimminy up. He was passed out. With unknown strength I carried him through the door and outside. All kinds of paranoid thoughts crossed my mind: who is it? Who's hurt? Then ... is he coming after me? She warned me about this accident ... who's hurt?

I put Jimminy on the rear car seat. I turned around and the

rock star was standing by the gate. Tears still running down his face. I panicked. I was the only one who knew about his negligence in her death ... it had been covered up ... That was why the black magician had been blackmailing him and he had almost killed her ... and he had wanted to kill her ... What if he put some weird curse on me now that I knew what had happened? Imagine a court case? I knew Maria didn't blame him, but it wouldn't look good in court. It would ruin his career ... He began walking towards the car. I dropped the keys. I fumbled for them. He was very close. I wanted to scream, 'Leave me alone!' I floored it.

I drove fast – where to? Where to? I kept hearing a message in my head. Someone screaming and a woman talking; I couldn't figure it out.

Finally I stormed into my house. The answer-machine was blinking. I pressed play.

'There is a man lying on the ground here, his name is Al. He gave me your phone number. They are taking him to the Cedar Sinai Hospital ...' and the woman with the screaming baby went back to helping Al.

9
Alchemy

'Is there a lot of blood?'

'Yes,' the stranger on the other end of the cell answered. I could barely hear her because of her screaming baby.

'How does it look?'

'The paramedics are taking him to hospital now. Cedar Sinai.'

It was then that I realised that the screaming that sounded like an infant was in fact Al, in agony.

Without thinking, I dialled Astrid's machine. Left a message. Al's had an accident. Meet me at Cedar Sinai. I got there in fifteen minutes. Astrid was already standing there.

'Come on,' she said, and she went around to the side door, the ER door, 'Staff Only' it said at the entrance. She pushed the double doors open. Told me to wait outside. She ran into the paramedics who had scraped Al off the road and brought him in.

'How does it look?' she asked.

'He's fractured his skull so – not good.'

I tore in behind her. Astrid turned around and before I could open my mouth she said, 'He's doing great.' She lied. I was so grateful for that lie.

I went in. Apparently there was a man under the blood-soaked sheets, but there were dents and confusion where his legs had been, and the sheets were stained red. I was overcome with a sense of complete calm. Again he screamed, this time in terrible, inarticulate pain, and then his eyes seemed to stare at some invisible force in front of him; they were fixed and black and vacant – I could hear the nurse relaying the details to the approaching surgeon:

'Run over by a black Honda, low impact – any other car and he'd be dead. Thrown up in the air by thirty feet or so, we estimate; legs broken in six places, below the knee; shoulder broken; seems coherent, no brain damage we know of ... It was a hit and run.'

I went into white shock when I heard that. And my thoughts came so fast. Someone had run him over and left him on the road to die. Someone had actually done that. I thought I was going to throw up, I felt such despair that someone could do that ... leave him in a pool of blood, like an animal, screaming in agony, to die. A hit and run. Where had he run to? Could I find him? Could I try and psychically track him down? Then all those thoughts left me in a blinding flash of clarity. He's gone. You will never find him. I knew it was him. I hoped it was a man in alcoholic black-out who was oblivious to what he had done – that might make it understandable, at least. At the same time, if it was someone who knew what he had done, I knew he would wake up every day with more guilt and fear ... I had to stop this. No good would ever come from trying to understand this; I was not the scorekeeper; his karma, his destiny, had crushed Al's body and my dreams, my dreams of a future husband, the father of my child? Oh God, please ...

Then Al passed out. I stared at him – I had never told him how I really felt about him, that it was him I loved from the moment I had first seen him … and now it was too late … He had been snatched away by the City of Angels, and I was going to be left without him for the rest of my life. He had tried to reach me, he had literally sent me his heart on a postcard, and I had rejected it.

'I'm so sorry,' I kept saying it. 'I'm sorry I didn't call you after you sent me that beautiful card … I'm so sorry … please come back …'

The nurse was looking at me with wide, perplexed eyes. She couldn't feel his soul – hovering, deciding, finished yet – or more? She couldn't feel his fate: would he go through the door, the portal to the other world, to the light, to the relief of a white bright Spirit world, or would he drift back to his body and the rest of his life?

'He's unconscious,' she said gently.

He was. That's why I could tell him the truth. I was holding his hand. I saw it all in a millisecond: he was about to die and I saw his life flashing … His first love, a black and white rabbit; then Martha Roberti, the girl he had a crush on at fourteen; his father's funeral; a standing ovation at Sundance; his mother's funeral; a story he was writing called *Beautiful Truth*; a moment of happiness standing on a bridge in New York with the sun shining gold and a white frost in Central Park; then a picture of my face looking at him, laughing; then just stars – flying, flying towards peace – we were losing him now …

He was yanked out of my hand. The metal rail of the hospital bed moved and I was left standing alone. Alone in the hospital room. An arm went around me: it was Astrid. 'We need to wait now. I'm going to get you some food.'

I took the lift, past the baby ward. Past women holding newborns. Pictures of bliss. Went to the fifth floor. It was 9 p.m. We had to wait. I sat there for thirty minutes. What a night. I couldn't catch up with it. He had seen me as his life was flashing past – nothing could be worked out tonight. Just pray. Never felt so calm. Out of my hands. I could only hold hands and see.

10 p.m. Jimminy arrived. White-faced. Terrified. Desperately hungover and groggy. He called everyone I had on my cell phone and just said, 'Please pray for Al, he's had an accident.'

I called the rabbi who I had helped on a kidnapping case; he prayed in Yiddish. Astrid called Bambi and Cindy; they did the rosary. The Indian palmist did Sanskrit chants; the Buddhists did 'Nam yoho renge kyo'; Ziers's guru gang did 'Om namah shivaya'; I even called my friend who had become a Scientologist, who did some bizarre ceremony. Finally I called Diana. Too scared. In case it was bad news.

'It's in God's hands, darling. His soul is in his hands, in Spirit's hand.'

I wanted Spirit to lose their grip on his soul, and let it fall back to earth for us to have more time. Please. Had I run out of favours? Were they used up on Steve? I didn't have any bargain to make this time, just the truth – my unknown lover is leaving. Give him back to me, please, give him back. I could hear myself praying ... but I could see nothing ... Was I being protected from knowing he wasn't going to make it? Why wouldn't Spirit tell me what was going to happen? So many times I had seen futures played out like films of lives; but I couldn't see his and I couldn't see for mine – and there was no ours; would there ever be? Pray for us now and at the hour of our death – all I could hear; I only knew it from the poem ... if I got it wrong would that mean it wouldn't work? Nothing, nothing you can do; not in the realms of magic now, in the realms of grace ...

All the while Jimminy sat with Astrid and me. He called a doctor friend of his. Didn't tell us much. We wouldn't know about brain damage until he woke up. Jimminy bought chicken noodle soup from the deli across the street, and Astrid and he picked out all the chicken and pretended it was vegetarian – thought I wouldn't care any more, but more than ever, I didn't want to be near death in any way, even a chicken's.

Another group of three were in the waiting room with us. Parents and the wife's sister, maybe. None of us could speak to each other, but we all knew why we were there.

By 4.30 a.m. there was still no news. And the stress, the strain, the unbearable waiting loosened something in all of us, in our minds, in our beings. Astrid was cried out, I was prayed out, and Jimminy was hungover and shattered – he had seen a poltergeist, drunk a bottle of whisky and hadn't slept for a day and a half. We started doing Marx Brothers sketches and laughing strangely, wildly, hysterically. We were lying on the floor at this point, not sleeping but exhausted, looking out of the window at the dawn. I even said a prayer that if Al was meant to go home, to Spirit, I would accept that.

Then suddenly the swing doors opened. A ridiculously handsome surgeon came out into the lobby. He looked like a soap-opera doctor – you could ski down his white coat from his cheekbones; I was so tired I was almost hallucinating.

'Is he OK?'

The young doctor we were all staring at was tall and in charge. And we all knew it. Al had pulled through the night.

'He'll be OK.'

'Is there brain damage?'

'We don't know yet. He's in a coma. We have to wait for him to wake up. At that point we can operate again. His skull has impacted his brain and until he regains consciousness we won't know if there's been any brain damage.'

'You should all go to sleep now. Why don't you take your wife and her sister home.' Jimminy smiled.

'No, that's us,' said another trio, who had been waiting behind us.

The surgeon turned to the next people waiting for him to give them back a life. And we all knew.

'Dr Stewart will be out in a minute.'

The way Dr Stewart opened the door was very different from the way our doctor had walked out. Our Dr Newton had bounced out like a young warrior. Stewart was bowed. Bowed to the inevitability of death.

'I'm sorry ...' he said, and the woman, the mother, I could see her legs fall from underneath her and a strange and terrible cry came from her mouth. Her husband stood so still, I wondered if he'd ever have the courage to breath again. We walked past and I felt her son's soul fly over us, out through the window, like Peter Pan, forever young for them, back home.

I walked out into the cold dawn, and sat looking out of the car window at the City of Angels, thanking them. I don't know exactly what for – that the paramedics got there in minutes; that the woman with the cell had stood in front of the oncoming traffic to protect him and had called me; for the surgeon that had saved him; that Al still had a chance. And I prayed for the unknown parents dead son's soul. I couldn't close my eyes when I prayed and I felt Al open his. He didn't know where he was. Neither did the mother's son. Al was back on earth, and Peter – for that was his name – was in the invisible realms.

By the time I got home, Mishka and Twiglet were there at the gate, hungry, oblivious, wanting to be touched. Jimminy came in and made a bed on the sofa. Astrid slept in his bed. I had forgotten how to think at this point. I just sighed and, unable to sleep, got up and cleaned the entire house, did Jimminy's laundry and folded it on his bed – it was the only thing I had any control over.

The next day, we were summoned to the ER room. Not like the series. Everyone here was dying. Not many happy endings. Al was lying on his bed. His body had swollen up to twice its normal size and he looked like a prehistoric warrior. Unconscious. But fighting. A strange little wire with a red light was attached to his finger – I thought it had been chopped off. Growing out of his legs were metal gates and constructs. New bionic on the outside. A gaping red wound zigzagged down his legs. I looked at him and he was in his body. I wondered how conscious he was. If he could hear us. The nurse explained to us that being in a coma is still a mystery to the medical profession. So yes, all vital signs were suggesting a stable condition, but in matters of the brain everything was very relative. Relative to what? Relative to God's plan for him, I thought. Jimminy and Astrid looked hopeful at the news. They went to get coffee for me.

I looked at the nurse. She knew that I knew he was still in a critical condition.

'And in case of bad news, we have to ask this question: is there a priest?' she said. 'Or a rabbi, or a minister?'

'I am the priest,' I said. 'I'm the priest for him.' And I was ready to be.

'Thank you,' said the nurse. 'I had to ask, it's procedure.'

I nodded.

'I'm sorry to interrupt you.' A small woman with brown hair and glasses was tugging at my sleeve, 'But I overheard you say that you were a priest?'

Oh God. What was I going to say?

'Well, yes, I am – a minister, sort of. Why?'

'My father hurled a phone at the minister of his church once ...' She seemed dazed, dazed with grief and confused. She went on, 'You're legally ordained?'

'Yes.'

'I need you to speak to my father. He's dying, and he won't speak to us about it. I'm his daughter, and he won't speak to me or my mother. He was a very famous psychiatrist. I think he's used to having all the answers, and now, well, he doesn't believe in anything very much – and I just want him to know he's going somewhere. Please can you help him – talk about God? Give him faith? I promise he won't throw a phone at you. He doesn't have the strength ...'

I smiled. I don't know where it came from, but a calm, polite, 'Yes, of course,' came out of my mouth.

'He hates organised religion ...'

'I won't mention anything specific.'

She took me into the hospital room. A very thin man with bright blue eyes was lying on the bed. His hand hung over the side of the bed like a bird's claw, with almost no flesh on it. He was returning to Spirit. The daughter whispered something to him. Then she turned to me: 'I'll leave you alone.'

I sat down next to him.

Then she whispered, 'Just let him know there's something else out there,' and she closed the door.

'Hello,' I said, gently.

'Do you want me to believe in God?' he asked sharply.

'I don't want anything from you.'

He seemed to relax when I said that. Something in him let go.

'I came in because your daughter—'

He waved his hand impatiently. 'Are you going to charge for a session?'

'No. I don't want to charge you for anything.'

The most astonishing thing happened: his face, which had been contorted with tension and anger, dissolved into sobs – not quiet decent, well-behaved tears, but loud, noisy, racking sobs. When they ceased, I picked up his hand. It felt like the most natural thing in the world. And he let me.

'My daughter says you believe in other worlds. I don't believe in any of that.'

'Then let's not talk about that. Let's talk about what we love.'

And, holding his hand rather than seeing what was going to come, his future, I knew we needed to look back, give him time to talk about what he was leaving. Paris. I felt Paris in his hand.

'I love Paris,' I said.

'My favourite city. I was there after the war. I loved a woman there once.'

And we were both quiet. Both seeing her in our mind's eye. Not his devoted wife, but the lost love that needed to be remembered before he died. Then I saw a boat.

'I lived on a boat in Paris.'

'I was on a boat in the war. Before I became an analyst. We're not allowed to tell people not to believe, you know, but I don't.'

'Hmm,' I said, thinking of his mother, standing at the end of his hospital bed, waiting for him. 'What did your mother think of that? Your beliefs?'

'Are you a shrink?' he said sternly. 'You sound like a shrink – I thought you were from God, a priest?'

I guess it was like a shrink session. I didn't tell him I could see his mother waiting for him, to welcome him home, to a place he didn't believe in. I suddenly felt intensely moved, and privileged, and honoured to be by his side. We both knew he was dying, that the unbearable pain of leaving was not going to be taken away by anyone.

'How do you feel this God?' he asked.

'There were beautiful churches when I visited Vienna one New Year's Eve; I felt God in the beauty of it, everyone doing the waltz, the snows …' I felt in his hand that Vienna was his other favourite place. He carried it with him in the lines of his hands.

'Vienna. I loved Vienna. And the Sachertorte was delicious – but what's the connection between chocolate and God?'

'Aren't they the same thing?' I said, smiling.

'I can't talk to my daughter, I can't talk to my wife – they want me to be … they want me to feel …'

'I don't want anything from you,' I said.

And again, he started to sob. It was a strange, harsh sound, but he was breaking underneath.

'Have you ever seen an angel?' he asked.

'No, I don't think I have.'

'Well, you have or you haven't.'

'I haven't.'

'I had a patient once. She had been in a concentration camp, and she was telling me about her child who the Germans had killed, and I saw her, sitting in my armchair, in my study, in front of me, and around her were a pair of wings, golden wings – I saw an angel.'

We said nothing.

'I couldn't tell her. I am – I was – a very well-respected analyst. I couldn't tell her …' He was exhausted. All the talking.

Then he clutched my hand and said, 'Will an angel come for me if I don't believe in them?'

'I expect so.'

'You don't seem certain of your divinity, of your ideas. That's a good thing. I can trust that.'

'Well, I've had some extraordinary experiences,' I said, 'which made me – forced me – to abandon everything I've ever believed, and that has helped me.'

'Was that grace?'

'I think so. I think so.'

'Was it beautiful? To have your ideas ... washed away. Is God in the beautiful things?

I didn't know quite what to tell him. I tried to feel into the moment, into his heart, to say the right thing.

'I think trees are the most beautiful things, and they are the nearest to God that I can see.'

'I am giving my money when I die to a tree-planting scheme. When I was in the concentration camp, there were no trees, so this I am going to leave behind.'

'So you are leaving God behind, even if you don't believe.'

'And I used to think the birds were angels, and they carried away the souls of the dead – I saw them, and I knew they were carrying away the souls of the dead, to somewhere else ...'

And then the strangest thing happened. The hospital window was open, and from out of the blue California sky, a tiny emerald hummingbird flew to the bunch of flowers on the window sill, then hovered there. We both stared, then I started to cry. I couldn't believe it, and neither could he. He tried to gesture and so did I, then, just as suddenly, it disappeared back into the sky from whence it had come. He shook his head. We didn't need to say anything.

'Thank you,' he said. 'Thank you.' And I wasn't sure if he

was thanking me, the bird or God – all of us or none of us. And it didn't matter.

He patted my hand.

Walking out of the psychiatrist's room, I knew he was on his way to heaven, but I had no idea if Al was on his way back to earth. I had to do something constructive, however outlandish, to try and steer him in the right direction, safely back to earth. It was almost as if I went into an altered state, like a warrior, and I was like Ed Harris in that movie where he was trying to land a rocket. I was trying to land a soul back in its body – I couldn't do it alone, and what fuelled me, as it had Ed, was the phrase, 'Failure is not an option.' It wasn't hubris, although it might have sounded like it; it was just my attempt to make something certain, knowing that it was impossible. I viewed the terrain. The Western doctors were doing what they could; it was time for Eastern wisdom to come in, the alternative healers. I would launch a celestial offensive. I would become a field marshal of healers. I had to take action and there were no Spirit whispers. Spirits weren't telling me anything about Al's fate. Almost as if they didn't care, but I knew that wasn't true. I wasn't a new friend to them, we had history. A long history. They wouldn't betray me, would they? No. If they were silent, I was convinced there was a lesson for me to learn from their silence. So I combated doubts I had by commencing a full-scale holistic assault and a round-the-clock healing attack.

The Agape Church (the hippest Science of Mind LA church) said prayers for him in their evening services, and a reiki master came every morning and transmitted healing with ancient Tibetan symbols. The afternoons were for the guest-star healers. One day

I had a past-life regressionist tell me Al had been a Roman general, and his karma was to pay – in this life – for his mindless slaughtering of innocents in that past life. This was his penance, that he had chosen, and it was his choice to return to his body or not, once he had finished fighting on the astral planes. I ruled out nothing and was willing to try anything to bring him back to earth. I had spent so much time trying to contact heaven and Spirit, perhaps even secretly felt like this life was something to endure until the splendour and ease of returning to Spirit, where it all felt so ideal and full of love. But now all I wanted was to be on the earth and make a life with Al when he came round. It was a deep knowing that my mind couldn't dispute.

The next afternoon an aromatherapist rubbed lavender on his temples. The following afternoon I found a professional foot-rubber, who used exotic 'rebalancing' oils that smelt of Jesus' crib, all frankincense and myrrh. The day after that he brought his friend, the 'humming girl'. She told me she believed in uncon-ditional love and that was why she was here. The real story was that she was trying to get a record deal and thought that if she practised some unconditional love by giving healing to Al, God would give her what she wanted. Her singing petitions to God to heal Al always had a coda which included a detailed breakdown of how much she wanted in the bank by when, for her singing career. Impatient at having to endure this, I politely suggested that she drop the 'unconditional' part of her pitch, as it was clearly a conditional deal with the divine. She turned on me and told me very peevishly that God was clearly punishing me for my sins, which was why my man was ill and I should repent. The only thing I came to repent was inviting her into Al's bedroom and anywhere near me as, moments later, she jabbed at my chest, crying, 'Jesus will invade your heart!' After that we rushed in a

Balinese 'clapper and bell-ringer,' who 'space cleared' the negative energy that the 'humming girl' had left behind. Honestly, what had Jesus done to deserve some of his followers? He was so much more forgiving and understanding than me. I prayed for his help to stop judging his followers for being judgemental, and to save Al.

After this little episode I lined up various groups to do 'absent healing'. No loons in the room. I was completely indiscriminate. Everyone was at it again. I had Christians praying, Catholics counting rosaries, Hindus chanting and Scientologists doing their secret thing. I felt better, as if all bases were covered. Even Brick caught the healing fever and sent an Australian model/soap star, all six foot four of him, to visit every day to give an invigorating massage. He would come in straight from surfing on Venice Beach, sunburnt and muscly, and so gorgeous that all the nurses would congregate in Al's room to watch the hunk's healing-hands sessions. They showed no interest in any of the other short, stumpy, bearded, worthy healers I had parading in. One particularly smitten nurse suddenly developed 'tension headaches', which required the soap star to massage her temples sensuously. Love and healing must have been in the air, as they ended up eloping and getting married in Hawaii. They sent a coconut from there, saying, 'Thank you Al, for getting us together.' I put it on the end of his bed. I felt it was a sign that he would get better.

The day the coconut ended up on Al's bed, I decided it was time to talk to my parents. Just tell them what was going on. I hadn't wanted to tell them too much – obviously, due to our secret psychic ancestry, they were used to my life being weird, but even I felt like I was an episode of *The Twilight Zone*. I imagined Mummy at Marks and Spencer, bumping into the Kent neighbours. 'What's your daughter up to?' Mrs Beeching would ask, as they chose cereals. 'Oh, she chats to dead people, and then in her time off she hovers round a Hollywood hospital, trying to bring the soul of her boyfriend back into his body.' And, it being England, Mrs Beeching would say, 'How lovely!' and Mummy would be viewed with suspicion over plums at the harvest festival.

And here was my insane reasoning: if I behaved as if Al were going to get well, then he would. I was prepared to make a complete fool of myself, to call my parents and tell them about this man that I had met, who might even be 'the one', then he might just wake up and *be* the one. Because the clarity that near-death experiences bring you is astonishing, even if they're someone else's. I had felt my mortality that night. And what was important to me. Maybe I was gripped by 'magical thinking' (Astrid's therapist's take, I'm sure); maybe I was suffering from post-traumatic stress syndrome (Jimminy's theory, courtesey of the latest Oprah), to think that Al was my love and that he would, against the odds, survive. The odds at that time were 75 per cent against a full recovery.

I sat in front of the phone for a good five minutes. Twiglet and Mishka sat with me – thank God for them, puppies who just wanted attention and love as usual, who insisted I get up at dawn to take them out for their walk.

Make the call. As long as I got Mummy first. Of course my father answered.

'How are you, darling?'

'Daddy, I've met someone.' He knew by my tone of voice that it was important.

'What does he do?'

'He used to be an actor.'

'Oh.' Not a very happy oh. 'What does he do now?'

'Now he writes and directs.'

A pause. 'Has he been married before?'

'Yes. Three times.'

'How old is he?'

'Umm, he's fifteen years older than me.'

'Politics?' he said, with a hint of desperation in his voice.

'Practically a communist.'

Grasping at straws, he asked, 'Is he healthy?'

'Well, he's a recovering alcoholic and he had cancer years ago.'

'Right. I see.'

'And actually, right now, he's in a coma.'

'I think I'd better put your mother on.'

Mummy had gathered only that there was a new man, and she had her own questions.

'Does he like animals?'

'Oh Mummy, he loves animals. He has a white wolf called Lupe ...'

'Is he American?'

'Sort of. His parents are both Italian. But they're dead, sadly.'

'Does he speak any languages?'

'Four. All fluently. Spanish, Portuguese, English and Italian.'

'And what does he look like?'

'He's beautiful – he looks like Al Pacino and Dudley Moore all rolled into one.'

'Does he love what he does?'

'He adores it.'

'And does he love you?'

'I have a feeling he does, Mummy. I have a feeling he does.'

'And does he know you're psychic?'

'His mother was a spiritualist.'

'He's one of the family, darling. When can we meet him?'

'Well it's a little bit tricky at the moment, as he's in a coma.'

My mother's optimism was not to be doused by a small inconvenience like a coma. 'Can he hear you? When you speak? They say that, don't they?'

'They do. And I think he can, Mummy.'

'Good, darling, I'll say prayers for you. And when he wakes up, ask him what he likes to eat. You can always ask him things telepathically. Auntie Violet used to do that.'

'Really? Mummy, I know this sounds mad,' Mummy was listening very intently, 'but I don't think being psychic's a curse any more. I think it's a gift.'

I heard an excited rustle of paper, then a strange squeak on the answer machine – Mummy was always pressing the button and was even more technologically ignorant that I was.

'Got to go, darling!'

'Oh, bye – bye Mummy.' But she was still there, on speaker phone.

'Mummy? Mummy?' She couldn't hear me.

'Look, darling, she said it! See, like it says in my letter from my great grandfather Jack!' She was talking excitedly to my father. 'Mummy?!' I was yelling – a letter from her great grandfather Jack? The only one I knew of was from five generations ago, the one in the photograph – the President of the Spiritualist Association.

'She said it! "It's a gift, not a curse!" Now I have to send her the letter!! Those were Jack's instructions.'

I tried one last time – 'Mummy?! But it was useless. I could hear her bustling around and the crackle of paper.

'He sounds a bit worrying,' said my father, 'this bloke in a bed with no money and without a proper job.'

'He sounds marvellous!' said my mother – and then she must have hit the box again as it all went quiet.

What on earth was Mummy talking about? Great grandfather Jack and letters? I actually felt a bit worried about them. However insane LA was, maybe being out in the middle of the English countryside wasn't' good for my parents. Too many frosts. It had gone to their heads, being locked out without the sun – maybe they had that sun deprivation disease, seasonal affective disorder; they were clearly disordered, I should get them out here. Must make plans to do that. The phone went again. God if only I could stay under the blanket a little longer.

'Astrid!'

'I'm at the Grove! I tell you, you're really missing out.'

'I'll live.'

'What about Al – how is he?'

'Same.'

'And psychically?'

'Not sure. I feel like he can hear us, and maybe helping all of it is – showing him it's a friendly world – all these healers coming in and helping him for nothing – shows him that people do things just to be nice. That it's a kind world.'

'That's great.' I heard her lighten up.

'Listen, did you hear? Lara went to the nut house! She started doing intensive work on that script, your part, *How Did It Feel?* ...'

I loved my friends, they always referred to it as my part. She carried on:

'It sent her over the edge!'

'How do you know?'

'Big-star-tiny-body was in rehab with her.'

'I thought rehab was for people coming off drugs?'

'Lara knew she'd have fun there, everyone goes now, it's the coolest thing. And Big-star-tiny-body comes out today and wants to see you, for a reading or something. I told her about Al and that you were at the hospital, so she said forget it, but she may come by to say hi.'

'Lara went nuts?'

'Oh yeah. She thought she was an alien, ended up in Burbank asking some suburban couple if they could hold her pod before she went home to Mars ... very creepy.'

'Poor thing.'

I felt really bad now. Was I to blame? Why the hell had I told her to do *How Did It Feel?* in that psychic reading? More to the point, why had Spirit told her? She'd ended up mad.

'Yeah, my therapist says deep subjects like the one in your film, they trigger healing crises ... although the *National Enquirer* didn't call it that of course.'

'Speaking of ... and how is your sister?'

'Great. Is everyone we know mentally ill, mad, in rehab or hospital?' she asked.

'Is everyone we know here in the entertainment industry?' I replied

'Yes, probably ...'

'Then yes!'

'Oh, and we missed one: prison.'

'What? Who's in jail?'

'Brick. He screwed some coke dealer and "borrowed" from Lara's paycheque to pay him back. She found out, and now she's in rehab she's insisting on scrupulous honesty. She'll have trouble finding a new agent in Hollywood if that's her criteria. Although Brick's only doing a short stint in jail, and is going down to rehab himself – not for the drug problem but to try and get his clients back.'

I sighed.

'What's the psychic POV on all that?' asked Astrid, always curious.

'I guess hospitals and jails are almost like karmic clearing houses. It looks really bad from the world's point of view – breakdowns, addiction, imprisonment – but from the soul's point of view, it's a healing, isn't it? Most people aren't going to change without a really big shock, are they?'

'Is smoking a healing?' said Astrid, inhaling. 'A crisis that leads to health? Eventually?'

'You mean after yellow teeth and crows' feet and lung-cancer scares?'

'Changing the subject swiftly … You know what, your scary law suit from Lara – you were one of twenty, by the way – she's dropped all charges.'

'Thank God for that. One down …'

'You'll stay in the States. Don't worry about that.'

'How do you know?'

'I just have a feeling.'

We laughed, I heard Astrid smoke two more cigarettes and I sat looking out of the window. At last Twiglet and Mishka were friends. That was something. And tomorrow it was winter solstice, 21st December. The day that marks the return of the sun; the Mesopotamians started a twelve-day festival of renewal on that day. It was a turning-point day, when the light would win over the darkness again. And that night I had a feeling something special was going to happen the next day. Al was a good Catholic as a boy after all – he might want to wake up for Christmas.

Winter solstice. I put on a red dress with scarlet shoes and set off to the hospital. Sat in my usual seat next to Al. Read him a poem: 'It may not always be so' by e e cummings. Then went out to the nurses' station to get some water. Looked up and saw Big-star-tiny-body walking towards me, and the surprise was that she was with Lara. Of course, they were both just out of rehab. I felt rather afraid. I'd done readings for plenty of Americans just out of treatment, and everything became very serious. I was terrified that I would crack a joke and be labelled 'emotionally avoidant' when I was just being British. Maybe we were emotionally avoidant. Oh dear. They were bearing down on me.

'We need your help.'

'Right,' I said nervously. I couldn't help thinking how ironic it was that we were in the hospital: Al was in a coma, but their request was firstly for their own health, not the obviously sick person's, Al. I suspected a Brit would have started with, 'How's Al?'

Big-star-tiny-body actually looked great. She no longer had the body of a young girl with a large swollen head. She looked better. She grabbed me by the hand. Oh no. Not a reading now, please …

'I just want to say thank you. At the restaurant. You were the only one who told me the truth. You knew I'd just gone and barfed my lunch. And I really appreciate it.'

'Oh well, thank you for the thank you,' I said, feeling awkward.

'You're not used to receiving, are you?' said Lara. Oh no. I didn't want to be analysed.

'I'm not sure.'

'Well ... I think you give to others and you don't like it when other people give to you, because then it means you aren't needed. It's called co-dependence.'

'OK.' I just wanted to hide in a hole. And what I wanted to find out was what had happened – why she had gone mad? Or was that it? Maybe she was right: I was thinking about that because I was emotionally avoidant, or whatever she called it ... I preferred to abdicate to Spirit and not really feel. I was getting sucked into this analytical energy ... I felt confused. What did I want to say? I went all British and polite. Always a safe bet.

'Lara, I felt awful when I heard about your break—'

'Oh, when I'd flipped my lid! No hassle! Best thing that ever happened to me! I was wolfing down Valium and Oxycontin – no wonder I thought I was off to another galaxy ...'

Well, that was good, she seemed to have a sense of humour about it. Maybe I had misjudged them. But I still felt bad ... responsible somehow.

'When I told you to do the film, in the psychic reading for you on the set ... and then when Astrid told me ...' Oh no, I didn't want to get Astrid into trouble ...

'Go ahead,' said Lara.

'Well, she told me you said that the script ... must have set off ... your breakdown ...'

'And how did you feel about that?' said Lara, with a pene-trating, Valium-free stare.

I wanted to scream. Can't you tell, you stupid cow? I felt terrible! Guilty! Idiotic! Lost my faith in Spirit! But I tried to do it ... their way. What did I bloody feel?

'I felt ... happy because then I was in with a chance to play the part! Al had offered it to me before, and then, well, basically

I was replaced ... because you were ... who the investors wanted ... and I was pissed!'

And they whooped with joy! 'That's it! That's the truth!'

Oh my God, they loved it! I wasn't being at all 'spiritual' and they loved it. There were clearly some great advantages to being American and telling the truth.

'I mean, I did also feel worried for you, and sorry for you ... I guess ...' And I meant it.

'It was the best thing that ever happened to me. I was meant to read that script and I was meant to go la-la. Now I know the difference. It's hard in LA, you know, to tell the difference between the basic attitude needed to survive in the entertainment industry and to be totally nuts. Now listen. We have a proposition to make to you. Teach us how to be psychic. Can you?'

'Yes, I think I can. I mean, you're both imaginative, and we are all naturally psychic ...'

'And thank you. Your reading helped me. And I apologise for the law suit – I didn't really know what I was doing.'

'It's fine.'

'Would you like a hug?' she asked tentatively. We hugged like bears. 'And next time I hear a girl throwing up, I'll tell her– like you did with me, even though I hated you at the time.'

She embraced me again. And they both left, signing autographs as they went.

What a lesson. I had said what I really felt, and that was what made them want me to teach them about spiritual stuff. I felt a little shaky. And happy. The readings were kind of exhausting ... maybe I could be American and selfish ... Oh dear, I couldn't call them selfish. That was my British over-politeness. Maybe I could be American, like them, and do what I wanted – I could teach other people how to be psychic, and act as well, and even, if I really allowed myself to dream – that's what they did over here, they went for big silly dreams – I could write books and make films … and be happy! This made me burst into floods of tears. Oh God. It was all so confusing … but maybe that was what this was all about: I needed to be confused, and not be the know-it-all psychic who had all the answers …

'Big-star-tiny-body needs a new name.'

It was Jimminy, handing me a large coffee. He had bumped into her coming out of the hospital.

'Big-star-sexy-body?'

We nodded. I glanced back at Al's room nervously.

'You know, I know you want Al to get well, but why don't you just trust that he will? That whoever you hear your reading information from is in charge of it, and they will take care of him. Today's a special day, and I think you need a little break. You've been at this for two weeks almost – you need some fresh air and lunch at home.'

'You sound like my mother.'

'You know I'm the wise one.'

We walked away from Cedar Sinai and out into the afternoon sun.

'What we need,' said Jimminy, 'is a miracle. We don't need a healing, we need a miracle.'

I was plunged deep into thought. A miracle. A miracle. What was that? A spontaneous remission, I think they called it, when an illness or medical situation is suddenly reversed.

'Where are we going to find one?' I said, as we once again pounded the pavements, the only idiotic Brits trying to pretend we were in a civilised country where people walked.

'Ask your psychic guidance.'

'Oh Jimminy, I don't know if I have any left.'

'Well, I'll ask mine. I think we should go home, hang out with the dogs and have a nice cup of tea.'

'Oh, Jimminy, the place is such a mess ... I can't bear it ...'

'Don't worry about that.'

Distressed as I was about the pigsty state of the house, I really did want to leave the hospital for a bit. I got in the car with Jimminy.

'You know what Gurdjieff said?'

'Who?'

'Gurdjieff? Ouspensky? Armenian healer from the thirties?'

'Oh God, don't tell me some nut has been channelling him at the foot of Al's bed ...'

'No, no. It's from one of his books. He said something like "miracles happen when you change your way of thinking", and you only have to do the simplest thing to do that. He suggested that you change your normal route.'

'In your brain?'

'No, literally. If you normally drive down Sunset to get home, take Fountain.'

Jimminy swerved the car. 'Fine, we'll take Fountain.'

As we were driving down Fountain, one of the least beautiful streets in LA, we both glanced at a church on a street corner. The church door was open, a light was on, and we could see a circle of men were sitting round. It was a sort of hideous room. We were both fascinated though, and Jimminy drove into the parking lot. We both peered in. The lights were neon, the chairs were plastic, the coffee looked and smelt undrinkable. But the words we could hear, the words were to be Jimminy's salvation. The notice on the door said that it was an AA meeting. Jimminy looked at me. Without speaking, he went inside, and I went round to sit in the church's garden.

I didn't feel particularly drawn to go inside, so I sat under a tree outside and meditated. In a vision I saw Ishtara, Lakshmi and Tara, my neon guides, blue, pink and green, all pointing at something. They were pointing at my heart, and then I saw a big pink rose bloom from it; they picked it and put it in Al's hand. Then I saw a group of elderly people in the vision. They looked vaguely familiar – they had freckles and red hair and were dressed in old-fashioned clothes, Victorian style, or just after. One appeared to be the ringleader, Jack. In his hand he had an envelope, and then I heard, 'Trust.' Then a picture of a big red heart again, that looked like the Jim Dine one Al had sent me in the postcard. I opened my eyes. Jimminy was standing there with an old man, a salty sea-captain type, the one you'd trust if your boat was sinking. He couldn't have been more different from Jimminy – he was weathered, dressed in nondescript clothes – and I watched them as they exchanged numbers and Jimminy walked towards me with tears in his eyes.

'What is it, Jimminy?'

'This is a disaster!' But he was laughing. 'After all this – my life spent in pursuit of glamour – this is where I end up ...' He gestured to the dark church hall, 'And he said, "keep coming back" – I have to come back here!' But he was clearly very happy.

'Why?'

'It's just where I'm meant to be.' And then he turned and walked back towards the group of men and brought back his new mentor. The salty sea captain came towards me.

'I'm David and I'm an alcoholic.'

'Hello, David,' I said. 'I'm Lucinda and I'm psychic.'

He looked powerfully puzzled.

'Is there a twelve-step program for that? Is it something you are powerless over and your life has become unmanageable? That's the first step.'

'Yes!' I said. 'That's pretty much true.'

'Well, the step after that is, "Come to believe that a power greater than yourself could restore you to sanity."'

That's Spirit, I thought. But it didn't really make sense to me. Because the thing I was powerless over was the thing that would heal me. It was very peculiar. And the language was very 1950s and it sounded sort of Christian – but the energy in the words felt real and profound and true. And, most importantly, Jimminy was into it.

'Then once you've let something in that's bigger than your small mind—'

Jimminy was squinting. 'Whisky? Tequila? A dozen cold beers ...'

The sea captain loved that. 'No, no, a divine presence that helps you, heals you, not destroys you because you have an allergy to that stuff.'

'You know, I think I do. Although sometimes I think I don't ...' and he made the sea captain laugh again.

'And what happens after that?' I said, curious to find out what on earth these twelve steps were.

'You make a decision – well, here it is,' and he said it off by heart, because that was where it was living in him: 'Make a decision to turn your will and life over to the care of God as we understand God.'

'How can anyone understand God?' said Jimminy blearily.

The captain seemed to find that funny too.

But I knew what it meant to me: – my triumvate trio – female friends in Spirit – Ishtara, Lakshmi and Tara. Ishtara: the ancient Babylonian Venus, the goddess of Love, she who had to descend to hell before uniting with her soulmate; Lakshmi: my Indian mother, fuchsia pink and four-armed, bestower of material prosperity and spiritual liberation, still to me a wildly improbable combination but I had faith in her faith; and Tara: the Buddhist nun, green, the colour of the heart, the colour of compassion, the feminist of the bunch who had vowed to find liberation in female form. And the three of them with their eight hands had been pointing to my heart. They had not been pointing to my third eye, where I received psychic guidance; they had very clearly been pointing to my heart. Perhaps that was what I had to listen to. I wasn't sure what I was even listening for. Everything was always filtered through my psychic vision. Not through the eyes of my heart. But salty sea captain was an action kind of guy, and was starting in what he had called the miracle prayer, the third-step prayer.

The prayer sounded a little old-fashioned, but I knew I should show willing – any prayers were OK by me at the moment, especially if they could help Al. So, rather bizarrely, among the Chevrolets and pick-up trucks in the parking lot, Jimminy, the sea captain and I started saying this peculiar prayer. I didn't catch it all but I put my heart into it. 'God, I offer myself' – something something – 'take away my difficulties' – that was a good bit – then something about 'that victory over them' – I'd pray for victory over my difficulties and Al's – and then the last bit I caught was, 'May I do thy will always'. And we all got up from the parking lot. I wondered what Ishtara, Lakshmi and Tara wanted for me. What was their 'will' for me? A pink rose. Unconditional love, that was what pink represented.

Jimminy actually had tears in this eyes.

'Do you mind if I go and have coffee with the lads?' The sea captain hugged him and he went off to his band of men.

'I'll drop him back,' said David, and he turned to concentrate on Jimminy.

I somehow knew that the prayer we had all said, that had come from a desperate place in each of our hearts, was going to change us. Maybe it was even the miracle. I got in the car. Trust. Trust what? Spirit, I supposed. But that was a bit ridiculous when I thought about it. It was like praying and then hearing as your message, 'Pray.' I was doing that. Wasn't I? Trusting. I still hadn't heard any news from the immigration people. That wasn't good. Especially as it was the holidays. Oh God, I'd have to go back to England and get SAD, and be laughed at for failing. Why did prayer sometimes bring up its opposite in me … sheer terror?

I suddenly felt incredibly tired. I arrived home to a big bunch of flowers and SURPRISE! on the door. I opened it and the wreck of the past few weeks was unrecognisable. LOVE ASTRID was scrawled in her signature red lipstick on the mirror. The whole place was gleaming. And I had two new dogs. Instead of a yellow and dusty red pair, Mishka was laundry white and Twiglet a deep chocolate brown. And in Twiglet's mouth was an envelope, hand-delivered, with 'Happy Christmas' written on it. 'Thought you might want this for Christmas, picked it up from our lawyer.' Confirmation that Miss Clare has been awarded the extraordinary alien visa.

I was over the moon and dancing around the house singing, 'I'M AN EXTRAORDINARY ALIEN!' I had to go and tell Al.

I arrived at the hospital to find a buzz of activity around Al's door.

'What happened?' I asked my favourite nurse, Cathy.

'Have a look!'

He was sitting up.

'Just wait a moment. They have to check there's no brain damage, then they can operate on him, as his skull impacted his brain. If he can answer a few basic questions they'll do it almost immediately.'

The doctor came out. Shook my hand. 'We'll be taking your husband in to operate in about five minutes. If you just want to go and say hello. And we do want you to know it's a high-risk operation.' Cathy winked at me. 'I pretended you were his wife.'

The first thing I did was just hold his hand. And just to feel him hold it back made me believe in God.

'Hello,' I said.

'Hello,' he said back. And it was very familiar. It was here that he belonged. Back on earth.

'I'm starving. Do you have any chocolate?'

I shook my head with a silly grin I couldn't get rid of. 'I can go and get you some.'

'No, we haven't got long, have we?' he said, staring at me.

'Five minutes.' I smiled.

'I've been watching you.' And he smiled that smile.

'Watching – how?'

'It's as if I had a thousand eyes in my head, and I could see behind me and around me, and I watched you.'

'You were having an out-of-body experience?'

'I knew you'd have a name for it ... it felt great.'

'You feel like that when you go home, I think. But you decided to come back.'

Then he burst out with it: 'I did and – my God! – there are whole other worlds up there! I heard voices – I slipped out of my body ... I could see colours ... I even thought I saw an angel – Oh my God, they'll lock me up if I talk about this to anyone – I mean except you – but, you know – I have to tell you – I may be going back there now …'

'I know.' I couldn't think about that. I had to give him faith. In case he didn't make it back.

'What did you hear?'

'I saw how stupid I've been, running around obsessed with making it – making it my reason for living – and I missed you … I could hear you sometimes, when you were by my bed – the poem, I remember the poems, today's was "it may not always be so".'

Now I couldn't believe it.

'You don't believe it?'

I looked at him. 'Are you reading my mind?'

'I'm not reading it, it's just that, I can see people's thoughts, what people are thinking, like subtitles. Over their head.'

I am thinking of pink. I am thinking of a rose.

'Pink … flower … rose?'

'Oh my God, that's incredible! You know this has been written about? This happens to some people: you can get a blow on the head and become psychic.'

'Is it God's idea of a joke – give a cynical intellectual psychic powers?' he said, retaining his old-wolf cynicism, because it was a fur coat that kept him cosy.

'Do you want some of my clients? I need help.'

'No. We need to make our films. Do you want to do mine?'

'What film?'

'The film you came to America for, the film you said you'd die happy if you made …'

'Oh, that film!'

We had both heard the 'die happy' bit and felt the heaviness of what was about to happen. A long operation. Al wanted to keep talking, as if that would make him forget he might die.

'Funny. You realise how true that is, when – anyway, I asked you about it on the set that day. You told me you'd be doing the part.'

'I did?'

'You don't remember? I handed you a script and asked if I would get the actress I wanted for the lead. I wanted you. It was our film.'

'But you went to Lara and asked her to do it?' Why were we talking about this when we had so little time?

'No. Lara came up to me, and said you'd told her to do it.'

'But I didn't know it was *How Did It Feel?*. I was in a reading.'

'I didn't know that. I just thought you wanted her to do it because you didn't want to any more.'

'And I told you I was going to play the part?' Why was this so important to him?

'Listen, I was obsessed with the film. For the wrong reasons: recognition, making it. I forgot life. And one perfectly normal day, I stepped out on to the road and a car almost took it all away from me. But now, if I'm given another chance, I will make the film. We will make the film. But it won't make me. That's the difference from before.'

'Who taught you that?'

'Tinkerbell.' Why was he talking to Tinkerbell? Oh dear. Maybe there was brain damage.

'Only kidding. Fooled you. No, the truth is, if the vision you had was true, of us doing the film ... you know what that means ...'

I shook my head

'It means I'll live ... I'll be fine after the operation ...'

'He's coming to get you in about a minute,' said Cathy apologetically.

Al lowered his voice to a whisper, 'The doctor's worried, he was asking me questions and reassuring me all the time, but I could see over his head. This one is touch and go, but if it's go I'll meet you on Christmas Eve, at the Grove, under the tree at seven.'

'It's a deal,' I said, shaking his hand.

'And why is everyone obsessed with the Grove?' I couldn't help it. My last minute of conversation with him and this I had to know.

'It's sort of like up there,' he said, pointing up to heaven. 'Nothing looks real, and it's brightly coloured with fountains and music. It's the nearest we can get to heaven in LA.' We were running out of time.

'Were you whizzing around out of your body spying on me all the time?'

'Most of it. You really like chocolate, don't you?'

'Yes, I do.'

He looked at me closely. I tried to stop myself thinking anything, as I knew the state he was in – he read my mind.

'Do you know what I'm thinking?' he asked with a beautiful smile. I smiled back. I thought he was thinking what we'd both been thinking since we'd first met.

'Usually.'

'If I think it, you'll hear it, right? You hear?'

'Clairaudient, yes. That's where I go to naturally. It's faster than words, so let's do that. I'll start.'

He looked at me. I listened. Paused.

'That's a big question to ask telepathically.'

'Well …' I really couldn't help it but I thought for a second, about the prophecy, the prediction that the man I was going to be with was supposed to be a writer. Al wasn't that.

'You can't be serious,' he said, hearing my thoughts, and now he spoke out loud. 'You're worried about that? You're the prophet, aren't you? I've just come from all of that – we're the angels, you know. We're their angels, you know that? Their helpers. We're the ones who ultimately chose. That's the point, we have to listen to them, sure, but all they're telling us is how to listen to our hearts. You know that?'

'You know what? You come and meet me at the Grove at seven, under the tree, and then you'll know what the answer is. I trust you.'

'We need to take him now,' said Cathy with a grimace.

'I want you to see me looking like a man again. Standing up. Not a thing lying in a bed. Do you understand?'

I nodded. And it was said without a trace of pride. It was said because it was the truth.

'I'll see you on Christmas Eve.'

I left the hospital feeling exhausted. And once again I found myself handing over the fate of a man I loved to the gods. Nothing makes you feel more helpless than watching an iron trolley being rolled away down a hospital corridor. I'd watched it with Steve, and now with Al. Two men I'd loved. One then, the other now, and in between the whole of my time in Hollywood …

I must have walked a lot, because when I got home it was already dark. I didn't want to talk to anybody. I was beyond consolation. This was a solitary thing. And I still wasn't shown past the present. No hint. No voice. No visions. Just the wait. I crawled under the covers with Mishka and Twiglet and did something I have never done before – I watched children's cartoons, without the sound.

Time passed. Didn't sleep.

The ring of my cell phone was like a bell announcing the end of the rest break. I fumbled in the covers trying to find it. Didn't make it. Checked the message. It was buried. He had survived the night. And it was better if he wasn't disturbed for a couple of days. I fell into bed. And I slept for three whole days. I was so exhausted, and there were no dreams, no signs, just unconsciousness. I woke up on Christmas Eve at six o'clock in the evening. I had to be at the Grove at seven. He'd be there. And if he wasn't I didn't want to think about what that meant. I pulled on a red dress and headed out to a café; I had to eat, or I'd faint. I tripped over a strange-looking envelope on the steps that I had to take with me.

His question to me – would I? – well, that was I'd always wanted. Wasn't it? But why didn't he fit the prophecy? So off I went. This was so ridiculous. Of course I wanted to – he had just survived, for God's sake; Spirit had given him back, so I had to listen to them. But why had Spirit misled me with the prophecy? I'd built my life around them. Interpreting them. What now? I'd be a normal person, without insider info to keep me safe – love was far harder than police cases or haunted houses, and that was bad enough. Oh God, I was ruining it all. How could I explain to him? If I didn't have Spirit, if I didn't trust their prophecies, I had nothing – what was I? Who was there to love? I had worn my psychic powers as a great big shield in front of my heart. I was terrified.

Food. I wandered into a café. There was a beautiful girl standing behind the cake counter. Now? Now I had to talk to her and give a message. This was what I heard. What I felt. Was this not the height of martyrdom? Not to get my answer for me at the most important moment of my life, but to give a reading to someone else.

Do it! Do it! There as a long line of frustrated people waiting in the line with cell phones. Trust. I took a deep breath: 'Excuse me ...'

She knew I wasn't ordering a cake. Why now? Again catering to someone else's needs. Do it!

'I'm a psychic and I have a message for you.'

She sped around the cake counter.

'Do you mind if I hold your hand?'

She shook her head.

'You have a little boy who died – he is in Spirit, he's standing behind you.'

She mewed, a small sigh that only a mother who has lost a child as beautiful as the sun can utter.

'He's with you. He's pointing to your tummy. His old home. He says there's another child coming. You're wondering if it's him, his soul – he's with you in Spirit for ever he says but this is someone new. It's a girl. And you're not to feel guilty, you're not replacing him ... Oh, and one more thing, he wants you to travel with your camera. That's it.'

She took me by the hand, through the back of the restaurant with the pots and the pans. Into her office. To a wall of photographs she had taken. To a photograph of her dead son.

'This is my son. Isn't he lovely?'

A little boy who looked like a deer-eyed mischief-maker smiled back at me with secrets. Secrets that were his and his mother's life together. The best of friends.

'Now I have to tell you something,' she said. 'I found out this morning that I was pregnant. No one knows. So when you told me—' she started to cry now, 'that I was going to have a baby, that he knew – you see, I was in such a state, I ran into two friends, they gave me the card of a psychic. I thought about seeing her, but I don't really trust psychics. Anyway, when you walked in and then told me all that, it's just magical ... Spirit is talking through you.'

And I realised, not by thinking, or by analysing, that just by wandering around, full of feelings, that I had been in exactly the right place at the right time. And trusting. That was what being psychic was about. Not haunted houses and TV shows and press and famous people. Not even about prophecies. Just two people, connecting with each other, soul to soul. She had reminded me. I embraced her.

'Thank you! Thank you!'

'For what? It was you!'

I left the café, back towards Al. I didn't need that food. Just soul food.

'You dropped this!' The girl was running after me, holding the envelope. I noticed that on the back it said 'urgent', although I didn't remember having seen that the first time I had looked at it. I tore it open.

Dear Lucinda

 This letter may come as a bit of a surprise to you. I am your great-great-grandfather, Jack, and I was the head of the Spiritualist Association in Glasgow at the turn of the century. You may have seen photographs of me; I am a rather good-looking chap with red hair. By the time you get this letter, however, I will be in Spirit and the century will have turned again and a hundred years will have passed. You will be looking at the beginning of your new century.

I turned the letter over. It looked like it had been written over a hundred years ago. The writing was black and inky and spidery. I leant against a tree, completely mesmerised. I knew nothing was more important than reading this letter. In it was the clue I had been looking for. I walked as I read.

I am your family, even if you don't see me. I am your ancestor even if you don't feel me. I am your family and will always be with you. Love is the only thing that is real. Love has propelled me to write to you, a girl five generations away, to tell her I love her. It goes by so fast, this life, so fast, I am sitting here, as I write to you, looking out at the peacocks and the elephants in the garden of Chilham Castle, and I am an old man. I couldn't accept this gift that I know you have and I wasted so much time, too many times I could have helped someone and I didn't. I don't want that to happen to you. I may sound sad and full of regrets; I am not, I can only write this because I am profoundly in love with this great privilege called life. We're very interested in the East, as a clan, our family, and I have studied Buddhism. To be given a human life is the greatest honour we can ever be given. And my great honour is coming to a close, and I wanted to help someone, help someone I'd never even met, but who was linked to me through blood and love.

Five generations after me. That was what I was told. The next pyschic one. And your daughter will be psychic too. They tell me. Big brown eyes like the Galloway cows and the Indian gods. I love cows. Spent some time with Bernard Shaw, a spiritualist, followed his guidance and don't eat animals. Especially cows. You can do a lot with cheese you know. Eat it most meals. Shaw loves it too. He writes plays, you know. You are in that world too. You are a maker of things. Masks. I see masks. Books. And flying photographs, the talking pictures. And most of all I see love. Say yes to the man. He loves you. And say yes to the world. You are living in dark, dark times, but remember we are here. Remember your ancestors never forget you. Listen. Listen closely. I will be in a song. I will be in a poem. I will be in a stranger's glance. All of us who have passed through the veil of ignorance remember what is true. We are love. This is the truth. We are love. You and I. However old and helpless I may feel. I am dying, they tell me, of some tropical disease I picked up in the East, but let me tell you, it was worth it! The temples and things I saw. What I understood about the world. Life is short. So short. Do what makes you happy. Trust yourself. Give as if you were as boundless as the sea, because you are. Trust your heart. It never lies, Lucinda.

With the greatest respect and love,

Your great-great-grandfather Jack.

I was at the doors of the Grove. Crying. I was crying so hard I could barely see. But it looked so beautiful! Like a fairytale. A huge Christmas tree, silver lights, a full moon, and music was playing and the fountain was dancing in time to it. Everything was in harmony. As I walked through this mini-heaven, I saw what Astrid said was true. Everyone comes to the Grove. And I saw that what Jack had said was true. Love was inevitable, unavoidable and everywhere. Here we all were, not up the mountains meditating but doing everyday things, and it was everywhere.

Cindy and Bambi: the lesbian strippers were buying lamp-shades, setting up home together, and we had all given up on them, thought they were too damaged to find love. Shelby, from the wedding shower, so pregnant she could barely move; Astrid and Joan, Astrid was smoking and drinking coffee, Joan her sister roaring with laughter at something in the *National Enquirer*. Jimminy was talking earnestly to the salty sea captain, and Ziers was there too, all dressed up in Indian clothes, with a bhindhi, showing them both pictures of his new guru. In the corner, kissing in the shadows, were the supermodel and shit face, wildly in love. And there, by the bins, was Rubin, playing his cello with all his heart. He stopped and started talking to a woman who had been listening and it was Adam Sandler's fan! She was a little skinnier, and she had a dog, and they were both patting it and chatting.

Of course Al was there. Sitting on the bridge and waiting for me. I walked towards him – he looked as I remembered him from before, in his black Neapolitan suit – and the strangest thing was that as I walked, I had extreme déjà vu. I felt as if I was walking through past times, past lives, India, Italy, and every time it was him I had been walking towards, in a toga, in a bhindhi, in a ruff; it was always him.

'Now it's my turn to hold your hand. I'll tell you your future, if you want …'

'You will be loved by a wildly difficult man, who is tall, dark and handsome and from across the water – that's what they say, right?'

'That's what they say.'

'But it isn't a romantic dream, he's real.'

The fountains soared; Al went down on one knee.

I looked at him. Yes was already engraved on my soul. Yes had been engraved on my spirit before I was born. I just made it real. Yes.

To our surprise, giant snowflakes poured down on to our

heads. The fountains started dancing and a song, Frank Sinatra's 'I Was Born to Love', started playing on the sound system so that everyone could hear it. It was the most ridiculously kitsch and beautiful of moments.

'I'm a writer as well … I wrote our film,' said Al.

'You wrote it? So you lied?? You lied!'

'I live in Hollywood, what can I say?'

'The truth!'

'I tell that in the films. My life will always be confusing. It's only in films and books that everything can make sense.'

I looked at him solemnly. 'Is this—'

'This is the last lie I will tell you …'

And it was. And I could feel the Spirit who had first shared the prophecy with me smiling happily.

'Welcome to our new home,' he said.

'Welcome to Hollywood.'

And finally, finally we kissed.

Then, for some mysterious reason, the lights suddenly went out and the piped music stopped – it was as if the circuits had been blown by an excess of emotion. It was dark. And then the most beautiful thing. In the dark, Rubin started playing his cello. It was haunting – no ghosts, heart-haunting – and we all listened. And then Astrid lit up, and gradually everyone else lit their lighters too. And looking around, that was when I finally realised, holding my tall dark stranger's hand – although tall was exaggerating a bit, my small dark handsome man's hand – that whenever you were, whatever the enviroment, wherever you come from, locked in cages of whatever kind as a child, whatever you were up to now, love was possible.

The snow had stopped too. A big fat full moon, a real one, was there, once the fake one had been turned off. I was with a man who was next to me, there were no tricks, and he loved me – freckles, cheese-eating, all of it; weird witch, actress, writer to be, all of it – and we had said yes. Finally we had said yes. And I thanked all those who had gone before us, my great-great-grandfather and his clan, all of those around me, my friends furry and otherwise, and I thanked all those who were yet to come. I was a psychic. I couldn't help it. I could feel the future. But just for now, everything was perfect just as it was.

The End